Mathematics of Time Series Forecasting

Build Robust Time Series Forecasting Systems in Python Using Mathematical Theory, Statistical Modeling, Machine Learning, and Deep Learning

Dr. Sulekha AloorRavi

www.orangeava.com

First Published: March 2026

Published By: Orange Education Pvt Ltd, AVA®

Address: 9, Daryaganj, Delhi, 110002, India

275 New North Road Islington Suite 1314 London,
N1 7AA, United Kingdom

ISBN (PBK): 978-93-49887-66-4
ISBN (E-BOOK): 978-93-49887-68-8

Scan the QR code to explore our entire catalogue

www.orangeava.com

Get a Free eBook

We hope you're enjoying your recent book purchase! Your feedback is incredibly valuable to us and helps other readers discover books that truly make a difference.

If you found this book useful or enjoyable, we'd greatly appreciate it if you could leave a short review with a 5-star rating on Amazon. Your review supports our work and allows us to reach more learners worldwide.

As a thank-you, we're happy to offer you a **free digital copy of this book** plus a **30% discount code** for your next purchase on our official websites:

www.orangeava.com

www.orangeava.in (For the Indian Subcontinent).

☑ **How it works:**

Leave your review on Amazon, take a screenshot of the confirmation or use the following link to submit the claim and email it to **info@orangeava.com.** Once received the required detail, we will send your rewards within 24 hours, **along with one month free subcription to the book on AVA SkillShelf!**

Claim Form
https://rebrand.ly/4d2477

Thank you for your support—it truly means a lot to us.

Downloading the code bundles and colored images

Please follow the links or scan the QR codes to download the **_Code Bundles and Images_** of the book:

https://github.com/ava-orange-education/Mathematics-of-Time-Series-Forecasting

The code bundles and images of the book are also hosted on **_https://rebrand.ly/a278e4_**

In case there's an update to the code, it will be updated on the existing GitHub repository.

Errata

We take immense pride in our work at **Orange Education Pvt Ltd,** and follow the best practices to ensure the accuracy of our content to provide an indulging reading experience to our subscribers. Our readers are our mirrors, and we use their inputs to reflect and improve upon human errors, if any, that may have occurred during the publishing processes involved. To let us maintain the quality and help us reach out to any readers who might be having difficulties due to any unforeseen errors, please write to us at:

errata@orangeava.com

Your support, suggestions, and feedback are highly appreciated.

Dedicated to

My loving Husband,
Dileep,
My Strength and Support System.

About the Author

Dr. Sulekha AloorRavi is a data science and analytics leader with extensive experience in time series forecasting, applied artificial intelligence, and quantitative modeling. Her career spans leadership roles in global financial services, where she has built and scaled data-driven forecasting frameworks that blend mathematical precision with business impact.

With deep expertise across asset management, financial markets, and enterprise analytics, Sulekha has designed AI-powered decision systems for investment analysis, client intelligence, and revenue optimization. Her work integrates classical statistical modeling with modern machine learning and deep learning approaches to forecast complex, real-world phenomena with high accuracy and interpretability.

With a doctorate in Artificial Intelligence (AI), Dr. Sulekha has made significant contributions to the fields of predictive modeling and advanced analytics. Her doctoral research focused on developing innovative investment strategies through AI and machine learning.

Beyond her leadership roles, Sulekha is an educator, mentor, and thought leader in the field of Artificial Intelligence and Machine Learning. Through her writing, she aims to make advanced mathematical and AI concepts accessible to practitioners, researchers, and students.

In this book, *Mathematics of Time Series Forecasting*, she brings together the disciplines of mathematics, statistics, and artificial intelligence, offering readers a structured and practical guide to understanding and forecasting time-dependent data, from foundational models to cutting-edge deep learning architectures.

An accomplished author, Dr. Sulekha has published two books on time series analysis and metaprogramming, reflecting her commitment to bridging academic depth with real-world implementation.

About the Technical Reviewer

Dileep Vuppaladhadiam is an accomplished leader in the field of Artificial Intelligence and Machine Learning (AI/ML) with a remarkable 18-year track record of shaping the industry. His expertise spans a wide spectrum of domains, including solution design, data architecture, data engineering, data science, and the practical application of artificial intelligence and machine learning technologies.

Throughout his career, Dileep has played a pivotal role in deploying cutting-edge AI/ML-based applications, employing rigorous data science methodologies to empower data-driven decision-making. His achievements include the successful implementation of numerous AI/ML solutions, both on-premises and in cloud environments, delivering substantial business value.

Dileep's academic journey is equally impressive, encompassing accounting, economics, finance, business administration, data science, artificial intelligence, business analytics, and business intelligence. His commitment to education extends beyond his own studies, as he has also served as a dedicated coach, mentor, and faculty member, inspiring and guiding countless aspiring data scientists.

His professional footprint spans diverse sectors, including Manufacturing and Industrial, Information Technology, Banking, Finance, Retail, Travel and Tourism, as well as Consulting. Dileep has had the privilege of leading Research and Development, Technical Consultancy, and Support teams, bringing innovative solutions to renowned organizations such as IBM, Capgemini, Barclays, HSBC, HomeCredit, Mindtree, and Infosys.

Currently, he holds the prestigious position of Vice President at Wells Fargo, where he plays a pivotal role in guiding the global enterprise towards achieving unparalleled business value. Dileep's focus centers on harnessing the power of robust and scalable data engineering and data science approaches tailored to the modern business landscape.

Acknowledgments

I am deeply grateful to my family for their unwavering support, patience, and encouragement throughout the journey of writing this book. Their love and understanding have been my greatest strength, allowing me to dedicate countless hours to research, writing, and refinement. To my spouse, Dileep, whose faith in me never faltered, and to my nephew, Sai Sathvik, whose laughter and boundless energy brought light to my long days, I owe my heartfelt gratitude.

I thank them for their many sacrifices, for understanding the late nights and weekends spent immersed in work, and for being my constant source of inspiration. Their belief in me has been the quiet force behind every page of this book. I am forever indebted to their unconditional love and encouragement.

My sincere thanks to the publishers for their guidance, professionalism, and unwavering support throughout the publishing process. Their commitment to quality and dedication to creating meaningful resources for readers have been instrumental in shaping this book into its final form.

Finally, to the readers, I offer my deepest appreciation. Thank you for choosing this book as a companion in your journey to learning time series analysis. Your curiosity and passion for learning inspire me to continue exploring, teaching, and writing. I hope these pages empower you to uncover patterns in data, forecast with confidence, and approach every analytical challenge with clarity and creativity.

Preface

Time is the most intricate dimension of data. Every transaction, temperature reading, market movement, or sensor output is a snapshot in time. This book, *Mathematics of Time Series Forecasting*, is written for those who wish to decode that story. The book blends mathematical theory with computational practice, aiming to help readers not only build forecasting models but also understand the science that makes them work.

The book bridges classical statistics and modern artificial intelligence, showing how timeless mathematical principles still underpin even the most advanced forecasting architectures. It introduces readers to the continuum between stochastic processes, ARIMA-family models, and deep learning networks, with each concept supported by mathematical derivations and real-world Python implementations. The goal is to empower professionals, researchers, and learners to model uncertainty with precision and interpretability.

Hence, whether you are a data scientist, financial analyst, engineer, or researcher, this book will guide you through the complete forecasting journey, from mathematical intuition to practical implementation. Each chapter is structured to balance theory, intuition, and application, ensuring that readers build both conceptual clarity and coding proficiency.

Chapter 1 lays the mathematical foundation of time series analysis by introducing stochastic processes, which model uncertainty and temporal dependence. It explores discrete and continuous processes such as Markov Chains, Poisson Processes, Brownian Motion, and Random Walks, providing the conceptual bridge between probability theory and real-world forecasting applications.

Chapter 2 explains the concept of stationarity, its types, and its critical role in forecasting accuracy. Readers will learn to identify and handle non-stationary behavior through detrending, differencing, and transformations that make the data suitable for model training.

Chapter 3 introduces the first set of statistical tests to verify whether a time series is stationary. Covering visual inspection, the K-S Test, and the Dickey-Fuller family, it demonstrates how to interpret test results, and translate them into practical pre-processing actions for forecasting models.

Chapter 4 introduces more powerful and complementary statistical tests such as the Phillips-Perron, KPSS, DF-GLS, and Ng-Perron tests. These approaches offer refined detection of non-stationarity, addressing autocorrelation, heteroskedasticity, and structural complexity in real-world datasets.

Chapter 5 explores advanced econometric tools including the Schmidt-Phillips, Variance Ratio, Zivot-Andrews, and Leybourne-McCabe tests. Each test is discussed with mathematical rigor, and demonstrated through examples to handle structural breaks and complex stochastic behavior.

Chapter 6 covers data parsing, indexing, resampling, handling irregularities, detrending, deseasonalizing, and variance-stabilizing transformations, forming the essential pre-modelling pipeline for any forecasting task.

Chapter 7 introduces the core forecasting architectures such as AR, MA, ARMA, ARIMA, SARIMA, and Exponential Smoothing models. It details their mathematical formulations, assumptions, and implementation in Python, building the foundation for all future model comparisons and enhancements.

Chapter 8 presents Machine Learning (ML) methods such as Decision Trees, Random Forests, and XGBoost, along with deep learning architectures like LSTMs. It emphasizes reframing time series problems into supervised learning format, and illustrates how these models capture non-linear and long-term dependencies.

Chapter 9 extends forecasting to multivariate systems where multiple time-dependent variables interact dynamically. It covers Vector Autoregression (VAR), Vector Error Correction Models (VECM), and deep learning-based Multivariate LSTMs, showing how to model complex interdependencies across variables for higher predictive accuracy.

Thus, writing this book has been a journey of translating years of applied learning, mathematical exploration, and practical experimentation into a structured guide for professionals and students, alike. Hence, whether you are decoding financial markets, optimizing energy systems, or uncovering behavioural trends, may these chapters empower you to see patterns in time not as randomness, but as rhythm. Every dataset tells a story as this book is an invitation to understand and forecast it with clarity, rigor, and creativity!

DID YOU KNOW

Did you know that Orange Education Pvt Ltd offers eBook versions of every book published, with PDF and ePub files available? You can upgrade to the eBook version at **www.orangeava.com** and as a print book customer, you are entitled to a discount on the eBook copy. Get in touch with us at: **info@orangeava.com** for more details.

At **www.orangeava.com**, you can also read a collection of free technical articles, sign up for a range of free newsletters, and receive exclusive discounts and offers on Print Books and eBooks.

PIRACY

If you come across any illegal copies of our works in any form on the internet, we would be grateful if you would provide us with the location address or website name. Please contact us at **info@orangeava.com** with a link to the material.

ARE YOU INTERESTED IN AUTHORING WITH US?

If there is a topic that you have expertise in, and you are interested in either writing or contributing to a book, please write to us at **business@orangeava.com**. We are on a journey to help developers and tech professionals to gain insights on the present technological advancements and innovations happening across the globe and build a community that believes Knowledge is best acquired by sharing and learning with others. Please reach out to us to learn what our audience demands and how you can be part of this educational reform. We also welcome ideas from tech experts and help them build learning and development content for their domains.

REVIEWS

Please leave a review. Once you have read and used this book, why not leave a review on the site that you purchased it from? Potential readers can then see and use your unbiased opinion to make purchase decisions. We at Orange Education would love to know what you think about our products, and our authors can learn from your feedback. Thank you!

For more information about Orange Education, please visit **www.orangeava.com**.

Table of Contents

CHAPTER 1
Introduction to Time Series and Mathematical Foundations

Introduction

Time series analysis is a vibrant field of study focused on exploring how data points evolve over time. In this book, we delve into the mathematical foundations of time series analysis and forecasting. This book will focus on looking at practical examples and real-world applications of time series data, along with step-by-step instructions to apply them using Python.

Whether you are a data scientist, data analyst, data engineer, or Python programmer who works on data that deals with time, you will benefit from the chapters of this book. In this opening chapter, we lay the mathematical groundwork necessary to understand and apply advanced time series methods.

We will start this chapter by introducing the concept of a stochastic process, which models uncertainties and variations inherent in time-dependent data. By treating a time series as a realization of a stochastic process, we will gain powerful tools throughout this chapter to characterize and predict the behavior of time series data.

By the end of this chapter, readers will be able to understand the foundational role of stochastic processes in modeling time series data, distinguishing between discrete and continuous time/state formulations, and recognizing how randomness is systematically captured in dynamic systems. The readers will also be able to identify and differentiate key types of stochastic processes, including Markov Chains, Poisson Processes, Brownian Motion, and Random Walks, and grasp their mathematical formulations and real-world applications.

Structure

In this chapter, the following topics will be covered:

- Overview of Stochastic Processes
  - Discrete and Continuous Time
  - Discrete and Continuous State
- Types of Stochastic Processes
  - Markov Chains
  - Poisson Process
  - Brownian Motion
  - Random Walk
- Comparison of Stochastic Processes

Overview of Stochastic Processes

Stochastic processes are mathematical models that help in understanding or defining systems that evolve over time with randomness. These processes are fundamental to modeling time series data since time series data is often random, uncertain, and has a lot of variability. This section covers a detailed explanation of stochastic processes, their mathematical concepts, and their importance in time series analysis.

Discrete and Continuous Time

The simple definition of a stochastic process is that it is a collection of random variables indexed by time. It can be mathematically defined as follows.

$$X_t : t \in T$$

X_t is a random variable for each time point t, in the index set of T.

T represents continuous or discrete time.

Discrete-time Process

A discrete-time stochastic process is a type of stochastic process where the evolution of a system or phenomenon is observed at specific, separated points in time, typically indexed by integers (for example, t = 0, 1, 2, ...). At each time step, the process takes on a value from a set of possible outcomes, and this value is governed by some underlying probability distribution that may change over time or depend on past values. This kind of process is ideal for modeling phenomena where data is naturally collected at regular intervals, such as daily stock prices, monthly sales, or hourly temperature readings. The index set T in a discrete-time process can be counted. Example: t = 0, 2, 4, 6,...10

Continuous-time Process

The index set T in a continuous time process cannot be counted. For example: t can be between 0 and ∞.

Let us look at these concepts with a simple traffic story of a metropolis on a busy Monday morning. The streets of a metropolis are busy with cars, taxis, and buses, each hurrying to work or school. It is always a challenge for traffic engineers to model and predict ever changing congestion of these streets. Let us turn to stochastic processes and their mathematical frameworks to capture the randomness in how traffic evolves from moment to moment.

In this traffic story, let us consider X_t as the number of cars travelling past a traffic signal at time t. Over the course of a single day, the traffic increases and decreases, reflecting the unpredictable nature of the real-life road conditions. In this case, we can choose to either measure the number of cars in a discrete time interval, such as every 15 minutes, or on a continuous time basis, such as every second throughout the day.

To understand this further, let us simulate the traffic scenario by defining the traffic rate as a mathematical function.

Code:

```
def traffic_rate(time_minute):
    if 0 <= time_minute < 360:
        return 2
    elif 360 <= time_minute < 540:
        return 10
    elif 540 <= time_minute < 900:
        return 5
    elif 900 <= time_minute < 1140:
        return 12
    else:
        return 3
```

In the preceding code, we have defined the code for the traffic rate as a function of time. This function, **traffic_rate**, determines the rate of traffic (how many cars are arriving per minute) at a given time of day. It divides the day into different time periods (such as morning, afternoon, evening, and so on) and assigns a specific traffic rate to each period. For example, if the time period is between 0 and 360, then the number of cars per minute is returned as 2. Thus, traffic rate is a simple function that returns the number of cars on the road at any point in time, depending on what time of the day it is.

In the next step, let us simulate the traffic at discrete time intervals.

Code:

```
def simulate_discrete_traffic(interval=15, total_minutes=1440,
seed=None):
    if seed is not None:
        np.random.seed(seed)

    times = list(range(0, total_minutes, interval))
    car_counts = []

    for t in times:
        lam = traffic_rate(t) * interval
        arrivals = np.random.poisson(lam)
        car_counts.append(arrivals)
    return times, car_counts
```

The preceding code simulates traffic flow over a day in discrete time intervals, for example, 15 minutes. It calculates how many cars arrive during each interval, if cars arrive randomly but follow a certain pattern at certain hours of the day. The peak hours of the day will have more cars, whereas regular hours will have fewer. The results are returned as two lists: **`times`** will consist of time intervals, and **`car_counts`** will consist of the corresponding number of cars.

In the preceding code, we have used the Poisson distribution to randomly generate the number of cars arriving at that interval. The Poisson distribution is often used to model random events (such as car arrivals) that happen independently at a known average rate.

Now that we have defined the discrete traffic simulation, let us write a function to visualize it and understand what the traffic would look like.

Code:

```
def plot_traffic(times, car_counts, title="Traffic Simulation"):
    plt.figure(figsize=(10, 5))
    plt.plot(times, car_counts, marker='o', linestyle='-',
label='Cars Arriving')
    plt.title(title)
    plt.xlabel('Time (minutes)')
    plt.ylabel('Number of Cars')
    plt.grid(True)
    plt.legend()
    plt.show()
```

In the preceding code, **`plot_traffic`** is used to visualize the results of a traffic simulation. It takes data about when cars arrive (**`times`** and **`car_counts`**) and creates a line graph to show how the number of cars changes over time. It is like drawing a picture of the traffic flow throughout the day. It creates a line graph with time on the x-axis and the number of cars on the y-axis.

This graph would help us to see:

- When traffic is heavy (for example, during rush hour).
- When traffic is lightest (for example, late at night).
- How traffic changes over time.

With all the required functions defined, let us now bring the discrete traffic simulation to life by calling the functions that have been defined so far.

Code:

```
discrete_times, discrete_counts = simulate_discrete_traffic(
    interval=15,
    total_minutes=1440,
    seed=42
)
print('Discrete Times', discrete_times)
print('Discrete Counts', discrete_counts)
```

The output of the simulated data is displayed as follows:

```
Discrete Times [0, 15, 30, 45, 60, 75, 90, 105, 120, 135, 150,
165, 180, 195, 210, 225, 240, 255, 270, 285, 300, 315, 330, 345,
360, 375, 390, 405, 420, 435, 450, 465, 480, 495, 510, 525, 540,
555, 570, 585, 600, 615, 630, 645, 660, 675, 690, 705, 720, 735,
750, 765, 780, 795, 810, 825, 840, 855, 870, 885, 900, 915, 930,
945, 960, 975, 990, 1005, 1020, 1035, 1050, 1065, 1080, 1095,
1110, 1125, 1140, 1155, 1170, 1185, 1200, 1215, 1230, 1245, 1260,
1275, 1290, 1305, 1320, 1335, 1350, 1365, 1380, 1395, 1410, 1425]
Discrete Counts [28, 34, 23, 32, 36, 24, 27, 29, 32, 26, 29, 25,
31, 32, 27, 33, 22, 26, 27, 31, 21, 17, 28, 36, 142, 135, 160,
158, 160, 145, 165, 144, 143, 159, 167, 133, 82, 82, 75, 70, 89,
73, 68, 69, 91, 78, 83, 88, 70, 68, 73, 63, 93, 75, 98, 75, 69,
78, 56, 89, 164, 187, 169, 175, 185, 158, 173, 187, 180, 186,
188, 206, 174, 204, 170, 194, 46, 55, 42, 48, 47, 35, 46, 48, 49,
41, 48, 48, 34, 40, 55, 51, 46, 38, 40, 48]
```

Let us further look at the overview and plot of the simulated data as follows:

```
print("=== Discrete-Time Simulation (every 15 min) ===")
print(f"Number of observations: {len(discrete_times)}")
print(f"Total cars over the day: {sum(discrete_counts)}")
print(f"Average cars per observation: {np.mean(discrete_
counts):.2f}")
print(f"Max cars in a single interval: {max(discrete_counts)}\n")
```

```
plot_traffic(discrete_times, discrete_counts, "Discrete-Time Traffic
(Every 15 min)")
```

The preceding code simulates traffic over a full day (24 hours) and then analyzes and visualizes the results. It uses the **simulate_discrete_traffic** function to generate the data, calculates summary statistics such as total cars, average cars, and maximum cars in an interval, and finally creates a graph to show how traffic changes over time.

Output:

```
=== Discrete-Time Simulation (every 15 min) ===
Number of observations: 96
Total cars over the day: 8147
Average cars per observation: 84.86
Max cars in a single interval: 206
```

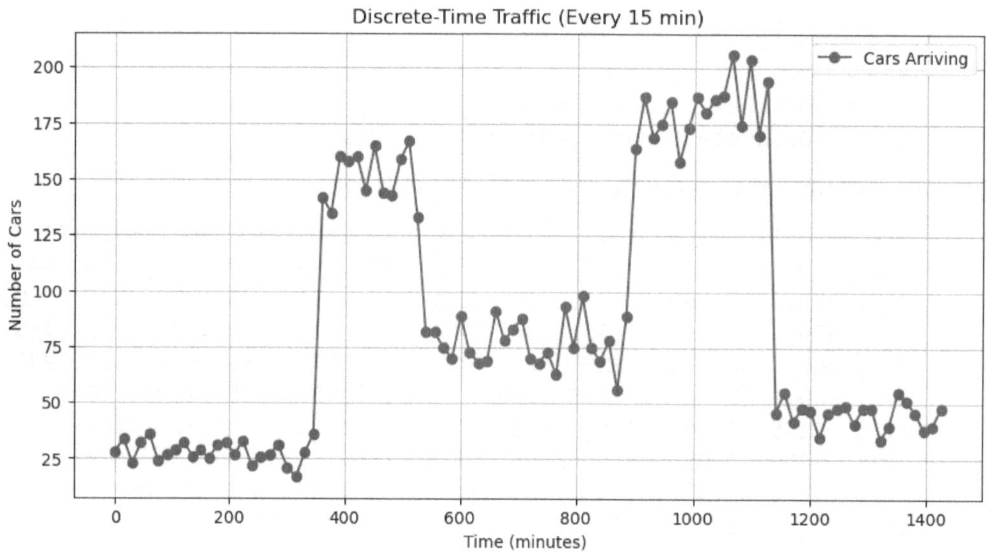

Figure 1.1: *Discrete Time Traffic*

Figure 1.1 depicts the traffic captured at every 15-minute interval over a day of 24 hours. *Figure* 1.1 is a great example of a time series analysis for discrete data. The **discrete_times** that represent discrete time intervals of 15 minutes and **discrete_counts** that represent the number of cars arriving at each interval are a classic example of time series data, where each data point is tied to a specific time.

Let us now create a similar example for continuous time process and review the traffic application of time series further.

Code:

```
def simulate_continuous_traffic(delta=1, total_minutes=60, seed=None):
    if seed is not None:
        np.random.seed(seed)

    steps = int(total_minutes / delta)
    times = [delta * i for i in range(steps)]
    car_counts = []

    for t in times:
        lam = traffic_rate(int(t)) * delta
        arrivals = np.random.poisson(lam)
        car_counts.append(arrivals)
    return times, car_counts
```

In the preceding code, **simulate continuous traffic** simulates traffic flow over time in a more detailed way compared to the discrete time process simulation example. Instead of looking at traffic in fixed intervals (such as every 15 minutes), it simulates traffic in very small-time steps (for example, every 1 minute or even every second). This gives a more continuous view of how traffic changes over time.

Continuous traffic data is also generated using the Poisson distribution. It uses randomness to model car arrivals but follows a pattern defined by **traffic_rate(t)**. This function simulates traffic in very small time steps (for example, every minute), giving a more detailed view of traffic flow.

With all the required functions defined, let us now bring the continuous traffic simulation to life by calling the functions that have been defined so far.

Code:

```
continuous_times, continuous_counts = simulate_continuous_traffic(
        delta=1,
        total_minutes=60,  # 1 hour
        seed=42
    )
print('continuous_times',continuous_times)
print('continuous_counts',continuous_counts)
```

The output of the simulated data is displayed as follows:

```
continuous_times [0, 1, 2, 3, 4, 5, 6, 7, 8, 9, 10, 11, 12, 13,
14, 15, 16, 17, 18, 19, 20, 21, 22, 23, 24, 25, 26, 27, 28, 29,
30, 31, 32, 33, 34, 35, 36, 37, 38, 39, 40, 41, 42, 43, 44, 45,
46, 47, 48, 49, 50, 51, 52, 53, 54, 55, 56, 57, 58, 59]
continuous_counts [4, 1, 3, 3, 1, 2, 1, 1, 2, 2, 1, 0, 4, 2, 1, 3,
2, 6, 1, 1, 2, 2, 1, 3, 4, 1, 3, 1, 4, 4, 2, 0, 0, 2, 2, 2, 1, 5,
4, 0, 1, 2, 2, 0, 2, 2, 3, 1, 0, 2, 2, 1, 3, 2, 3, 2, 0, 2, 1, 1]
```

Let us further look at the overview and plot of the simulated data as follows.

```
print("=== Continuous-Time Simulation (every 1 min) ===")
print(f"Number of observations: {len(continuous_times)}")
print(f"Total cars over the hour: {sum(continuous_counts)}")
print(f"Average cars per minute: {np.mean(continuous_counts):.2f}")
print(f"Max cars in a single minute: {max(continuous_counts)}\n")

plot_traffic(continuous_times, continuous_counts, "Continuous-Time
Traffic (Every 1 min, 1 hour)")
```

The preceding code simulates traffic flow over 1 hour in 1-minute intervals (continuous time steps) and then analyzes and visualizes the results. It uses the **simulate_continuous_traffic** function to generate the data, calculates some summary statistics such as total cars, average cars, and maximum cars in an interval, and finally creates a graph to show how traffic changes over time.

Output:

```
=== Continuous-Time Simulation (every 1 min) ===
Number of observations: 60
Total cars over the hour: 116
Average cars per minute: 1.93
Max cars in a single minute: 6
```

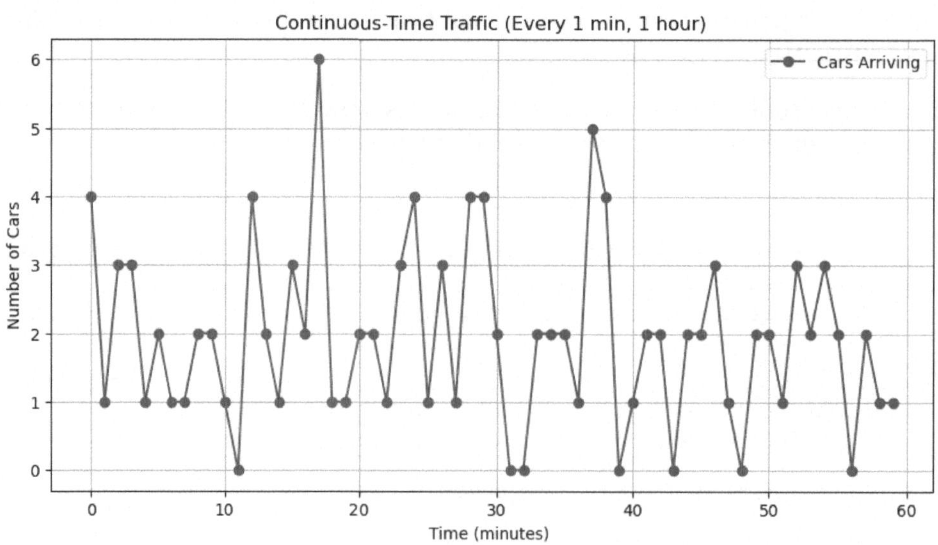

***Figure 1.2:** Continuous Time Traffic*

Figure 1.2 depicts the traffic captured at every 1-minute interval over 1 hour. *Figure* 1.2 is a great example of a time series analysis for continuous data. The **continuous_ times** that represent continuous time intervals of every 1 minute and **continuous_**

`counts` that represent the number of cars arriving at each interval are another classic example of time series data, where each data point is tied to a specific time.

Both the discrete time process and continuous time process examples covered in this section for traffic simulation can be used to:

- **Simulate traffic patterns:** Since it generates realistic data about how many cars arrive at different times of the hour or a day.
- **Analyze traffic:** Since it calculates useful statistics such as total cars, averages, and peak traffic.
- **Visualize traffic:** Since it creates a graph to make it easy to see trends, such as rush hours or quiet times.

This example lays the groundwork for more advanced time series analysis techniques, such as forecasting, decomposition, and statistical modeling.

Discrete and Continuous State

Now that we have looked at the time aspect of stochastic processes, let us further look at the State space concept of the stochastic processes.

For the same traffic stochastic processes, $X_{t,}$ the state space is the set of all possible values for the number of cars that X_t can have at any time t.

How State impacts traffic modeling?

Like time, the State space can also be classified into two types:

For instance, if we are tracking the length of the queue, such as the number of cars waiting at a traffic signal, then the discrete state space comes into the picture.

On the other hand, if we are tracking speed, position, or travel time, then the **`continuous`** state space comes into the picture.

Discrete-State

The discrete state space is countable. For example, {0, 1, 2, 3,...} represents the number of cars in a queue at a traffic signal.

The number of cars in a traffic signal can be written in a discrete state as:

$$Xt+1= Xt+ At+1-Dt+1$$

`Xt {0, 1, 2, …}` is the discrete state or the length of the queue at a traffic signal during time t.

`At+1` is the number of cars arriving at the traffic signal during the interval [t, t+1].

`Dt+1` is the number of cars departing the traffic signal during the interval [t, t+1].

To understand this further, let us simulate the discrete state space of our traffic example further by defining its mathematical function.

```
Code:
def simulate_discrete_queue(num_steps=50, lambd=2.0, capacity=3,
seed=None):
    if seed is not None:
        np.random.seed(seed)

    X = np.zeros(num_steps+1, dtype=int)

    for t in range(num_steps):
        arrivals = np.random.poisson(lambd)
        departures = min(X[t], capacity)
        X[t+1] = X[t] + arrivals - departures

    return X
```

In the preceding code, the function **simulate_discrete_queue** simulates a traffic signal system where cars arrive randomly at the signal. The traffic signal allows a fixed number of cars to pass during each time step. It also tracks how the number of cars waiting changes over time.

This function can be used in applications where we want to:

- Model traffic flows at intersections.
- Optimize traffic signal timing to reduce congestion.
- Predict how many cars will be waiting during peak hours.

Now that we have defined the discrete queue simulation, let us write a function to visualize it and understand what the traffic would look like.

Code:

```
def plot_queue(X, title="Discrete-State Queue Length"):
    plt.figure(figsize=(8, 4))
    plt.step(range(len(X)), X, where='post', marker='o')
    plt.title(title)
    plt.xlabel("Time Step")
    plt.ylabel("Number of Cars")
    plt.grid(True)
    plt.show()
X_discrete = simulate_discrete_queue(num_steps=30, lambd=2.0,
capacity=3, seed=42)
print('Discrete data',X_discrete)
```

The output of the simulated data is displayed as follows:

```
Discrete data [0 4 2 3 3 1 2 1 1 2 2 1 0 4 3 1 3 2 6 4 2 2 2 1 3
4 2 3 1 4 5]
```

Let us further look at the overview and plot of the simulated data as follows:

```
plot_queue(X_discrete, "Number of Cars in a Discrete-State Queue")
```

In the preceding code, our goal is to visualize how a line of cars at a traffic signal changes over time. The **plot_queue** function does exactly that—it creates a graph to show the number of cars waiting at the signal during each time step. The function takes a list of numbers (X) representing the number of cars waiting at the signal over time and turns it into a step-by-step graph.

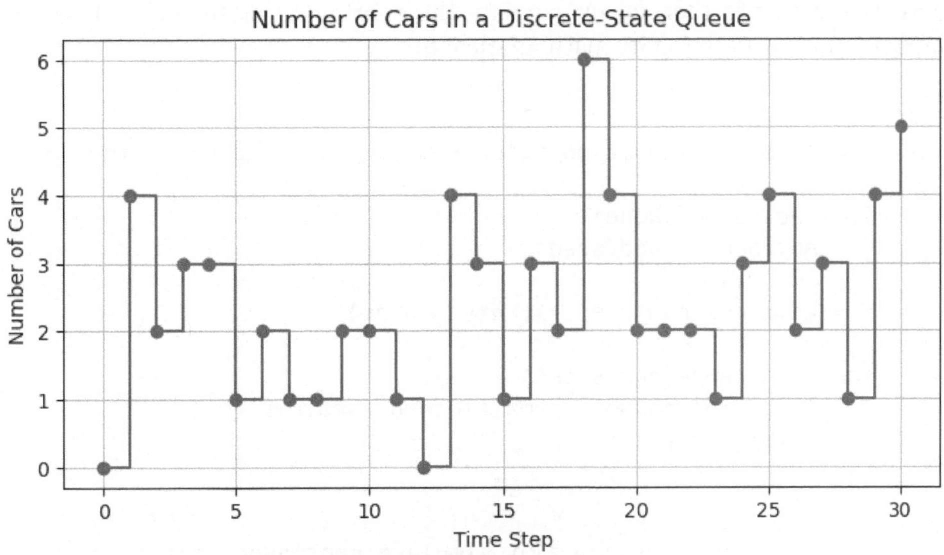

Figure 1.3: *Discrete State Queue*

Figure 1.3 shows:

- How the line of cars grows and shrinks.
- When the traffic signal lets cars through.
- How long the queue gets during peak times.

Let us now create a similar example for the continuous state process and review the traffic application of time series further.

Continuous State

The continuous space is an uncountable set, and it is usually referred to as R. For example, the exact location of the car on a highway can vary over a continuous range of real numbers.

The position of a car (in miles or kilometers) in continuous state space can be represented as:

$$Y_{t+1} = Y_t + Z_{t+1}$$

where:

$Y_t \in R$ the car can be in any real-valued position along the highway,

$Z_{t+1} \sim N(\mu, 2)$ is a normally distributed "step" that could capture acceleration, deceleration, or random fluctuations.

To understand this further, let us simulate the continuous state space of our traffic example further by defining its mathematical function.

Code:

```
def simulate_continuous_position(num_steps=50, mu=0.2, sigma=0.5,
seed=None):
    if seed is not None:
        np.random.seed(seed)

    Y = np.zeros(num_steps+1, dtype=float)

    for t in range(num_steps):
        step = np.random.normal(loc=mu, scale=sigma)
        Y[t+1] = Y[t] + step

    return Y
```

In the preceding code, the function **simulate_continuous_position** simulates real-world randomness in the movement of a car speeding up and slowing down unpredictably. The car's movement is random but follows a general trend (for example, it tends to move forward but sometimes slows down or even reverses slightly). The randomness is modeled using a normal distribution since it is a common distribution observed in most of the situations of daily traffic.

Now that we have created a function to track the position of the car on the highway over time, let us further create a function to visualize how far the car has traveled at each time step.

Code:

```
def plot_position(Y, title="Continuous-State Position"):
    plt.figure(figsize=(8, 4))
    plt.plot(range(len(Y)), Y, marker='o', linestyle='-')
    plt.title(title)
    plt.xlabel("Time Step")
    plt.ylabel("Position (miles)")
    plt.grid(True)
```

```
    plt.show()
Y_continuous = simulate_continuous_position(num_steps=30, mu=0.2, sigma=0.5, seed=42)
print('Y_continuous', Y_continuous)
```

The output of the simulated data is displayed as follows:

```
Y_continuous [0.         0.44835708 0.57922493 1.10306919 2.06458412 2.14750744
 2.23043896 3.22004537 3.80376273 3.76902554 4.24030556 4.20859671
 4.17573184 4.49671297 3.74007285 3.07761393 2.99647017 2.69005461
 3.04717827 2.79316624 2.28701439 3.21983877 3.30695062 3.54071472
 3.02834063 2.95614927 3.21161056 2.83611377 3.22396278 3.12364344
 3.17779656]
```

Let us further look at the overview and plot of the code as follows.

```
plot_position(Y_continuous, "Car Position in a Continuous-State in a highway")
```

In the preceding code, the **plot_position** function takes a list of positions of the car at different time steps as input and turns it into a line graph.

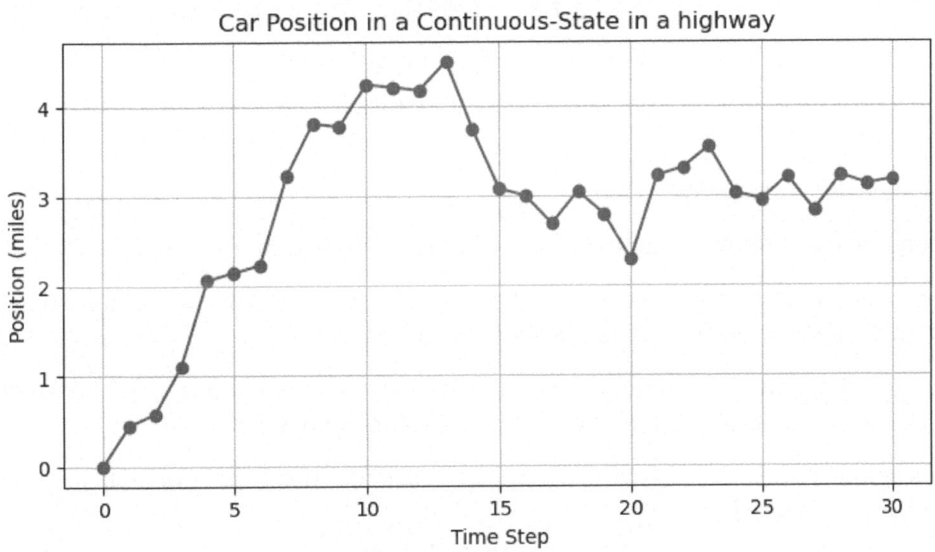

***Figure 1.4**: Continuous State Position*

Figure 1.4 shows:

- How the car's position changes over time.
- Whether the car is moving forward, backward, or staying still.
- The randomness or smoothness of the car's movement.

Now that we have looked at the time and state aspects of stochastic processes, let us further look at the type of stochastic processes that help in understanding the randomness of time series data.

Types of Stochastic Processes

The common types of stochastic processes, along with their mathematical workings, are discussed in this section.

Let us look at the common types of stochastic processes as follows:

1. Markov Chains
2. Poisson Processes
3. Brownian Motion
4. Random Walks

Markov Chains

A Markov chain is a type of stochastic process that satisfies the Markov property:

$$P(X_{n+1}=j \mid X_n=i, X_{n-1},\ldots, X_0)=P(X_{n+1}=j \mid X_n=i)$$

The probability of moving to a future state depends only on the current state and not on history.

From the traffic example,

X_n denotes the number of cars at a traffic signal at time step n.

The probability distribution of the number of cars at the next time step, X_{n+1}, depends only on X_n and not on the past states of the queue.

For simplicity of this example, let us make use of a simple set {0,1,2,3}. The model in this case has four states: state of 0 cars, 1 car, 2 cars, and 3 cars.

Let us define a transition matrix P, where each entry captures the probability of moving from state i to state j.

$$P_{i,j}=P(X_{n+1}=j \mid X_n=i)$$

A hypothetical transition matrix for this will look like:

$$P=\begin{bmatrix} 0.5 & 0.4 & 0.1 & 0.0 \\ 0.2 & 0.4 & 0.1 & 0.1 \\ 0.1 & 0.3 & 0.4 & 0.2 \\ 0.0 & 0.2 & 0.4 & 0.4 \end{bmatrix}$$

In this example $P_{1,2}=0.3$, which means that there is a 30% chance of going from 1 car to 2 cars in the next time step.

To understand this further, let us simulate the Markov chains on our traffic example further by defining its mathematical function.

Code:

```
def simulate_markov_chain(transition_matrix, initial_state, num_
steps=20, seed=None):
    if seed is not None:
        np.random.seed(seed)

    num_states = transition_matrix.shape[0]
    states = [initial_state]

    for _ in range(num_steps):
        current_state = states[-1]
        probs = transition_matrix[current_state]
        next_state = np.random.choice(num_states, p=probs)
        states.append(next_state)

    return states
```

In the preceding code, **simulate_markov_chain** function simulates the Markov chain that moves between different states by taking the probabilities of state change in the transition matrix as input.

Let us define the transition matrix as follows:

Code:

```
transition_matrix = np.array([
    [0.5, 0.4, 0.1, 0.0],
    [0.2, 0.4, 0.3, 0.1],
    [0.1, 0.3, 0.4, 0.2],
    [0.0, 0.2, 0.4, 0.4]
])
```

Let us further call the **simulate_markov_chain** function and review the results.

Code:

```
states = simulate_markov_chain(transition_matrix, initial_state=0,
num_steps=20, seed=42)
print('Simulated states', states)
print("=== Markov Chain Simulation for Traffic Queue ===")
print("Transition Matrix:\n", transition_matrix)
print("Simulated State Sequence:", states)
```

The preceding code generates the following output.

Code:

```
Simulated states [0, 0, 2, 2, 2, 1, 0, 0, 1, 2, 2, 0, 2, 3, 2, 1, 0,
0, 1, 1, 1]
=== Markov Chain Simulation for Traffic Queue ===
```

```
Transition Matrix:
 [[0.5 0.4 0.1 0. ]
 [0.2 0.4 0.3 0.1]
 [0.1 0.3 0.4 0.2]
 [0.  0.2 0.4 0.4]]
Simulated State Sequence: [0, 0, 2, 2, 2, 1, 0, 0, 1, 2, 2, 0, 2, 3,
2, 1, 0, 0, 1, 1, 1]
```

Simulated state sequence is the simulated sequence of the number of cars transitioning from one state to another based on the probability matrix.

Let us define a function to visualize how the Markov chain states behave.

Code:

```
def plot_markov_chain_states(states, title="Markov Chain States Over
Time"):
    plt.figure(figsize=(8, 4))
    plt.step(range(len(states)), states, where='post', marker='o')
    plt.title(title)
    plt.xlabel('Time Step')
    plt.ylabel('Queue Length')
    plt.ylim(-0.5, max(states) + 0.5)
    plt.grid(True)
    plt.show()
plot_markov_chain_states(states, title="Number of Cars at a Traffic
Signal (Markov Chain)")
```

The preceding code takes a list of states from a Markov Chain simulation as inputs and creates a step plot.

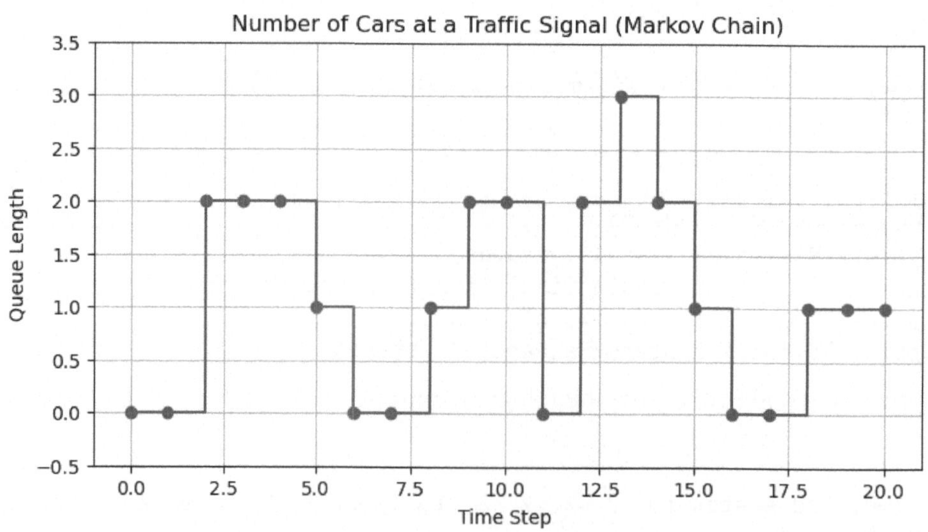

Figure 1.5: *Markov Chain State Space*

Figure 1.5 demonstrates the number of cars simulated by the Markov chain at each time step.

Having discussed Markov chains as one type of stochastic process, we now turn to another type—the Poisson process.

Poisson Process

A Poisson process is a stochastic process that models the number of cars arriving or events occurring at any point in time.

In a Poisson process, the rate is the rate at which events happen at any point in time. In this case, the number of cars arriving at the traffic signal at any unit of time is calculated at the rate of λ cars per unit time. It can be defined as follows.

$$Nt-Ns \sim Poisson(\lambda t-s)$$

where:

> **N(t)** is the number of cars arriving at time t, and
>
> **N(s)** is the number of cars arriving at time s

For $0 \leq s \leq t$.

Similarly, the number of arrivals in the interval (0,t) will be:

$$Nt \sim Poisson(\lambda t)$$

This can be rewritten into the Poisson probability function as follows:

$$PNt=k=(\lambda t)kk!\ e-\lambda t$$

where:

P(k) = the probability of k arrivals in an interval, and

λt = mean number of arrivals in an interval.

Properties of Poisson Process

The following are the two most important properties of the Poisson process that make it ideal for simulating the car arrivals at a traffic signal:

- **Memoryless Arrivals:** The car arrivals according to the Poisson process will occur randomly over time with no memory of how long it has been since the last arrival.
- **Stationary Increments:** During a stable period over the day, the arrival rate might roughly be constant over time.

To understand this further, let us simulate the Poisson Process on our traffic example further by defining its mathematical function.

Code:

```
def simulate_poisson_process(rate, max_time, seed=None):
    if seed is not None:
        np.random.seed(seed)

    arrival_times = []
    current_time = 0.0

    while True:
        interarrival = np.random.exponential(scale=1.0/rate)
        current_time += interarrival

        if current_time > max_time:
            break
        arrival_times.append(current_time)

    return arrival_times
```

In the preceding code, **simulate_poisson_process** function simulates car arrivals at a traffic signal over a period of time. It models the arrivals as a Poisson process, which is a common way to describe random events such as cars arriving at a certain average rate. It takes in **rate** as one of the inputs, which is the average number of cars arriving per unit of time. It also takes in **max_time** as input, which is the total time for this simulation. This function returns a list of arrival times for the cars. The time between arrivals follows an exponential distribution, which is a key property of Poisson processes.

Code:

```
rate = 2.0
max_time = 10.0
seed = 42

arrivals = simulate_poisson_process(rate, max_time, seed=seed)
print("Number of arrivals:", len(arrivals))
print("Arrival times:", arrivals)
```

This function can be called by providing the required inputs for **rate**, **max_time**, and **seed** (random seed value).

Output:

```
Number of arrivals: 23
Arrival times: [0.23463404498842955, 1.7396947604471902,
2.398067607219915, 2.8545388841078916, 2.939351319339065,
3.024149465296367, 3.0540688496007076, 4.059684281840678,
4.51922535865431, 5.134850389506606, 5.145250043506175,
6.897028781085331, 7.790243552762669, 7.909587365387142,
```

```
8.009926859761974, 8.111232571178101, 8.29260943590834,
8.664573351338767, 8.947341884728935, 9.119453381005906,
9.592638817955805, 9.667756082319475, 9.840513838320676]
```

The **simulate_poisson_process** function has generated the time of arrivals as output.

In the next step, let us define a function to plot the Poisson process.

Code:

```
def plot_poisson_arrivals(arrival_times, max_time):
    fig, ax = plt.subplots(figsize=(8, 1.5))

    ax.hlines(y=1, xmin=0, xmax=max_time, color='black')
    for t in arrival_times:
        ax.plot(t, 1, marker='o', color='red')

    ax.set_ylim(0.8, 1.2)
    ax.set_xlim(0, max_time)
    ax.set_xlabel("Time")
    ax.set_title("Poisson Process Arrivals")
    plt.show()
plot_poisson_arrivals(arrivals, max_time)
```

In the preceding code, the function **plot_poisson_arrivals** visualizes the car arrival times generated by the **simulate_poisson_process** function. It creates a timeline plot where each car arrival is marked as a red dot along a horizontal line. This makes it easy to see when cars arrive over time.

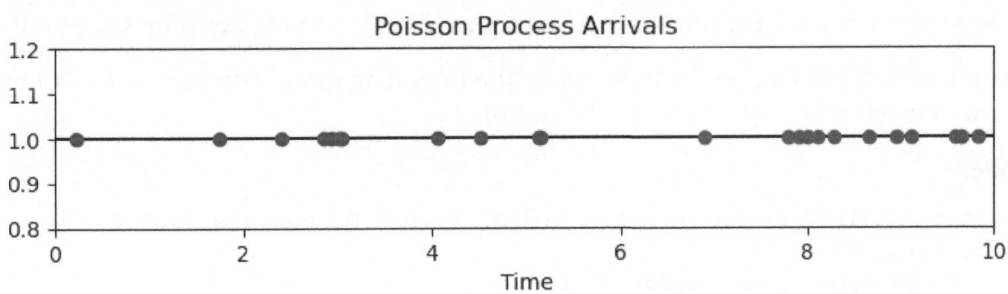

Figure 1.6: *Poisson Process Arrivals*

Figure 1.6 shows a **timeline** plot of car arrival times. It uses a horizontal line to represent time and red dots to mark arrivals. This plot helps to visualize the random events of car arrivals at a traffic signal.

Randomness in discrete time intervals is well captured by the Poisson distribution. The Poisson distribution is suitable for both discrete and continuous time series data. Let us further look at another stochastic process that is well-suited for continuous time intervals and continuous states.

Brownian Motion

Brownian motion or Wiener process is a stochastic process that can be used to understand the randomness in continuous-time and continuous-state time series data.

Standard Brownian motion is defined as follows:

Let Wtt≥0 be a standard Brownian motion. Then, for each increment Δt:

$$Wt+\Delta t- Wt \sim N(0, \Delta t)$$

Over multiple increments:

$$Wt = k=1n(Wtk- Wtk-1),$$

where:

each (Wtk- Wtk-1) - increment is independent, and

~ N(0, tk- tk-1) - increments are normally distributed.

The randomness in Brownian motion can be either positive or negative, and it can be unpredictable. For our traffic example, this randomness can go only in a positive direction since the movement of a car on a highway is in a forward direction. The Brownian motion, being the randomness in continuous-state and continuous-time, can be applied to either the speed or the position of the car. Even though the movement of vehicles in traffic is strategic and is not totally uncertain and not a Brownian example, we will apply this concept to understand Brownian motion in general, since it is one of the stochastic processes that can impact time series data.

To understand this further, let us simulate the Brownian motion on our traffic example further by defining its mathematical function.

Code:

```
def simulate_brownian_motion(total_time=1.0, num_steps=1000,
seed=None):
    if seed is not None:
        np.random.seed(seed)

    dt = total_time / num_steps
    times = np.linspace(0, total_time, num_steps+1)

    increments = np.sqrt(dt) * np.random.randn(num_steps)

    W = np.zeros(num_steps+1)
    for i in range(1, num_steps+1):
        W[i] = W[i-1] + increments[i-1]

    return times, W
```

In the preceding code, the function **simulate_brownian_motion** simulates Brownian motion, also called a Wiener process. In the context of traffic, this code is for modeling the random fluctuations in the position of the car in traffic flow over time. The function returns two arrays: one for the time points and one for the corresponding values of the Brownian motion.

This function can be called by providing the required inputs for **total_time**, **num_steps**, and **seed** (random seed value).

Code:

```
times, W = simulate_brownian_motion(total_time=1.0, num_steps=1000,
seed=42)
print("=== Brownian Motion Simulation ===")
print(f"Final time: {times[-1]}")
print(f"Final position W(1.0) = {W[-1]:.4f}")
print(f"Mean of increments (should be close to 0): {np.mean
(np.diff(W)):.4f}")
print(f"Var of increments (should be close to dt): {np.var
(np.diff(W)):.4f}")
```

The **simulate_brownian_motion** function has generated the time and positions of the car as output.

```
=== Brownian Motion Simulation ===
Final time: 1.0
Final position W(1.0) = 0.6113
Mean of increments (should be close to 0): 0.0006
Var of increments (should be close to dt): 0.0010
```

In the next step, let us define a function to plot the Brownian motion.

Code:

```
def plot_brownian_motion(times, W, title="Brownian Motion
Simulation"):
    plt.figure(figsize=(10, 4))
    plt.plot(times, W, label="W(t)")
    plt.title(title)
    plt.xlabel("Time")
    plt.ylabel("Position (W(t))")
    plt.grid(True)
    plt.legend()
    plt.show()
plot_brownian_motion(times, W)
```

In the preceding code, the function **plot_brownian_motion** visualizes the results of a Brownian motion simulation. It takes the time points and the corresponding values of the Brownian motion as input and creates a line graph to show how the position of the car changes over time. This makes it easy to see the random fluctuations of the process.

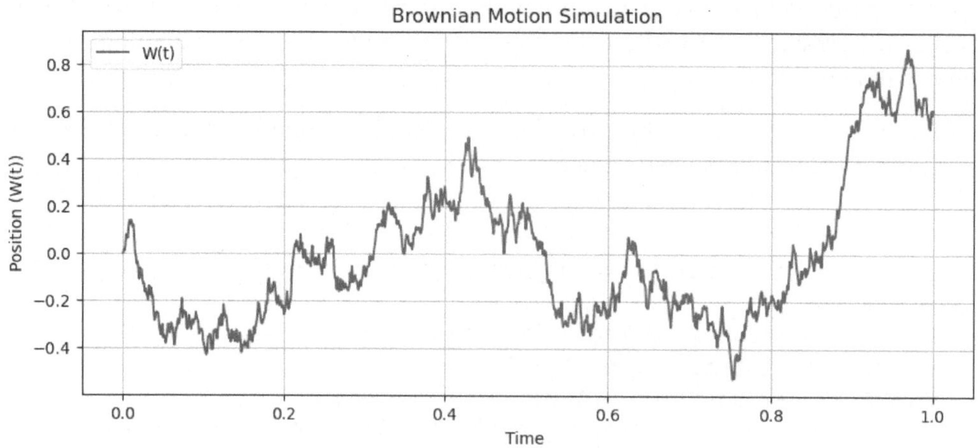

Figure 1.7: *Brownian Motion Arrivals*

Figure 1.7 shows a line graph of Brownian motion over time, with time on the x-axis and the position of the car due to Brownian motion on the y-axis.

Randomness in continuous time intervals and continuous state is well captured by Brownian motion. Let us further look at another slightly different stochastic process that is also well-suited for discrete time intervals, but can also be used for continuous time.

Random Walk

Random walk is one of the simplest stochastic processes and is suitable for discrete time intervals for capturing features such as speed and position of the car, rather than arrivals. In Random walk, each new state depends on the previous state plus some random increment.

Random walk can be defined as follows:

$$X_{t+1} = X_t + S_{t+1}$$

where, S_{t+1} is a random variable and each step in a state space can either move forward or backward.

Similar to the Brownian movement, the Random walk is also not a real-life scenario for the traffic example, but will be covered for conceptual understanding of one of the possible stochastic processes.

Let X_t be the position of a car at discrete time steps t = 0, 1, 2,...

$$X_{t+1} = X_t + S_{t+1}$$

where:

X0 is the initial position of the car,

St+1 is a random step where,

`St+1= {+1, with probability p,-1, with probability (1-p).`

To understand this further, let us simulate the Random Walk on our traffic example further by defining its mathematical function.

Code:

```
def simulate_random_walk(num_steps=50, p=0.5, seed=None):
    if seed is not None:
        np.random.seed(seed)

    positions = np.zeros(num_steps + 1, dtype=int)

    for t in range(1, num_steps + 1):
        step = 1 if np.random.rand() < p else -1
        positions[t] = positions[t-1] + step

    return positions
```

In the preceding code, the function **simulate_random_walk** simulates a 1-dimensional random walk. For a car moving in traffic, at each step, it can either move forward (+1) or backward (-1). The direction it moves is assumed to be random, but the probability of moving forward is given by p. This function returns the positions of the car at each step.

This function can be called by providing the required inputs for **num_steps**, probability, and seed (random seed value).

Code:

```
positions = simulate_random_walk(num_steps=50, p=0.6, seed=42)
print("Final position:", positions[-1])
```

The **simulate_random_walk** function has generated the positions of the car as output.

```
Final position: 18
```

In the next step, let us define a function to plot the Random walk.

Code:

```
def plot_random_walk(positions, title="Random Walk of a Vehicle"):
    plt.figure(figsize=(8, 4))
    plt.plot(positions, marker='o', label='Position')
    plt.axhline(y=0, color='gray', linestyle='--', alpha=0.5)
```

```
        plt.title(title)
        plt.xlabel("Time Step")
        plt.ylabel("Block Number")
        plt.grid(True)
        plt.legend()
        plt.show()
    plot_random_walk(positions, "Car's Random Walk Along City Blocks")
```

In the preceding code, the function **plot_random_walk** visualizes the results of the random walk simulation of a car in our traffic example. It takes the positions of the car at each time step as input and creates a line graph to show how the position changes over time. This makes it easy to see the random movement of the car.

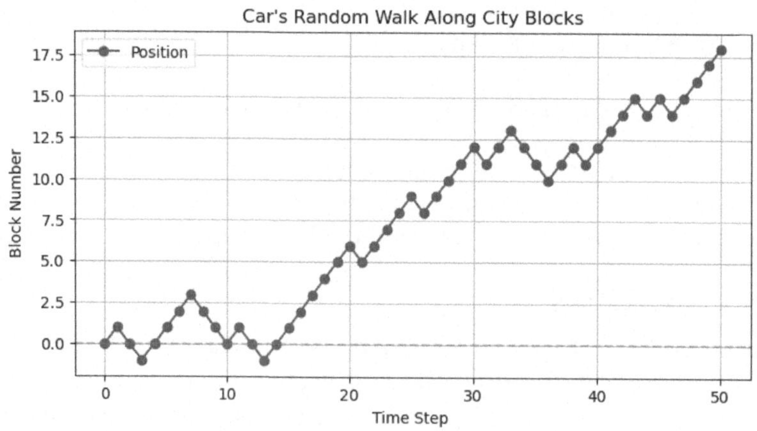

***Figure 1.8**: Random Walk Positions*

Figure 1.8 shows a line graph of Random Walk over discrete time steps with time on the x-axis and the position of the car due to Random Walk on the y-axis.

Comparison of Stochastic Processes

Having explored each stochastic process in detail, Markov chains, Poisson processes, Brownian motion, and random walks, this final section consolidates their key differences and unifies their theoretical foundations. These processes vary in their treatment of time (discrete versus continuous), state space (discrete versus continuous), and the nature of their randomness (memoryless transitions, event-driven jumps, Gaussian noise, or binomial steps).

Let us make a quick comparison of all the 4 types of stochastic processes covered in this chapter.

Characteristic	Markov Chain	Poisson Process	Brownian Motion	Random Walk
Time Domain	Discrete or Continuous	Discrete or Continuous	Continuous	Discrete
State Space	Discrete	Discrete (Counts)	Continuous	Discrete (typically integers)
Markov Property	Yes	Not required, but can be embedded	Not strictly, but can be embedded	Yes
Nature of Increments	Depends on transition probabilities	Stationarity and independent	Independent and normally distributed	Independent with probability p for +1 and 1-p for -1

Table 1.1: *Comparison of Stochastic Processes*

All these types of stochastic processes form the basis of measuring time series data and are further used in applications of forecasting time series and performing predictive analytics on the data. By understanding how data evolves, whether it arrives at random intervals as in Poisson, fluctuates continuously as in Brownian, or updates in discrete steps with memoryless transitions as in Markov, we can build models to predict future values or states.

Conclusion

In this chapter, we learned about an overview of the mathematical foundations of time series data, and we looked at the applications of stochastic processes with a traffic example.

We also looked at the concepts of discrete and continuous time and state in the domain of time series. We compared 4 different types of stochastic processes and analyzed them with examples as well as codes.

In the next chapter, we will look at the mathematical concepts behind data analysis, preparation, and visualization of time series in Python with examples and code.

References

- Komkov, V. and Dannon, V. (1991) Random walk simulation of chemical reactions represented by nonlinear reaction-diffusion equations, ZAMM - *Journal of Applied Mathematics and Mechanics / Zeitschrift für Angewandte Mathematik und Mechanik*, 71(3), pp. 103–110. Available at: https://doi.org/10.1002/zamm.19910710302.

- Trajstman, A.C. (2002) A Markov chain model for Newcastle disease and its relevance to the intracerebral pathogenicity index, *Biometrical Journal*, 44(1), pp. 43–57. Available at: https://doi.org/10.1002/1521-4036(200201)44:1<43::aid-bimj43>3.0.co;2-3.
- Addison, P.S., Qu, B., Nisbet, A. and Pender, G. (1997) A non-Fickian, particle-tracking diffusion model based on fractional Brownian motion, *International Journal for Numerical Methods in Fluids*, 25(12), pp. 1373–1384. Available at: https://doi.org/10.1002/(sici)1097-0363(19971230)25:12<1373::aid-fld620>3.0.co;2-6.
- Anderson, D.R., Sweeney, D.J., Williams, T.A., Camm, J.D., and Cochran, J.J. (2019) *Statistics for Business & Economics*. 14th edn. Boston: *Cengage Learning*, pp. 258–260.

Chapter 2
Preparing Time Series Data

Introduction

Stationarity is one of the most fundamental ideas in time series analysis. The idea behind the stationarity of a time series data is that the statistical properties of a process, such as the mean, variance, and autocorrelation of the time series, stay consistent over time. We can think of it as a process that does not undergo dramatic changes as time progresses. This means that the behavior of such time series remains stable and predictable. This stability is incredibly valuable because it makes analyzing and modeling time series far more manageable. Many widely used models, such as ARIMA, rely on the assumption of stationarity or require us to tweak the data through techniques such as differencing or de-trending before the model can be applied effectively.

In the real world, the time series captured data rarely conforms to perfect stationarity. Trends, seasonal patterns, or sudden shifts caused by economic, environmental, or social factors often disrupt the stability of a time series. For example, external macroeconomic factors can suddenly spike stock prices. Hence, stationarity of a time series need not always be strong. Time series data can show patterns of alternate forms of stationarity, which will be explored in this chapter.

In this chapter, we will take a deep dive into the different types of stationarity: strict (strong) stationarity, weak (covariance) stationarity, trend stationarity, and difference stationarity. We will then break down their mathematical definitions and highlight why they matter in real-world applications. Thus, whether we are dealing with financial data, climate records, or sales trends, understanding these concepts will help in making sense of the time series and prepare it for analysis.

By the end of this chapter, readers will be able to differentiate between various types of stationarity in time series, including strict stationarity, weak stationarity, trend stationarity, and difference stationarity, understanding their definitions, distinctions, and implications for modeling. The readers will also be able to understand the mathematical formulation behind each type of stationarity and how they translate to real-world time series behavior in domains such as finance, climatology, and economics.

Structure

In this chapter, the following topics will be covered:

- Types of Stationarity
  - Strict (Strong) Stationarity
  - Weak (Covariance) Stationarity
  - Trend Stationarity
  - Difference Stationarity

Types of Stationarity

Stationarity is one of the most important concepts in time series analysis. It plays a key role in helping us understand and model data that evolves over time. This section covers different types of stationarity that can be observed in time series data.

Strong Stationarity

Among the different types of stationarity, Strong Stationarity is the most desired form for a perfect time series dataset. Strong stationarity is also known as Strict Stationarity. A time series is considered strongly stationary if the joint distribution of any group of observations stays the same, no matter how far we shift it in time. In simpler terms, this means that every statistical feature of the series, whether it is the overall shape of its distribution, its average value, its variability, or even how its values relate to each other over time, remains constant.

Imagine looking at the time series data today, yesterday, or a year from now; its underlying behavior would look statistically identical. While strong stationarity represents an ideal form of consistency, it is often too strict to be fully satisfied by real-world data.

Trends, seasonal patterns, and other irregularities usually get in the way. Despite this, strong stationarity is very valuable as a theoretical concept. It provides a solid foundation for mathematical analysis and supports many key results in fields such as stochastic processes and econometrics, even if we rarely encounter it in practice since a strong stationarity data is highly consistent in nature.

An example of strong stationary data can be: The daily returns of the USD or EUR rate calculated as percentage changes, in stable economic environments, since they tend to hover around a stable average with consistent variability, as long as there are no major economic shifts.

Mathematical Explanation

Strong stationarity can be defined as follows:

Imagine a stochastic process $\{X_t\}$. $\{X_t\}$ is considered to be strongly stationary if for any number of time points $t_1, t_2, ..., t_k$ and for any time shift τ, the joint cumulative distribution function (CDF) of the observations at times $t_1, t_2, ..., t_k$ is identical to the joint CDF at times shifted by . The joint CDF captures the combined behavior of multiple random variables. It tells us how likely it is that all the variables will simultaneously take on values less than or equal to certain thresholds. The joint CDF captures the combined behavior of multiple random variables. It tells us how likely it is that all the variables will simultaneously take on values less than or equal to certain thresholds.

This can be mathematically defined as follows:

$$F_{X_{t_1},X_{t_2},...,X_{t_k}}(x_1,x_2,...,x_k) = F_{X_{t_1+\tau},X_{t_2+\tau},...,X_{t_k+\tau}}(x_1,x_2,...,x_k)$$

This means the probability structure of the process is invariant under time shifts, ensuring that all statistical properties remain consistent over time. This condition holds true for any arbitrary selection of times and any shift .

It is worth noting that this is much more demanding than weak stationarity, which only requires certain properties of the time series data to stay constant over time. Strong stationarity goes further, ensuring that every statistical aspect of the process, including higher-order moments and complex dependencies, remains unchanged. This makes it a much more comprehensive and theoretically powerful concept, even if it is rarely fully met in real-world datasets.

Implementing the Math as a Python Function

In this section, let us write Python code to check if a time series is strongly stationary. As seen earlier, strong stationarity means that the statistical properties of the series do not change over time.

To perform this, we will first split the series into segments and compare their distributions. If the distributions are similar across segments, we assume the series is approximately strongly stationary.

The Empirical Cumulative Distribution Function (ECDF) is a way to estimate the true cumulative distribution of a dataset. It tells us the proportion of data points that are less than or equal to a given value. Let us define the ECDF function as follows:

Code:

```
def empirical_cdf(data, x):
    count = 0
    for point in data:
        if point <= x:
            count += 1
    return count / len(data)
```

In the preceding code,

- For a given value x, the **empirical_cdf** function counts how many points in the data are less than or equal to x.
- It then divides this count by the total number of points to get the proportion, which is the probability.
- For example, if data = [1, 2, 3, 4] and x = 2, the ECDF at x = 2 is 0.5 because half the data points are ≤ 2.

The next function calculates the maximum difference between the ECDFs of two segments. This is similar to the Kolmogorov–Smirnov (K–S) test, which compares two distributions. The Kolmogorov–Smirnov (K–S) test will be discussed in the upcoming chapters of this book.

Code:

```
def max_ecdf_diff(segment1, segment2):
    combined_data = segment1 + segment2
    combined_data.sort()
    max_diff = 0
    for x in combined_data:
        ecdf1 = empirical_cdf(segment1, x)
        ecdf2 = empirical_cdf(segment2, x)
        diff = abs(ecdf1 - ecdf2)
        if diff > max_diff:
            max_diff = diff
    return max_diff
```

In the preceding code,

- The two segments are combined into one sorted list.
- For each point in the combined list, the ECDF is computed for both segments.
- The maximum absolute difference between the two ECDFs is then calculated.
- The maximum difference then tells us how far apart the two distributions are.

The next function checks if the time series is approximately strongly stationary by comparing the distributions of its segments.

Code:

```
def is_strongly_stationary(series, n_segments=3, threshold=0.1):
    series = list(series)
    segment_length = len(series) // n_segments
    segments = []
    for i in range(n_segments):
        start = i * segment_length
        if i == n_segments - 1:
            segments.append(series[start:])
        else:
            segments.append(series[start:start + segment_length])
    for i in range(n_segments):
        for j in range(i + 1, n_segments):
            max_diff = max_ecdf_diff(segments[i], segments[j])
            if max_diff > threshold:
                return False
    return True
```

In the preceding code,

- The input time series data is split into **n_segments**.
- For each pair of segments, the maximum ECDF difference is computed using **max_ecdf_diff**.
- If the maximum difference exceeds a threshold, the series is considered non-stationary.
- If all segment pairs have differences below the threshold, the series is approximately strongly stationary.

Real-World Example

Consider daily average temperature data collected at a specific weather station over multiple years. Climate scientists and meteorologists often seek patterns and changes in climate behavior over extended periods.

In an ideal scenario with no climatic trends or seasonality, daily temperatures would statistically behave the same way over different intervals, reflecting strong stationarity. Practically, however, seasonal cycles, global warming trends, or unusual climate events typically violate strict stationarity.

To empirically verify if temperature patterns remain statistically invariant over different segments, for example, for comparing distributions across years or seasons, we can perform an approximate strong stationarity test as described.

Python Implementation for Strong Stationarity Check on Temperature Data

In this example, let us generate synthetic daily temperature data for over 3 years, add a realistic seasonal pattern, and then check for stationarity. Let us also demonstrate how to handle seasonality by applying seasonal differencing and re-checking stationarity.

In the following code, we will create a synthetic dataset that mimics daily temperature readings over 3 years.

Code:

```
import numpy as np
import matplotlib.pyplot as plt
np.random.seed(0)
days_per_year = 365
total_years = 3
total_days = days_per_year * total_years
```

Let us further generate baseline temperature as follows.

Code:

```
baseline_temperature = np.random.normal(20, 3, total_days)
```

In the preceding code,

The baseline temperature is generated using a normal distribution with:

- Mean = 20°C as average temperature.
- Standard deviation = 3°C as variability in temperature.

This represents the stationary part of the data, as it fluctuates randomly around 20°C.

Let us then generate a seasonal component as follows.

Code:

```
seasonal_component = 10 * np.sin(2 * np.pi * np.arange(total_days) /
days_per_year)
```

In the preceding code,

A seasonal pattern is added to simulate real-world temperature changes over the year:

- The pattern is modeled using a sine wave with an amplitude of 10°C.
- The sine wave completes one full cycle every 365 days, mimicking the annual rise and fall of temperatures.

Let us further combine the baseline data with the seasonal component.

Code:

```
temperature_data = baseline_temperature + seasonal_component
```

In the preceding code,

- The final temperature data is created by adding the baseline temperature and the seasonal component.
- This makes the data non-stationary because the mean temperature changes over time due to the seasonal pattern.

Let us review the generated temperature data by visualizing it.

Code:

```
plt.figure(figsize=(12, 4))
plt.plot(temperature_data)
plt.title('Synthetic Daily Temperature Data with Seasonal Pattern')
plt.xlabel('Days')
plt.ylabel('Temperature (°C)')
plt.show()
```

The preceding code plots the synthetic temperature data to visualize the seasonal pattern.

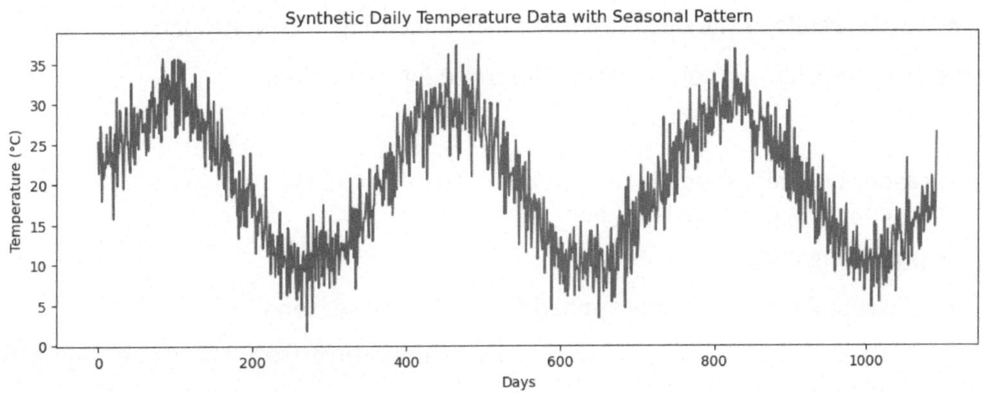

Figure 2.1: *Temperature with Seasonality*

In *Figure* 2.1,

- The x-axis represents days over 3 years.
- The y-axis represents temperature in °C.
- The plot shows a wavy pattern due to the seasonal component, with random fluctuations around it.

In the next step, let us check for approximate strong stationarity in the temperature data that has a seasonal component.

Code:

```
stationarity_result = is_strongly_stationary(temperature_data, n_
segments=5, threshold=0.2)
print(f"Approximate Strong Stationarity of raw data: {stationari-
ty_result}")
```

In the preceding code,

- The **is_strongly_stationary** function checks if the raw temperature data is approximately strongly stationary:
- It splits the data into 5 segments and compares their distributions using the ECDF (Empirical Cumulative Distribution Function).

Output:

```
Approximate Strong Stationarity of raw data: False
```

In the preceding output,

- Since the data has a strong seasonal pattern, the distributions of the segments will differ significantly.
- This results in the output being False, indicating non-stationarity.

In the next step, let us apply seasonal differencing to the data.

Code:

```
seasonally_adjusted_data = temperature_data[days_per_year:] -
temperature_data[:-days_per_year]
```

In the preceding code,

- Seasonal differencing is applied to handle the seasonality.
- Seasonal differencing subtracts the temperature from the same day in the previous year.
- For example, the temperature on day 366 is subtracted from the temperature on day 1, day 367 from day 2, and so on.
- This removes the seasonal pattern, leaving behind the stationary part of the data.

Let us further plot the seasonally adjusted data.

Code:

```
plt.figure(figsize=(12, 4))
plt.plot(seasonally_adjusted_data)
plt.title('Seasonally Differenced Temperature Data')
plt.xlabel('Days')
plt.ylabel('Differenced Temperature (°C)')
plt.show()
```

In the preceding code,

- The x-axis represents days. It shows 2 years of data, since the first year is used for differencing.
- The y-axis represents the differenced temperature in °C.

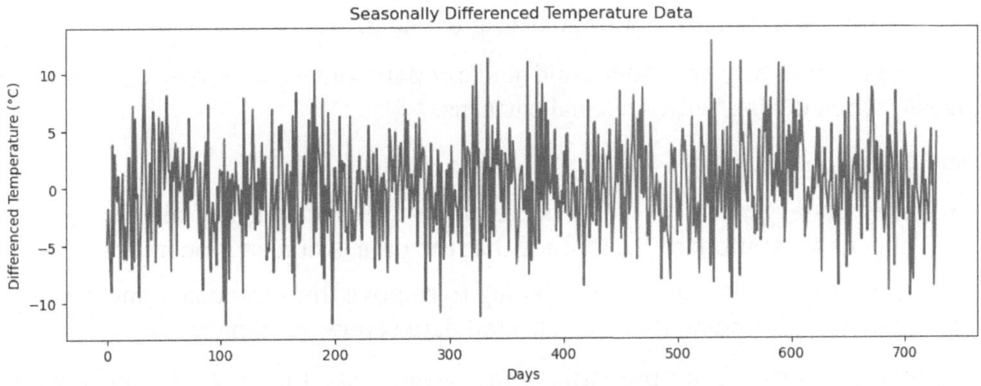

Figure 2.2: *Seasonally Adjusted Data*

The plot in *Figure* 2.2 shows random fluctuations, indicating that the seasonal pattern has been removed.

Let us further recheck the stationarity of adjusted temperature data.

Code:

```
stationarity_result_adjusted = is_strongly_stationary(seasonally_
adjusted_data, n_segments=5, threshold=0.2)
print(f"Approximate Strong Stationarity of seasonally adjusted:
{stationarity_result_adjusted}")
```

In the preceding code,

- The function **is_strongly_stationary** checks if the seasonally differenced data is approximately strongly stationary:
- It splits the adjusted data into 5 segments and compares their distributions.

Output:

```
Approximate Strong Stationarity of seasonally adjusted: True
```

In the preceding output,

- Since the seasonal pattern has been removed, the distributions of the segments will be similar.
- The results indicate that the output is True, indicating strong stationarity.

This example demonstrates how to:

- Simulate realistic time series data with seasonality.
- Check for stationarity and identify non-stationarity caused by seasonality.
- Handle seasonality using seasonal differencing.
- Re-check stationarity after adjusting the data.

This is a practical way to understand and prepare time series data for modeling, especially when dealing with seasonal patterns.

To summarize,

- This code generates synthetic temperature data with a seasonal pattern, checks for stationarity, and finds that the data is non-stationary.
- It then applies seasonal differencing to remove the seasonality and re-checks stationarity, finding that the adjusted data is now stationary.

This process is crucial for preparing time series data for analysis and modeling, especially when seasonality is present.

Strong or strict stationarity is a key concept in time series analysis, serving as a theoretical gold standard. It requires that the statistical properties of a time series, such as its distribution, mean, and variance, remain completely unchanged no matter how far we shift it in time. This level of consistency makes it a powerful tool for simplifying theoretical work. However, in the real world, data rarely meets these strict conditions. Trends, seasonal patterns, and sudden changes often disrupt the stability of time series, making strong stationarity more of an ideal than a reality.

Because of this, we often rely on approximations or weaker forms of stationarity, such as covariance stationarity, which only requires the mean, variance, and autocovariance to stay constant over time. With this understanding, let us dive into the concept of Weak Stationarity.

Weak Stationarity

At its core, stationarity represents a fundamental assumption in time series analysis that a dataset's statistical properties remain consistent throughout time. Among the various forms of stationarity, weak stationarity, also known as covariance stationarity, serves as the most practical and widely used version in applications.

Weak stationarity simplifies the strict requirements of strong stationarity by focusing on just two key characteristics:

- A constant mean that does not drift over time.
- A stable covariance structure where relationships between points depend only on their time separation or lag and not their absolute position.

More specifically, a time series qualifies as weakly stationary when it meets three essential conditions:

- **Constant central tendency:** The average value remains unchanged throughout the series.
- **Stable dispersion:** The variance maintains a consistent and finite magnitude.
- **Lag-dependent relationships:** The covariance between observations depends exclusively on their time difference.

This balanced approach makes weak stationarity, particularly valuable for real-world applications. It provides sufficient stability for reliable modeling and forecasting while remaining flexible enough to accommodate many practical datasets. This explains why foundational time series models such as ARMA and ARIMA are built on weak stationarity assumptions. They capture enough consistency for meaningful analysis without imposing unrealistic constraints on the data.

The distinction between weak and strong stationarity, ultimately reflects a practical compromise in statistical modeling. We maintain enough structure to draw valid conclusions while acknowledging that real-world data rarely satisfies ideal theoretical conditions.

Mathematical Explanation

Week stationarity can be defined as follows:

A stochastic process $\{X_t\}$ is considered weakly stationary if it meets three key mathematical conditions:

Constant Mean:

$$E(X_t) = \mu, \textit{for all } t$$

Constant Variance:

$$Var(X_t) = \sigma^2, \textit{for all } t$$

Autocovariance depends only on Lag:

$$Cov(X_{t,} X_{t+h}) = \gamma(h), \textit{for all } t, h$$

Here, is the autocovariance function, which measures how strongly a value at time relates to a value, steps ahead.

Weak stationarity ensures that a time series maintains statistical consistency in its mean and variance. This makes it suitable for modeling and forecasting. Strong stationarity imposes stricter distributional requirements while weak stationarity provides a more flexible but robust foundation for time series analysis.

Implementing the Math as a Python Function

In this section, let us write Python code to check if a time series is weakly stationary. As seen earlier, Weak stationarity means that some of the statistical properties of the series do not change over time.

To perform this, we will first write a code that helps determine if a time series is weakly stationary by examining whether its mean and variance remain roughly constant over time.

Let us first start with defining two helper functions to calculate the mean and variance.

Code:

```
def compute_mean(data):
    total = 0
    for value in data:
        total += value
    return total / len(data)
```

In the preceding code,

- The function **compute_mean** is a simple function that calculates the average of a dataset.
- It first adds up all the numbers.
- Then, it divides the sum by the number of data points.

In the next step, let us define another function to compute the variance.

Code:

```
def compute_variance(data):
    mean = compute_mean(data)
    total = 0
    for value in data:
        total += (value - mean) ** 2
    return total / (len(data) - 1)
```

In the preceding code,

- The function **compute_variance** measures how spread out the data is around its mean.
- It first calculates the average of the data by calling the function **compute_mean**.
- And then for each value, computes its squared deviation from the mean.
- Finally, it averages the squared deviations.

In the next step, let us define a function to check if a time series is weakly stationary.

Code:

```
def is_weakly_stationary(series, segments=3, mean_thresh=0.1,
var_thresh=0.1):
    n = len(series)
    seg_len = n // segments
    means = []
    variances = []

    for i in range(segments):
        start = i * seg_len
        end = (i + 1) * seg_len if i != segments - 1 else n
        segment = series[start:end]
        means.append(compute_mean(segment))
        variances.append(compute_variance(segment))

    mean_range = max(means) - min(means)
    var_range = max(variances) - min(variances)

    if mean_range > mean_thresh or var_range > var_thresh:
        return False
    else:
        return True
```

In the preceding code,

The function **is_weakly_stationary** checks if a time series is weakly stationary.

1. In the first step, the function compares the mean and variance across different segments of the data by:
    a. Dividing the time series data into equal segments.
    b. For example, if the data size is 300, then the series splits into 3 segments of 100 points each.
2. In the next step, the Segment Statistics are calculated by:
    a. Computing the mean and variance of each segment and
    b. Storing them in means and variances lists.
3. In the next step, check for consistency of the segments by:
    a. Calculating the mean and the range (max - min) of the segment.
    b. Checking if the range exceeds a predefined mean threshold.

If the mean is drifting, the series is non-stationary.

4. Similarly, check for consistency of the variance of each segment by:
    a. Calculating the variance and the range (max - min) of the segment.
    b. Checking if the range exceeds a predefined variance threshold.

If the variance is large, then there is unstable volatility in the series, and it is non-stationary.

5. If both the mean and variance ranges are within thresholds,
    a. then the series is weakly stationary.
    b. Otherwise, it is non-stationary.

Let us review this implementation further by applying it to an example.

Real-World Example

In this example, let us understand the importance of time series analysis in the demand and supply of household electricity. For energy providers, accurately predicting electricity demand is fundamental to maintaining grid stability and operational efficiency. Electricity demand patterns naturally follow predictable cycles since they have daily work rhythms, weekly routines, and seasonal changes. At the same time, they are vulnerable to sudden fluctuations from heat waves, cold snaps, or any major weather events.

While raw consumption data shows these inherent variations, making it non-stationary makes it effective to work with.

It can help in:

- Calculating hourly deviations from typical daily patterns.
- Applying day-over-day differencing.
- Removing predictable seasonal components.

We can transform the data into a weakly stationary series that is suitable for statistical modeling. This processing step is crucial because it allows utilities to:

- Generate reliable short-term load forecasts.
- Optimize power generation scheduling.
- Make informed energy trading decisions.
- Plan infrastructure investments strategically.

Data can be made more stable through weak stationarity and can help the utility grid operators gain better predictive accuracy that is needed to balance demand and supply in real-time.

Python Implementation for Weak Stationarity Check on Electricity Data

In this example, let us generate synthetic electricity demand data to demonstrate weak stationarity. Let us start by defining a function to generate electricity demand data synthetically for 365 days.

Code:

```
def generate_electricity_demand(days=365):
    import random
    random.seed(42)
    demand_data = []
    base_demand = 5000
    for day in range(days):
        daily_variation = random.uniform(-100, 100)
        demand = base_demand + daily_variation
        demand_data.append(demand)
    return demand_data
```

In the preceding code,

- The function **generate_electricity_demand** creates realistic daily demand values over a specified period, and it is defaulted to 1 year.
- It uses a base demand of 5000 MW, which is typical for a medium-sized city.
- It sets a random seed for reproducible results.
- It also adds random daily fluctuations between -100 and +100 MW to simulate natural variability.

Code:

```
electricity_demand = generate_electricity_demand()
electricity_demand[0:10]
```

In the preceding code, the **generate_electricity_demand** function is called, and the output is generated.

```
Output:
[5027.885359691577,
 4905.002151044533,
 4955.005863673824,
 4944.642147629765,
 5047.294242832802,
 5035.339897484582,
 5078.435913540969,
 4917.387766525883,
 4984.384363937054,
 4905.959443887614]
```

The preceding output represents a weak stationary scenario by design:

- The mean of the data is kept constant at ~5000 MW.
- The variance is bounded with a controlled fluctuation range.
- The data is generated with no trends or seasonal patterns for simplicity.

Let us now check if the generated data is weakly stationary.

Code:

```
stationarity_result = is_weakly_stationary(
    electricity_demand,
    segments=4,
    mean_thresh=100,
    var_thresh=1000
)
print(f"Is the synthetic electricity demand data weakly stationary?
{stationarity_result}")
```

In the preceding code, we have used the **`weak_stationarity_test`** function to check mean and variance consistency across segments.

The data parameters have been set with reasonable thresholds as follows:

- Mean variation ≤ 100 MW across segments.
- Variance variation ≤ 1000 MW^2 across segments.

Output:

```
Is the synthetic electricity demand data weakly stationary? True
```

In the preceding output, the stationarity test has resulted in being true for the synthetic data.

This example demonstrates how to:

- Simulate realistic time series data with stationarity.
- Check for stationarity and identify weak stationarity caused by seasonality.

This is a practical way to understand and prepare time series data for modeling, especially when dealing with seasonal patterns.

To summarize,

- This code generates synthetic electricity data with a weak stationarity pattern, checks for stationarity, and finds that the data is weakly stationary.

Weak stationarity serves as an important concept in time series analysis. It provides us with practical and realistic conditions under which many statistical models perform accurately. While many real-world datasets exhibit trends, seasonal patterns, or variability that violate strict or strong stationarity, transformations and analysis over shorter periods often yield weakly stationary segments.

Ultimately, understanding and verifying weak stationarity helps us to apply appropriate modeling techniques confidently, enhancing the accuracy and reliability of predictions and insights drawn from temporal data. With this understanding, let us proceed further with exploring trend stationarity.

Trend Stationarity

Trend stationarity is the next important concept in time series analysis. This is particularly useful when dealing with data that exhibits persistent trends over time. A time series is said to be a trend-stationary if the series can be expressed as:

- The sum of a deterministic trend component, such as linear, quadratic, or polynomial trends, and
- A stationary stochastic component whose statistical properties, such as mean, variance, and autocorrelation, are constant over time.

Assuming trend-stationary time series, such as a predictable upward climb. For example, a company's sales are growing steadily at 5% per year. While the numbers keep getting bigger over time, the way they grow follows consistent patterns we can work with.

The key insight is that if we can identify and remove that predictable trend, what is left behind behaves like a regular stationary series with:

- A steady average
- Consistent variability
- Reliable relationships between data points

This is powerful because:

- We can model the trend separately, like a simple linear growth, for instance.
- The leftover stationary part works with standard forecasting tools.
- When we make predictions, we can add the trend back in for accurate results.

Mathematical Explanation

Any time series data X_t, is considered trend stationary if it can be represented as:

$$X_t = \mu(t) + Y_t$$

where:

$\mu(t)$ is a deterministic trend function, and it can be a linear or a polynomial function, and

Y_t is a stationary stochastic process with the following properties:

- $E(X_t) = 0$, the mean is constant over time.
- $Var(Y_t) = \sigma^2$, the variance is constant over time.
- $Cov(Y_t + T_{t+h}) = \gamma(h)$, covariance depends on lag h

A linear trend stationary process is an example of trend stationarity, and it can be defined as follows:

$$X_t = \alpha + \beta t) + Y_t$$

The trend stationarity of a time series data can be determined by following the steps:

1. Estimate the deterministic trend component through linear regression.
2. Remove this estimated trend from the data.
3. Test the residual series for stationarity.

If the residual data is stationary, then the original data is expected to be trend stationary.

Implementing the Math as a Python Function

In this section, let us write Python code to check if a time series follows trend stationarity. With trend stationarity, the time series data is expected to follow a specific trend, such as linear, quadratic, or polynomial trends.

To perform this, we will first write a code that helps determine if a time series follows trend stationarity.

Let us start by defining a simple function to calculate the mean of the time series data.

Code:

```
def mean(data):
    total = 0
    for value in data:
        total += value
    return total / len(data)
```

In the preceding code,

- The function **mean** is a simple function that calculates the average of a dataset.
- It first adds up all the numbers.
- Then, it divides the sum by the number of data points.

In the next step, let us define another function to estimate the trend of the time series data.

Code:

```
def estimate_trend(series):
    n = len(series)
    sum_x = sum_y = sum_xx = sum_xy = 0

    for t in range(n):
        x = t
        y = series[t]
        sum_x += x
        sum_y += y
        sum_xx += x*x
        sum_xy += x*y
    slope = (n * sum_xy - sum_x * sum_y) / (n * sum_xx - sum_x**2)
    intercept = (sum_y - slope * sum_x) / n
    return intercept, slope
```

In the preceding code,

- The function **estimate_trend** calculated the linear trend of a time series dataset.
- It finds the best-fitting straight line through the input data points by calculating the slope and the intercept.

In the next step, let us define a function to remove the estimated trend from the series.

Code:

```
def remove_trend(series, intercept, slope):
    detrended = []
    for t in range(len(series)):
        trend = intercept + slope * t
        detrended.append(series[t] - trend)
    return detrended
```

In the preceding code,

- The **remove_trend** function takes the time series data as input, along with slope and intercept.
- It goes through each data point and calculates the trend at that point in time.
- It then subtracts the trend from the actual data.
- The remaining values in the series will then be considered as the detrended series.
- This will help in reviewing the true variations in the data without the impact of the trend.

In the next step, let us check the stationarity of the residual data.

Code:

```
def check_stationarity(residuals, segments=3, mean_thresh=100, var_
thresh=1000):
    n = len(residuals)
    seg_len = n // segments
    means = []
    vars = []

    for i in range(segments):
        start = i * seg_len
        end = (i + 1) * seg_len if i < segments - 1 else n
        seg = residuals[start:end]
        seg_mean = mean(seg)
        seg_var = mean([(x - seg_mean)**2 for x in seg])
        means.append(seg_mean)
        vars.append(seg_var)
    mean_diff = max(means) - min(means)
    var_diff = max(vars) - min(vars)
    if mean_diff > mean_thresh or var_diff > var_thresh:
        return False
    else:
        return True
```

In the preceding code,

- The function **check_stationarity** takes the residual data as input and examines if the data is stationary.
- It splits the data into segments and calculates the mean and variance for each segment.
- It calculates the difference between the maximum and minimum values of both mean and variance.
- It checks if the differences are greater than the predefined thresholds and returns as False for stationarity if the differences are greater for either the mean or variance, since it denotes that the data is not stable.

In the next step, let us define a function to test the data for trend stationarity.

Code:

```
def is_trend_stationary(series):
    intercept, slope = estimate_trend(series)
    residuals = remove_trend(series, intercept, slope)
    return check_stationarity(residuals)
```

In the preceding code,

- The function **is_trend_stationarity** takes in the time series data as input and performs all the steps needed to test trend stationarity of the data.

- It first calls the **estimate_trend** function, which returns the slope and intercept of the time series data.
- It then removes the trend of the data using the slope and intercept.
- It finally checks the stationarity of the data.
- If the residual data is stationary, then the original data is trend stationary.

Let us review this implementation further by applying it to an example.

Real-World Example

In growing urban areas, electricity consumption naturally increases over time due to fundamental drivers such as population expansion, economic activity, and technological adoption. This creates a clear upward trajectory, which we call a deterministic trend. However, when we look beyond this long-term growth, we often find that the short-term fluctuations around the trend caused by weather patterns, seasonal changes, or temporary usage variations exhibit stable statistical properties.

This combination makes electricity demand a classic example of a trend-stationary process.

We can isolate the stationary variations in the electricity consumption data by:

- Identifying the underlying growth trend through statistical analysis.
- Removing this deterministic component.

The ability to distinguish between structural growth and temporary variations gives energy providers a powerful framework for balancing reliability with economic efficiency in our evolving energy landscape.

Python Implementation for Trend Stationarity Check on Electricity Data

In this example, let us generate synthetic electricity demand data to demonstrate trend stationarity. Let us start by defining a function to generate electricity demand data synthetically for 365 days.

Code:

```
def generate_electricity_demand(days=365):
    import random
    random.seed(42)
    data = []
    intercept = 1000
    slope = 2
    for t in range(days):
        trend = intercept + slope * t
        noise = random.uniform(-50, 50)
        demand = trend + noise
        data.append(demand)
    return data
```

In the preceding code,

- The function **generate_electricity_demand** creates realistic daily demand values over a specified period, and it is defaulted to 1 year.
- We assumed the starting demand to be 1000 units and assigned it to the intercept.
- The slope is set to 2, assuming the daily growth is 2 additional units each day.
- Randomness is added to data as noise since the actual demand is not perfectly smooth.
- The function finally returns the synthetic data that has both trend and noise.

Code:

```
electricity_data = generate_electricity_demand(365)
electricity_data[0:10]
```

In the preceding code, the **generate_electricity_demand** function is called, and the output is generated as follows:

```
[1013.9426798457883,
954.5010755222667,
981.5029318369119,
978.3210738148823,
1031.6471214164012,
1027.6699487422911,
1051.2179567704845,
972.6938832629417,
1008.192181968527,
970.979721943807]
```

The preceding output represents a trend stationarity scenario by design.

Let us now check if the data generated is trend-stationary.

Code:

```
result = is_trend_stationary(electricity_data)
print(f"Is the synthetic electricity demand data trend stationary?
{result}")
```

In the preceding code, we have used the **is_trend_stationary** function to check the trend of the demand data.

Output:

```
Is the synthetic electricity demand data trend stationary? True
```

In the preceding output, the trend stationarity has resulted in being true for the synthetic data.

This example demonstrates how to:

- Simulate realistic time series data with trend stationarity.
- Check trend stationarity and remove trends within the data.

This is a practical way to understand and prepare time series data for modeling, especially when dealing with trends.

To summarize,

- This code generates synthetic electricity data with a trend stationarity pattern, removes the trend, and tests the stationarity of the data.

Trend stationarity is used for handling time series data, and it helps identify trends, especially in domains such as energy consumption, economics, and environmental monitoring. By identifying deterministic trends in the time series data and removing them from the original data, we can transform the time series data into simple stationary processes that can be forecasted effectively.

Difference Stationarity

Difference Stationarity is another important concept in time series analysis that describes a particular type of non-stationary process. A time series is called difference stationary if it can become stationary after differencing the data one or more times.

Difference stationarity contrasts with trend stationarity. In trend stationarity, a deterministic trend can be explicitly modeled and removed to achieve stationarity. By contrast, difference stationarity involves removing stochastic trends through differencing, revealing an underlying stationary process. The distinction is crucial because it determines the type of transformations needed, before applying standard forecasting models to time series data, ensuring robust predictions and reliable conclusions.

Mathematical Explanation

A time series X_t is difference stationary if there exists an integer d^{th} such that the difference of X_t is stationary.

$$\nabla^d X_t = (1-B)^d X_t$$

where:

- ∇ denotes the difference operator,
- B is the lag operator, and
- d is the order of differencing required to achieve stationarity.

Implementing the Math as a Python Function

In this section, let us implement differencing on the time series data to test if stationarity can be achieved.

To perform this, we will first write a code that helps determine if a time series follows stationarity after differencing.

Similar to the previous examples, let us start by defining a simple function to calculate the mean of the time series data.

Code:

```
def mean(data):
    total = 0
    for x in data:
        total += x
    return total / len(data)
```

In the preceding code,

- The function **mean** is a simple function that calculates the average of a dataset.
- It first adds up all the numbers.
- Then, it divides the sum by the number of data points.

In the next step, let us define another function to compute the variance.

Code:

```
def variance(data):
    mu = mean(data)
    total = 0
    for x in data:
        total += (x - mu)**2
    return total / (len(data) - 1)
```

In the preceding code,

- The function **variance** measures how spread out the data is around its mean.
- It first calculates the average of the data by calling the function **mean**.
- And then for each value, computes its squared deviation from the mean.
- Finally, it averages the squared deviations.

Code:

```
def difference(series, d=1):
    diff_series = series[:]
    for _ in range(d):
```

```
        diff_series = [diff_series[i] - diff_series[i - 1] for i in
range(1, len(diff_series))]
    return diff_series
```

In the preceding code,

- The difference function subtracts each value from the one before it.
- We can do this multiple (d) times for very strong trends.

In the next step, let us check if the time series is stationary.

Code:

```
def is_stationary(series, segments=3, mean_thresh=100,
var_thresh=1000):
    seg_len = len(series) // segments
    means = []
    variances = []

    for i in range(segments):
        start = i * seg_len
        end = (i + 1) * seg_len if i < segments - 1 else
len(series)
        segment = series[start:end]
        means.append(mean(segment))
        variances.append(variance(segment))
    mean_diff = max(means) - min(means)
    var_diff = max(variances) - min(variances)
    if mean_diff > mean_thresh or var_diff > var_thresh:
        return False
    return True
```

In the preceding code,

- The function **`is_stationary`** takes the time series data as input and examines if the data is stationary, similar to the Trend stationarity example.
- It splits the data into segments and calculates the mean and variance for each segment.
- It calculates the difference between the maximum and minimum values of both mean and variance.
- It checks if the differences are greater than the predefined thresholds and returns as False for stationarity if the differences are greater for either the mean or variance, since it denotes that the data is not stable.

In the next step, let us write the code to check for difference stationarity.

Code:

```
def is_difference_stationary(series, max_d=2):
```

```
    for d in range(1, max_d + 1):
        differenced_series = difference(series, d)
        if is_stationary(differenced_series):
            return True, d
    return False, None
```

In the preceding code,

- The function **`is_difference_stationary`** checks if a time series can be made stationary by applying differencing that removes trends by computing changes between consecutive values.

Let us review this implementation further by applying it to an example.

Real-World Example

The long-term increases in electricity demand can be stochastic, exhibiting random fluctuations rather than deterministic patterns, making the series potentially difference stationary. For instance, if electricity demand each month is influenced by random economic or demographic factors that cause persistent growth, differencing the data could remove the non-stationary trends. Once differenced, the resulting stationary data can be modeled and forecasted effectively using standard time series techniques, enabling utilities to better anticipate future electricity usage, optimize resources, and plan infrastructure investments.

Python Implementation for Difference Stationarity Check on Electricity Data

In this example, let us generate synthetic electricity demand data to demonstrate difference stationarity.

Code:

```
def generate_electricity_demand(months=60):
    import random
    random.seed(42)
    data = []
    demand = 1000
    for _ in range(months):
        random_growth = random.uniform(5, 15)
        demand += random_growth
        noise = random.uniform(-20, 20)
        data.append(demand + noise)
    return data
```

In the preceding code,

- The function **`generate_electricity_demand`** simulates monthly electricity demand for a growing city over time. It generates synthetic data that mimics real-world trends such as long-term growth and short-term randomness.
- We assumed the starting demand to be 1000 units.

- Randomness is added to data as noise since the actual demand is not perfectly smooth.
- The function finally returns the synthetic data that has both demand and noise.

Code:

```
electricity_data = generate_electricity_demand()
electricity_data[0:10]
```

In the preceding code, the **generate_electricity_demand** function is called, and the output is generated as follows:

```
[992.3946981934855,
1008.0729906942229,
1038.5772528068267,
1028.9086222921353,
1035.8421759613343,
1062.050878455982,
1055.055532656152,
1080.39853023061,
1089.3759045819247,
1079.159532180789]
```

The preceding output represents difference stationary data by design.

Let us now check if the data generated is difference stationary.

Code:

```
stationary_result, differencing_order = is_difference_stationary
(electricity_data)
if stationary_result:
    print(f"Data is difference stationary after differencing
{differencing_order} time(s).")
else:
    print("Data is not difference stationary within the given
differencing order.")
```

In the preceding code, we have used the **is_difference_stationary** function to check differencing and stationarity of the demand data.

If the data is stationary after differencing, the preceding code returns the value for differencing the data into a stationary series.

Output:

```
Data is difference stationary after differencing 1 time(s).
```

In the preceding output, the difference stationarity has resulted in being true for the synthetic data, with value for differencing the data into a stationary series as 1.

This is a practical way to understand and prepare time series data for modeling, especially when dealing with differencing.

To summarize,

- This code generates synthetic electricity data with a difference stationarity pattern, removes the difference, and makes the data stationary for further modeling usage.

Difference stationarity is an important and widely applicable concept in time series analysis. Recognizing difference stationary processes allows the time series data that is seemingly complex to be transformed and then further converting the series into simpler stationary forms suitable for accurate modeling and forecasting.

Conclusion

In this chapter, we learned about an overview of the stationarity of time series data, and we looked at the applications of stationary processes with examples.

We also looked at the concepts of strong and weak stationarity, followed by trend stationarity and difference stationarity. For each type of stationarity, we generated synthetic data and tested the concepts on each time series synthetic dataset.

In the next chapter, we will continue to look at the mathematical concepts behind data analysis, preparation, and visualization of time series in Python with examples and codes.

References

- Shumway, R.H. and Stoffer, D.S. (2017) *Time Series Analysis and Its Applications: With R Examples*. 4th edn. *Springer*.
- Hamilton, J.D. (1994) *Time Series Analysis*. *Princeton University Press*.
- Enders, W. (2014) *Applied Econometric Time Series*. 4th edn. *Wiley*.
- Brockwell, P. J. and Davis, R. A. (2016). *Introduction to Time Series and Forecasting* 3rd edn. *Springer*.
- Box, G. E. P., Jenkins, G. M., Reinsel, G. C. and Ljung, G. M. (2015). *Time Series Analysis: Forecasting and Control*. 5th edn. *Wiley*.
- Hyndman, R. J. and Athanasopoulos, G. (2021). *Forecasting: Principles and Practice*. 3rd edn. OTexts. Available online: https://otexts.com/fpp3/
- Taylor, J. W. (2010). Forecasting Electricity Demand Using Time Series Methods. *European Journal of Operational Research*.

CHAPTER 3
Tests for Stationarity - Part 1

Introduction

Understanding whether a time series is stationary is a critical first step in any time series analysis. As already seen in the previous chapter in detail, Stationarity implies that a series maintains constant statistical properties such as mean, variance, and autocorrelation over time. When this condition holds, time series models such as ARIMA, SARIMA, and VAR can produce reliable and interpretable forecasts. In contrast, non-stationary series, often characterized by trends, changing variance, or seasonal effects, require transformations before accurate modeling can be done.

This chapter focuses on various statistical tests developed to test stationarity. Each test provides a unique perspective on the structure and behavior of a time series. This helps us to determine whether the data exhibit unit roots, deterministic trends, or other non-stationary features. From classical methods such as the Augmented Dickey-Fuller (ADF) and Phillips-Perron (PP) tests, to complementary approaches such as the KPSS test, Schmidt-Phillips test, and Variance Ratio tests. In this and the upcoming chapters, we will explore how these tools detect different forms of stationarity or randomness.

We will not only explain the mathematical foundation of each test but also provide Python implementations from scratch, along with practical real-world examples and guidelines for interpreting results. Together, these insights will provide a better understanding of how to diagnose stationarity in various applied contexts in the real-world in domains including finance, economics, climate science, energy management, and many more.

By the end of this chapter, we will have a better understanding of how to identify and treat non-stationarity in time series data, ensuring that our models are both statistically sound and practically effective.

By the end of this chapter, readers will be able to grasp the importance of stationarity as a foundational assumption in time series modeling, and understand when and why transformations are necessary to render a non-stationary series suitable for forecasting. The readers will also be able to apply a range of statistical tests, including visual diagnostics, the Kolmogorov–Smirnov (K–S) test, and classical unit root tests such as the Dickey-Fuller and Augmented Dickey-Fuller (ADF) to detect various forms of non-stationarity in real-world data.

Structure

In this chapter, we will cover the following topics:

- Tests for Stationarity
    - Visual Inspection of Stationarity
    - Kolmogorov–Smirnov (K–S) Test
    - Dickey-Fuller (Original) Test
    - Augmented Dickey-Fuller (ADF) Test

Test for Stationarity

Stationarity is one of the most important concepts in time series analysis. It plays a key role in helping us understand and model data that evolves over time. This section covers different tests of stationarity that can be performed on time series data.

Visual Inspection of Stationarity

Visual inspection of stationarity is an intuitive yet critical first step in analyzing time series data. As already seen, Stationarity refers to the statistical stability of a time series, specifically, its mean, variance, and autocorrelation structure remain constant over time. Visual inspection involves graphically examining a time series to identify indications of non-stationarity, such as:

- trends,
- changing variability or heteroscedasticity,
- seasonality, and
- structural breaks.

Although formal statistical tests are essential for conclusive decisions, visual inspection helps us develop a preliminary understanding of the data, guiding subsequent analytical choices.

Visual inspection typically involves plotting the time series data and analyzing for:

- **Trends:** Systematic increases or decreases over time.
- **Seasonality:** Regular cyclical patterns occurring at fixed intervals (daily, weekly, monthly, annually, and so on).
- **Changing Variance:** Variability that increases or decreases over time.
- **Structural Breaks:** Sudden shifts or abrupt changes in the underlying pattern of the data.

This analysis helps us decide whether transformations such as differencing or detrending are required before applying forecasting or modeling techniques. In practice, visual inspection serves as an accessible initial diagnostic tool, especially useful in domains such as economics, finance, climate science, energy management, and so on.

Mathematical Explanation

Visual inspection does not directly rely on complex mathematical tests since it is more of an intuitive way of understanding stationarity in the time series data by visualizing it. However, the fundamental concept is grounded in the statistical properties of time series data.

As we know, Stationarity implies three core mathematical conditions, which are defined as follows:

Constant Mean:

$$E(X_t) = \mu, \quad \textit{for all } t$$

Constant Variance:

$$Var(X_t) = E[(X_t - \mu)^2] = \sigma^2, \quad \textit{for all } t$$

Time-invariant Autocovariance:

The autocovariance depends only on the lag and not on the absolute time.

$$Cov(X_t, X_{t+h}) = \gamma(h), \quad \textit{for all } t, h$$

where:

- **X** is the data point,
- **t** is the time point, and
- **h** is the time lag.

Visual inspection helps us intuitively assess these mathematical conditions by observing the following in the plots of the series:

- Deviations from a horizontal or flat pattern indicate a changing mean.
- Increasing or decreasing amplitude in fluctuations indicates changing variance.
- Cyclical patterns suggest seasonality or autocorrelation structures.
- Sudden changes suggest structural breaks, violating stationarity.

Implementing the Math as a Python Function

In this section, let us write Python code to calculate the rolling mean and rolling standard deviation. These statistics are also known as the moving average and moving standard deviation.

To perform this, let us write functions to compute rolling means and rolling standard deviations for a time series dataset.

Code:

```
def mean(series):
    return sum(series) / len(series)

def variance(series):
    mu = mean(series)
    return sum((x - mu) ** 2 for x in series) / len(series)

def rolling_stats(series, window):
    roll_mean = []
    roll_std = []
    for i in range(len(series)):
        if i < window - 1:
            roll_mean.append(None)
            roll_std.append(None)
        else:
            window_data = series[i - window + 1:i + 1]
            mu = mean(window_data)
            sigma = variance(window_data) ** 0.5
            roll_mean.append(mu)
            roll_std.append(sigma)
    return roll_mean, roll_std
```

In the preceding code,

- The function **mean** is defined to compute the average of a list of numbers.
- The function **variance** is defined to measure how spread out the data is around its mean.
- The function **rolling_stats** is defined to calculate moving averages and moving standard deviations over a specified window size.

Real-World Example

For this implementation, we will continue using synthetic data generation and generate data for electricity demand. This data usually exhibits daily, weekly, and annual cycles, trends due to growth, and occasional anomaly situations. It is important to perform a visual inspection of the data as a first step before applying other complex techniques.

Visual inspection of the data can help in identifying:

- Long-term trends, such as growing electricity usage over the years.
- Seasonal variations, such as increased demand during summers due to cooling requirements.
- Abrupt changes, such as shifts in consumption due to economic events.

Python Implementation for Visual Inspection of Electricity Demand Data

In this example, let us generate synthetic electricity demand data with realistic patterns and then analyze it using rolling statistics. Let us also demonstrate how to visualize this data to understand its properties.

In the following code, we will create a synthetic dataset that mimics daily electricity usage data over 90 days.

Code:

```
import matplotlib.pyplot as plt
import math
def generate_electricity_demand(days=90):
    demand = []
    for day in range(days):
        trend = day * 2  # upward trend
        seasonality = 20 * math.sin(2 * math.pi * day / 7)  #
weekly cycle
        noise = ((-1) ** day) * 5  # alternating fluctuation
        demand.append(100 + trend + seasonality + noise)
    return demand
electricity_demand = generate_electricity_demand()
electricity_demand[0:10]
```

In the preceding code,

- The **generate_electricity_demand** function is defined with a steady upward trend of +2 units per day, representing the growing city demand.
- The seasonality pattern is added to the data using a sine wave equation.
- Noise is added to the data using small alternating daily fluctuations.
- 100 units are considered the base demand.

The output of the generated data is displayed as follows:

```
[105.0,
112.6366296493606,
128.49855824363647,
109.67767478235116,
104.32232521764884,
85.50144175636353,
101.3633703506394,
109.0,
136.6366296493606,
132.49855824363647]
```

Let us further calculate the rolling statistics from the function **rolling_stats** defined in this section.

Code:

```
window = 7
rolling_mean, rolling_std = rolling_stats(electricity_demand,
window)
```

In the preceding code, the rolling statistics are computed with:

- A 7-day window is used to capture weekly patterns while filtering daily randomness.
- 7-day moving averages that smooth out daily noise.
- 7-day standard deviations that measure demand variability.

Let us visualize the data as follows.

Code:

```
plt.figure(figsize=(14, 6))
plt.plot(electricity_demand, label='Electricity Demand',
color='blue')
plt.plot([x if x is not None else 0 for x in rolling_mean],
label='Rolling Mean (7 days)', color='green')
plt.plot([x if x is not None else 0 for x in rolling_std],
label='Rolling Std Dev (7 days)', color='red')
plt.title('Visual Inspection of Electricity Demand - Time Series
& Rolling Statistics')
plt.xlabel('Day')
plt.ylabel('Demand (Synthetic Units)')
plt.legend()
plt.grid(True)
plt.tight_layout()
plt.show()
```

In the preceding code,

- Raw demand data showing all the ups and downs are captured in the blue line.
- Rolling means are captured in the green line that reveals the underlying trend through the noise.
- Rolling standard deviations are captured in the red line, and they will show the periods of high/low variability.

The preceding code plots the synthetic demand data to visualize the seasonal pattern as follows:

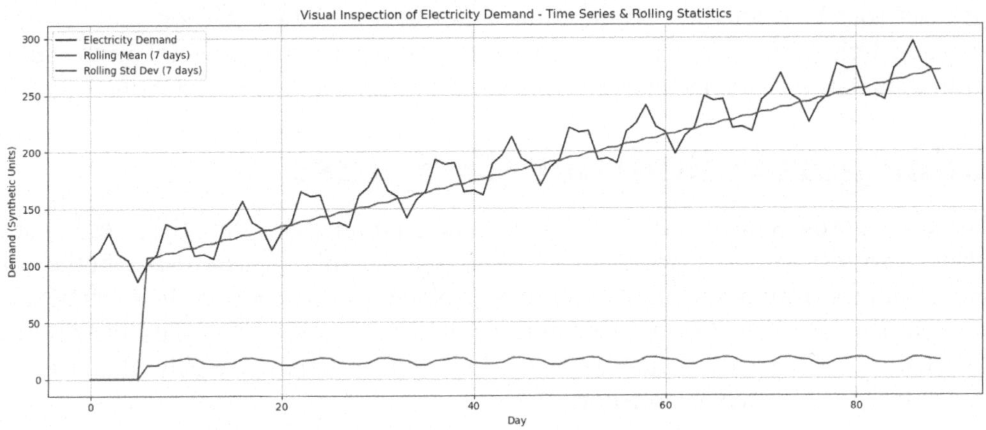

Figure 3.1: *Electricity Demand with Rolling Statistics*

In *Figure 3.1*,

- The base demand (in blue) shows an upward trend that increases steadily over time. The weekly fluctuations show a cyclical pattern.
- Rolling means (in green) show an underlying upward trend.
- Rolling standard deviation (in red) shows the amplitude of fluctuation increasing mildly, signaling possible non-constant variance.

This example helps us visually detect non-stationarity in the form of trend, seasonality, or changing variance before applying any formal stationarity tests.

This is a practical way to understand and prepare time series data for modeling, especially when dealing with seasonal patterns.

To summarize,

- This code generates synthetic electricity data with a seasonal pattern and checks for stationarity through visualization.
- It computes rolling statistics to understand the underlying patterns in the data.

This process is crucial for preparing time series data for analysis and modeling, especially when there is stationarity in the data.

Visual inspection of stationarity provides us with an accessible, intuitive approach for initial data exploration. While it does not replace formal statistical tests, visual inspection significantly aids the early detection of trends, seasonality, and structural breaks, guiding subsequent modeling and forecasting decisions.

In practice, combining visual inspection with formal stationarity tests and appropriate data transformations such as differencing or detrending ensures accurate modeling. Especially in fields such as electricity demand forecasting, visual inspection plays a crucial role in validating assumptions, interpreting data behavior, and ensuring robust analytical approaches. This intuitive step remains a fundamental best practice, reinforcing data-driven decision-making across various domains and industries.

Kolmogorov-Smirnov (K-S) Test

The Kolmogorov-Smirnov (K-S) Test is a non-parametric statistical test that is designed to test whether two datasets differ significantly. It also tests whether one dataset differs from a specified reference probability distribution. It is particularly powerful because it makes no assumptions about the underlying data distribution. This characteristic makes it suitable for various applications, especially when the data distribution is unknown or non-normal.

There are two main forms of the K-S test:

- **One-sample K-S test:** This tests if a given dataset follows a specified theoretical distribution.
- **Two-sample K-S test:** This tests if two independent samples come from the same continuous distribution.

The K-S test measures the maximum difference between the Empirical Cumulative Distribution Functions (ECDFs) of the datasets under comparison. If this maximum difference is statistically significant, we reject the null hypothesis in favor of the alternative hypothesis.

- Statistical significance means that the results are beyond a certain critical value.
- The null hypothesis is that the samples come from the same distribution.
- The alternate hypothesis is that the samples are drawn from different distributions.

The K-S test is extensively used in domains such as economics, climate studies, finance, environmental science, energy management, and so on, where comparing distributions, validating assumptions of stationarity or randomness is essential.

Mathematical Explanation

K-S test involves the comparison of Empirical Cumulative Distribution Functions (ECDF) and can be mathematically defined as follows:

Given a sample $X = \{X_1, X_2, \ldots X_n\}$, the Empirical Cumulative Distribution Function (ECDF), $F_n(x)$, is defined as:

$$F_n(x) = \frac{1}{n}\sum_{i=1}^{n} I(X_i \leq x)$$

where $I(\cdot)$ is an indicator function, equal to 1 if the condition is true and 0 otherwise.

For two samples, X of size n and Y of size m, with ECDFs $F_n(x)$ and $G_m(x)$, the K - S statistic $D_{n,m}$ is defined as the maximum absolute difference between these ECDFs.

$$Dn,m = xsup|Fn(x) - Gm(x)|$$

The null hypothesis for the two-sample test is that both samples are drawn from the same underlying distribution. The alternative hypothesis is that they come from different distributions.

The critical values or p-value for the K - S test statistic can be computed or obtained from K - S distribution tables, allowing us to determine statistical significance.

Implementing the Math as a Python Function

As we have seen earlier in this section, in the realm of statistical analysis, we often need to determine whether two datasets arise from the same underlying distribution. The Kolmogorov-Smirnov (K–S) test serves as our compass in this exploration, using a non-parametric method that compares empirical distributions without making restrictive assumptions about their shape.

In this section, let us write Python code to perform this two-sample K–S test from scratch.

The following is the step-by-step implementation of the test:

Code:

```
def ecdf(data, x):
    count = 0
    for point in data:
        if point <= x:
            count += 1
    return count / len(data)
```

In the preceding code,

- The empirical cdf function **ecdf** calculates what fraction of observations in the data fall below a threshold x.

- It also tells us how much of the data lies to the left of any given point.

Code:

```
def ks_statistic(data1, data2):
    combined = sorted(data1 + data2)
    max_diff = 0.0
    for point in combined:
        ecdf1 = ecdf(data1, point)
        ecdf2 = ecdf(data2, point)
        diff = abs(ecdf1 - ecdf2)
        if diff > max_diff:
            max_diff = diff
    return max_diff
```

In the preceding code,

- The function **ks_statistic** computes the maximum vertical distance between the two ECDFs.
- The difference quantifies how far apart the two distributions are at their most divergent point.

Code:

```
def ks_critical_value(n1, n2):
    from math import sqrt
    return 1.36 * sqrt((n1 + n2) / (n1 * n2))
```

In the preceding code,

- The function **ks_critical_value** calculates the threshold for statistical significance.
- The formula scales with sample sizes since the larger the datasets, the smaller the differences will be.
- The constant value of 1.36 is derived from the K-S table for.

Code:

```
def ks_test(data1, data2, alpha=0.05):
    n1 = len(data1)
    n2 = len(data2)
    D = ks_statistic(data1, data2)
    critical_val = ks_critical_value(n1, n2)
    reject_null = D > critical_val
    return D, critical_val, reject_null
```

In the preceding code,

- The function **ks_test** combines all the other functions needed to perform this test.

- It computes the observed divergence.
- It then determines the critical threshold.
- It finally returns the decision of whether the null hypothesis should be rejected.

Real-World Example

An important question in energy management is whether electricity demand during different periods, such as two consecutive years, follows the same statistical distribution. Using the K–S test, we can compare demand distributions across years to detect significant shifts due to growth, changes in consumer behavior, or policy impacts.

For example, suppose a utility wants to evaluate whether electricity demand distributions for the years 2023 and 2024 differ significantly. Performing a K–S test on monthly demand data for these two years helps determine if observed variations reflect underlying structural changes or simply random fluctuations.

Python Implementation for the K-S Test on Electricity Data

In this example, let us generate synthetic electricity demand data to demonstrate the K-S test for stationarity. This example will help us explore whether electricity consumption patterns have meaningfully changed between two consecutive years. This type of analysis will help energy providers to plan infrastructure investments and capacity adjustments.

```
Code:
def generate_electricity_demand(yearly_increase=50, months=12):
    import random
    random.seed(101)
    demand_year1 = [1000 + random.uniform(-50, 50) for _ in
range(months)]
    demand_year2 = [x + yearly_increase + random.uniform(-50, 50)
for x in demand_year1]
    return demand_year1, demand_year2
```

In the preceding code,

- Year 1 is simulated with monthly demand fluctuating around 1000 MW ±50 MW random noise, representing typical consumption volatility.
- Year 2 introduces a systematic yearly increase while preserving the same noise structure, denoting organic growth in demand.

Let us further generate the data.

Code:

```
year1_demand, year2_demand = generate_electricity_demand()
print("Year 1 demand:", year1_demand)
```

```
print("Year 2 demand:", year2_demand)
Output:
Year 1 demand: [1008.1152132504565, 969.4754495534137,
1046.525110706111, 1042.3976401676794, 996.7138678196974,
1016.347064453006, 971.4522969737968, 972.1696249526241,
978.8522433381256, 1019.2422745995318, 971.2376768358331,
1047.1105951353775]
Year 2 demand: [1015.1507616805729, 988.8041124265228,
1055.4114676896027, 1119.3868338286895, 1033.365365296701,
1063.5152908338596, 1004.0551236576313, 1035.9123168205679,
1019.2416764108581, 1040.0690450116333, 1014.2530804848323,
1077.5395763290896]
```

In the preceding output,

- Random seed helped in ensuring the reproducibility of the data.
- Noise parameter helped in capturing unpredictable short-term demand variations.

In the next step, let us call the non-parametric K-S test to objectively compare the two years' demand distributions.

Code:

```
D, critical_val, reject = ks_test(year1_demand, year2_demand)
```

In the preceding code, the test calculates:

- **D Statistic:** The maximum vertical distance between the two years' empirical CDFs. Larger values indicate greater divergence.
- **Critical Value:** The threshold for statistical significance (α=0.05). If D exceeds this, we reject the null hypothesis.

The null and alternative hypotheses are defined as follows:

- **Null Hypothesis:** Both years follow the same underlying demand distribution.
- **Alternative Hypothesis:** Demand distributions differ significantly.

In the next step, let us review the results of this test.

Code:

```
print("Kolmogorov-Smirnov Test for Electricity Demand (Year1 vs
Year2):")
print(f"K-S Statistic D: {D:.4f}")
print(f"Critical Value: {critical_val:.4f}")
if reject:
    print("Result: Reject null hypothesis (significant difference
detected).")
else:
```

```
    print("Result: Fail to reject null hypothesis (no significant
difference detected).")
```

In the preceding code,

- D value and critical value are printed.
- If reject=True, then the +50 MW increase reflects a systematic shift beyond random noise, suggesting the need for grid upgrades.
- If reject=False, observed changes could be random fluctuations, warranting monitoring but not immediate action.

Output:

```
Kolmogorov-Smirnov Test for Electricity Demand (Year1 vs Year2):
K-S Statistic D: 0.4167
Critical Value: 0.5552
Result: Fail to reject null hypothesis (no significant difference
detected).
```

In the preceding results,

- The K-S statistic D value shows the effective size of how stark the difference is.
- Comparison to the critical value determines statistical significance.
- The result has failed to reject the null hypothesis, indicating that there is no significant difference detected.

This example demonstrates how to:

- Simulate realistic time series datasets for electricity demand analysis.
- Define functions needed to perform the K-S test for stationarity.
- Handle randomness and noise in the data.
- Define and test the null and alternative hypotheses.

This is a practical way to understand and prepare time series data for modeling, especially when dealing with stationary data.

To summarize, this code:

- Generates synthetic datasets that mirror real-world electricity demand.
- Defines all the functions needed to perform the K-S test on the simulated data.
- Performs the test and interprets the results.

The Kolmogorov–Smirnov (K–S) test is an invaluable non-parametric statistical tool for comparing distributions without stringent assumptions about data normality or specific distributions. Its ease of interpretation, intuitive implementation through ECDFs, and robustness make it ideal for exploratory analysis in various disciplines.

In electricity demand analysis, as demonstrated, the K–S test helps utilities promptly identify shifts in consumption patterns. This helps in enabling proactive management and accurate forecasting of demand. Overall, the K–S test stands out as an essential technique for data-driven decision-making. It helps validate distributional assumptions, detect structural changes, and maintain operational efficiency across diverse fields.

Dickey-Fuller Test (Original)

The Dickey-Fuller (DF) Test, developed by David Dickey and Wayne Fuller, is one of the foundational statistical methods used to determine whether a time series contains a unit root, which would imply non-stationarity. A series is considered stationary if its mean, variance, and covariance structure remain constant over time. Non-stationary series typically exhibit trends, seasonality, or random walks, complicating analysis and forecasting.

The Dickey-Fuller test specifically examines the presence of a unit root in an autoregressive (AR) process of order one. This test serves as the basis for various extensions such as the Augmented Dickey-Fuller (ADF), Phillips-Perron (PP), and others. Understanding and properly conducting the original DF test provides a critical foundation for further advanced unit root analyses and time series modeling.

Mathematical Explanation

The original Dickey-Fuller test begins with the basic AR(1) model. Dickey-Fuller test can be mathematically explained as follows.

$$X_t = \rho X_{t-1} + u_t$$

where:

- X_t is the current observation,
- X_{t-1} is the previous observation,
- ρ is the autoregressive parameter, and
- u_t is an independent and identically distributed error term or white noise.

To test stationarity, the model is rewritten as:

$$\Delta X_t = (\rho - 1)X_{t-1} + u_t = \gamma X_{t-1} + u_t$$

where $\Delta X_t = X_t - X_{t-1}$.

Now, the hypothesis for testing becomes clearer.

Null hypothesis $(H_0): \gamma = 0$, which implies $\rho = 1$ (unit root/non-stationary).

Alternative hypothesis $(H_a): \gamma < 0$, indicating $\rho < 1$ (stationary).

The Dickey-Fuller test statistic is a t-statistic calculated as:

$$DF = \frac{\hat{\gamma}}{SE(\hat{\gamma})}$$

$\hat{\gamma}$ is the estimated coefficient from the Dickey-Fuller regression defined in this section.

SE $(\hat{\gamma})$ is the standard error of the estimate .

The Dickey-Fuller statistic (DF) is calculated by dividing the estimated coefficient $\hat{\gamma}$ by its standard error $SE(\hat{\gamma})$. The resulting value is similar to the t-statistic, which is typically used to test hypotheses about regression coefficients. However, an important distinction exists: although the DF statistic resembles a t-statistic, it does not follow the conventional t-distribution. This difference arises because, under the null hypothesis of a unit root (that is, the series is non-stationary), the test statistic has a unique distribution known as the Dickey-Fuller distribution.

Decision Rule:

If DF < critical value, reject the null hypothesis. The series is stationary.

If DF > critical value, fail to reject the null hypothesis. The series has a unit root (non-stationary).

Thus, the DF test statistic measures how strongly the series supports the unit root hypothesis and helps us decide whether the series is stationary or requires transformation for reliable analysis.

Implementing the Math as a Python Function

In this section, let us write Python code for a basic implementation of the Dickey-Fuller test statistic calculation.

Let us start by writing the code of the arithmetic mean as covered in many sections of this book.

Code:

```
def mean(series):
    return sum(series) / len(series)
```

In the preceding code,

- We have defined the function to calculate **mean** for a series of numbers.

In the next steps, let us define the function to calculate Ordinary Least Squares Regression.

Code:

```
def df_ols(y, x):
    n = len(y)
    x_mean = mean(x)
    y_mean = mean(y)
    numerator = sum((x[i] - x_mean)*(y[i] - y_mean) for i in
range(n))
    denominator = sum((x[i] - x_mean)**2 for i in range(n))
    beta = numerator / denominator
    residuals = [y[i] - beta*x[i] for i in range(n)]
    s2 = sum(e**2 for e in residuals)/(n - 1)
    se_beta = (s2 / denominator)**0.5
    t_stat = beta / se_beta
    return beta, t_stat
```

In the preceding code, the **df_ols** function performs several critical operations.

Covariance calculation is performed in this function to measure how changes in one variable correspond to changes in another. For example, tracking how electricity demand fluctuates with temperature changes.

Variance computation is performed by squaring deviations from the mean. This is to amplify significant variations while diminishing minor fluctuations.

This function produces two important outputs:

- **beta:** The estimated relationship between variables.
- **t_stat:** A measure of how reliable this relationship appears to be.

Let us now implement the Dickey-Fuller test.

Code:

```
def dickey_fuller_test(series):
    delta_series = [series[i] - series[i-1] for i in
range(1,len(series))]
    lag_series = series[:-1]
    gamma, df_stat = df_ols(delta_series, lag_series)
    return df_stat
```

In the preceding code,

- The purpose of the Dickey-Fuller test is to bring everything together in the context of time series analysis.
- It converts our input time series data into **delta_series**, which calculates the differences between consecutive points.
- It also calculates the lagged values (**lag_series**).
- Using **df_ols**, it examines whether current changes relate to previous levels.

- Finally, the Dickey-Fuller test statistic acts as a directive indication of whether the time series data is stationary or not.

Real-World Example

Electricity demand typically includes seasonal and trend components due to economic growth, demographic changes, or seasonal weather patterns. The Dickey-Fuller test helps analysts determine if the electricity demand series exhibits stationary behavior or contains stochastic trends requiring differencing or other transformations before modeling.

Accurate detection of stationarity is required for forecasting electricity consumption, optimizing generation capacities, planning infrastructure, and energy trading.

Python Implementation for DF Test on Electricity Data

In this section, let us implement the Dickey-Fuller test on synthetically generated electricity demand data to mimic the real-world application.

Code:

```
def generate_electricity_demand(T=50):
    demand = [1000]
    for t in range(1, T):
        demand.append(demand[-1] + 10 + ((-1)**t)*5)
    return demand
electricity_demand = generate_electricity_demand()
electricity_demand[0:5]
```

Output:

```
[1000, 1005, 1020, 1025, 1040]
```

In the preceding code,

- The function **`generate_electricity_demand`** is defined to generate synthetic electricity demand time series data that emulates the electricity consumption patterns of a growing urban center.
- The series begins at 1000 MW, representing the baseline electricity demand of a mid-sized city.
- This initial value anchors the simulation, reflecting typical residential, commercial, and industrial power needs.
- Each subsequent month, demand increases by 10 MW, capturing the city's expansion.
- The term **`((-1)**t)*5`** introduces alternating monthly variations of ±5 MW, capturing cyclical fluctuations.

Let us now perform the Dickey-Fuller test on the generated time series data.

Code:

```
df_statistic = dickey_fuller_test(electricity_demand)
```

In the preceding code,

The function **dickey_fuller_test** returns the Dickey-Fuller test statistic, a single number that quantifies evidence for/against stationarity.

Code:

```
df_critical_5pct = -2.93
print("Original Dickey-Fuller Test for Electricity Demand 
Series:")
print(f"DF Statistic: {df_statistic:.4f}")
print(f"Critical value (5% significance): {df_critical_5pct}")

if df_statistic < df_critical_5pct:
    print("Reject null hypothesis (series is stationary).")
else:
    print("Fail to reject null hypothesis (series has unit root/
non-stationary).")
```

In the preceding code,

- The Dickey-Fuller test statistic we computed is evaluated against statistical theory to draw a meaningful conclusion about our electricity demand time series.
- The critical value of -2.93 defines the 5% significance level critical value for the Dickey-Fuller test.
- The resulting test statistic is compared against the critical value to decide on the stationarity of the data.
- If the test statistic< critical value, the series is considered to be stationary.
- Otherwise, it is considered to have a unit root and be non-stationary.

The original Dickey-Fuller test is a relatively simpler statistical approach and is critical for the preliminary assessment of time series stationarity.

However, the Dickey-Fuller test has known limitations. It assumes independence in residuals and performs poorly in small samples or complex series with autocorrelation. Thus, more advanced tests such as ADF are often employed to complement or verify DF results.

Augmented Dickey-Fuller (ADF) Test

The Augmented Dickey-Fuller (ADF) Test is one of the most commonly used statistical methods to test for stationarity in time series data. Let us recall that stationarity implies that a series has constant mean, variance, and autocorrelation structure over time. Non-stationary series exhibit trends or structural changes that complicate forecasting and statistical inference. Identifying stationarity is crucial for choosing appropriate models in fields such as finance, economics, climatology, and energy management.

Specifically, the ADF test evaluates whether a time series contains a unit root. The unit root is a mathematical property that indicates non-stationarity. If a series has a unit root, it typically exhibits persistent trends or random walks. The Augmented Dickey-Fuller test extends the original Dickey-Fuller test by adding lagged difference terms to account for serial correlation. This makes it more robust and applicable to real-world data with temporal dependencies.

The practical significance of the ADF test lies in its widespread use for:

- validating modeling assumptions,
- informing data transformations such as differencing, and
- enabling robust forecasting and analysis.

Mathematical Explanation

ADF test is mathematically based on a regression model and can be defined as follows:

$$\Delta X_t = \alpha + \beta t + \gamma X_{t-1} + \sum_{i=1}^{p} \delta_i \Delta X_{t-i} + \epsilon_t$$

where:

- $\Delta X_t = X_t - X_{t-1}$ is the first difference of the time series,
- α is a constant and an intercept,
- βt is a deterministic time trend. This is an optional parameter of the model,
- γX_{t-1} tests for the presence of a unit root,
- $\sum_{i=1}^{p} \delta_i \Delta X_{t-1}$ represents lagged differences included to control for autocorrelation, and
- ϵ_t is the error term and assumed to be white noise.

Hypothesis testing for ADF is defined as follows:

- Null Hypothesis $(H_0): \gamma = 0$, the series has a unit root and is non-stationary.
- Alternate Hypothesis $(H_0): \gamma < 0$, the series does not have a unit root and is stationary.

To decide whether to reject the null hypothesis, we compare the calculated test statistic to critical values derived from Dickey-Fuller tables. If the calculated statistic is more negative than the critical value at the chosen significance level (for example, 5%), we reject the null hypothesis, concluding the series is stationary.

Implementing the Math as a Python Function

As we have seen earlier in this section, testing for stationarity can be performed on time series by testing if it contains a unit root, which indicates non-stationarity in the data. This can be done only by performing an ADF test on the data.

In this section, let us write a simplified yet comprehensive Python implementation of the Augmented Dickey-Fuller test.

Let us begin our journey with the simplest yet most powerful statistical tool, the arithmetic mean.

Code:

```
def mean(data):
    return sum(data) / len(data)
```

In the preceding code,

- The **mean** function captures the central tendency of data by summing all values and dividing by their count.

Let us further implement Ordinary Least Squares (OLS), a fundamental statistical technique for modeling relationships between variables.

Code:

```
def ols(y, X):
    n = len(y)
    X_mean = mean(X)
    y_mean = mean(y)

    numerator = sum([(X[i] - X_mean)*(y[i] - y_mean) for i in
range(n)])
    denominator = sum([(X[i] - X_mean)**2 for i in range(n)])

    beta = numerator / denominator
    alpha = y_mean - beta * X_mean

    residuals = [y[i] - (alpha + beta * X[i]) for i in range(n)]
    residual_variance = sum([res**2 for res in residuals]) / (n - 2)

    se_beta = (residual_variance / denominator)**0.5
    t_stat = beta / se_beta

    return beta, t_stat
```

In the preceding code,

- The **ols** function calculates the slope (beta) that minimizes the squared vertical distances between data points and the regression line.

- Computes the intercept (alpha), ensuring that the line passes through the mean of both variables.
- Derives a t-statistic to assess the slope's significance through:
  - Residual analysis or differences between actual and predicted values,
  - Standard error estimation, and
  - Hypothesis testing framework.

Let us further proceed with implementing the function for the ADF test.

Code:

```
def adf_test(series, lag=1):
    n = len(series)
    diff_series = [series[i] - series[i-1] for i in range(1, n)]
    lagged_series = series[:-1]

    for i in range(1, lag):
        lagged_diff = [diff_series[j-i] for j in range(i, len(diff_
series))]
        diff_series = diff_series[i:]
        lagged_series = lagged_series[i:]

    gamma, t_stat = ols(diff_series, lagged_series)

    return gamma, t_stat
adf_critical_value_5pct = -2.86
```

In the preceding code,

- The **adf_test** function answers an important question in time series analysis: does this data exhibit problematic trends?

It does this by:

- Creating differenced series to remove potential trends.
- Incorporating lagged terms to control for autocorrelation.
- Applying our OLS engine to test if the series exhibits a unit root.
- The test's goal is to examine whether past values meaningfully predict changes (the gamma coefficient) and to compare the t-statistic to critical values.
- The -2.86 threshold represents a simplified 5% significance level for rejecting the null hypothesis of non-stationarity.

Real-World Example

Let us continue with the Electricity demand example to perform an ADF test as well. As already reviewed in this chapter and in the previous one, Electricity demand patterns often exhibit non-stationary behavior due to trends of increasing usage over the years, seasonal patterns of high demand during summer/winter, and structural changes such as economic or demographic shifts. Determining whether electricity demand is stationary or not is critical, as non-stationary series require specific transformations before forecasting.

Python Implementation for ADF Test on Electricity Data

Let us assume that a utility company wants to analyze monthly electricity demand to ensure accurate long-term forecasts. Applying the ADF test helps identify if the series is stationary, guiding whether differencing or other transformations are necessary before modeling.

The first step for this application is to generate synthetic data that is non-stationary.

Code:

```
def generate_electricity_demand(months=50):
    demand = []
    base = 1000
    for t in range(months):
        value = base + t * 10 + ((-1)**t)*20
        demand.append(value)
    return demand
```

In the preceding code, the **generate_electricity_demand** function is defined with the following properties and computations:

- The base Consumption starts at 1000 MW, representing a mid-sized city's baseline need.
- Demand is increased by 10 MW monthly, indicating the city's expansion.
- The term **((-1)**t)*20** captures predictable fluctuations such as weekend versus weekday patterns.

Let us further generate the data.

Code:

```
electricity_demand = generate_electricity_demand()
electricity_demand[0:10]
Output:
[1020, 990, 1040, 1010, 1060, 1030, 1080, 1050, 1100, 1070]
```

In the preceding code,

- 50 months of electricity demand data are generated to run the ADF test.

Let us further call the function to run the ADF test.

Code:

```
gamma, t_stat = adf_test(electricity_demand)
print("ADF Test for Electricity Demand Series:")
print(f"ADF gamma coefficient: {gamma:.4f}")
print(f"ADF t-statistic: {t_stat:.4f}")
print(f"Critical Value at 5% significance: {adf_critical_
value_5pct}")

if t_stat < adf_critical_value_5pct:
    print("Result: Reject null hypothesis - series is
stationary.")
else:
    print("Result: Fail to reject null hypothesis - series is
non-stationary.")
```

In the preceding code, the **adf_test** function computes the following:

- The Gamma Coefficient is used to measure how strongly past values influence present changes.
- The t-statistic is used to quantify the evidence against non-stationarity.
- If the t-statistic plunges below -2.86, we declare the series stationary.
- Otherwise, we acknowledge its non-stationary nature.

Output:

```
ADF Test for Electricity Demand Series:
ADF gamma coefficient: -0.0392
ADF t-statistic: -0.9693
Critical Value at 5% significance: -2.86
Result: Fail to reject null hypothesis - series is
non-stationary.
```

The preceding output clarifies that the generated synthetic data has a unit root and is non-stationary in nature, and the need for transformations such as differencing.

This example demonstrates how to:

- Simulate realistic time series datasets for electricity demand analysis.
- Define functions needed to perform the ADF test for stationarity.
- Calculate the coefficients needed to perform the test.
- Define and test the null and alternative hypotheses.

This is a practical way to understand and prepare time series data for modeling, especially when dealing with stationary data.

To summarize,

- This code generates synthetic datasets that mirror real-world electricity
- demand.
- Defines all the functions needed to perform an ADF test on the simulated data.
- Performs the test and interprets the results.

The Augmented Dickey-Fuller (ADF) test remains a fundamental tool in time series analysis, widely used across domains for detecting stationarity. Its robustness, simplicity, and practical interpretability make it indispensable for the analysis of time series data.

For real-world applications, especially in electricity demand forecasting, identifying stationarity through the ADF test is important. This helps in guiding appropriate data transformations and modeling strategies. Accurate detection of stationarity enhances the effectiveness of predictive models. This, in turn, helps in informed strategic planning and decision-making across industries.

It is to be noted that the ADF test should be used in conjunction with visual inspections, other stationarity tests, and domain expertise to ensure robust conclusions and meaningful insights.

Conclusion

In this first part of the chapter, we explored foundational methods for assessing stationarity in time series data, each method offering unique insights into the underlying properties of a series.

We began with **Visual Inspection of Stationarity**, a critical yet intuitive step that helps identify evident trends, seasonal patterns, and shifts in mean or variance simply by observing plots of the data. Although visual inspection alone cannot conclusively determine stationarity, it is indispensable for guiding us towards the appropriate transformations and formal tests.

Next, we discussed the **Kolmogorov-Smirnov (K-S) Test**, a non-parametric method used to evaluate if a sample aligns with a particular theoretical distribution or to compare two distributions. While the K-S test is not specifically designed for stationarity testing, it offers valuable insights into the stability and consistency of distributions over time, complementing more specialized stationarity tests.

We then focused on the foundational **Dickey-Fuller (DF) Test**, the original statistical test specifically designed to detect the presence of unit roots. Understanding this test is important, as it lays the groundwork for many modern unit root tests. We highlighted how the DF statistic differs from a standard t-statistic, emphasizing the importance of specialized critical values due to its unique distribution under non-stationarity.

Building upon the DF test, the **Augmented Dickey-Fuller (ADF) Test** enhances accuracy by accounting for serial correlation in the data through the inclusion of lagged difference terms. The ADF test thus provides a more robust and realistic assessment of stationarity, particularly valuable when analyzing real-world economic, financial, or energy-related datasets that often exhibit autocorrelation.

Together, these methods form a comprehensive initial toolkit for detecting stationarity, offering both intuitive and rigorous analytical approaches. Employing them for the right use cases and scenarios helps us gain a nuanced understanding of the structure and behavior of time series data, guiding the critical decisions required for accurate modeling and forecasting.

In the next chapter, we will continue to understand more advanced tests for stationarity.

References

- Shumway, R.H. and Stoffer, D.S. (2017) *Time Series Analysis and Its Applications: With R Examples*. 4th edn. *Springer*.
- Hamilton, J.D. (1994) *Time Series Analysis*. *Princeton University Press*.
- Enders, W. (2014) *Applied Econometric Time Series*. 4th edn. *Wiley*.
- Hyndman, R. J. and Athanasopoulos, G. (2021). *Forecasting: Principles and Practice*. 3rd edn. OTexts. Available online: https://otexts.com/fpp3/
- Chatfield, C. (2003) *The Analysis of Time Series: An Introduction*. 6th edn. Boca Raton: *Chapman & Hall/CRC*.
- Massey Jr., F.J. (1951) The Kolmogorov-Smirnov test for goodness of fit, *Journal of the American Statistical Association*, 46(253), pp. 68–78. Available at: https://doi.org/10.1080/01621459.1951.10500769.
- Conover, W.J. (1999) *Practical Nonparametric Statistics*. 3rd edn. New York: *Wiley*.
- Dickey, D.A. and Fuller, W.A. (1979) Distribution of the estimators for autoregressive time series with a unit root, *Journal of the American Statistical Association*, 74(366), pp. 427–431. Available at: https://doi.org/10.1080/01621459.1979.10482531.
- Fuller, W.A. (1996) *Introduction to Statistical Time Series*. 2nd edn. New York: *Wiley*.
- Said, S.E. and Dickey, D.A. (1984) Testing for unit roots in autoregressive-moving average models of unknown order, *Biometrika*, 71(3), pp. 599–607. Available at: https://doi.org/10.1093/biomet/71.3.599.
- Maddala, G.S. and Kim, I.-M. (1998) *Unit Roots, Cointegration, and Structural Change*. Cambridge: *Cambridge University Press*.

CHAPTER 4
Tests for Stationarity - Part 2

Introduction

Time series data often lies at the heart of decision-making in many domains such as economics, finance, climatology, energy systems, and so on. A fundamental assumption in many time series models, especially those used for forecasting, inference, and exploratory analysis, is that the data are stationary. In the previous chapter, we explored foundational techniques such as the Dickey-Fuller and Augmented Dickey-Fuller (ADF) tests, as well as visual inspection methods and the Kolmogorov–Smirnov (K–S) test. These initial tools serve as the gateway for deeper investigation, especially when we encounter data with autocorrelation, heteroskedasticity, or ambiguous stationarity behavior.

This chapter builds upon that foundation by introducing a suite of more robust, complementary, and refined statistical tests that address the limitations of traditional methods. These tests not only offer improvements in power and reliability but also provide alternative formulations of the null hypothesis.

Together, they help answer an essential question: *Is the time series truly stationary*, or *is it just a statistical illusion*?

Classical unit root tests, such as the Dickey-Fuller family, test the null hypothesis that the series is non-stationary. If the test fails to reject the null hypothesis, it does not prove that the data is non-stationary. It just indicates insufficient evidence to claim otherwise. This asymmetry in hypothesis testing often results in failing to detect stationarity when it exists, causing type II errors. This can easily happen, especially in small samples or series with structural complexity.

To resolve this, we will need to perform complementary tests on the time series data. This chapter introduces and contextualizes such methods within a broader spectrum of stationarity testing.

The chapter begins with the Phillips-Perron (PP) test, followed by the KPSS test and Elliott-Rothenberg-Stock (DF-GLS) test. We then turn to the Ng-Perron test, followed by informal checks.

By the end of this chapter, readers will be able to understand the limitations of classical unit root tests such as Dickey-Fuller and ADF, especially in the presence of structural breaks, autocorrelation, or heteroskedasticity, and recognize the need for complementary testing strategies.

Structure

In this chapter, we will cover the following topics:

- Tests for Stationarity
  - Phillips-Perron (PP) Test
  - Kwiatkowski-Phillips-Schmidt-Shin (KPSS) Test
  - Elliott-Rothenberg-Stock (DF-GLS) Test
  - Ng-Perron Test

Test for Stationarity

Stationarity is one of the most important concepts in time series analysis. It plays a key role in helping us understand and model data that evolves over time. This section covers some of the complementary tests of stationarity that can be performed on time series data.

Phillips-Perron (PP) Test

The Phillips-Perron (PP) Test is a widely recognized statistical method used to test for stationarity in time series data. Like the Augmented Dickey-Fuller (ADF) test, the Phillips-Perron test checks for the presence of a unit root, indicating whether the time series is stationary or non-stationary.

Non-stationary data can exhibit trends, seasonality, or structural changes, which complicate forecasting and analysis. The Phillips-Perron test is particularly useful because it improves upon the Dickey-Fuller methods by adjusting for autocorrelation and heteroskedasticity in error terms through non-parametric statistical techniques.

Mathematical Explanation

The Phillips-Perron test considers the following regression equation, and it can be mathematically defined as:

$$\Delta X_t = \alpha + \rho X_{t-1} + \epsilon_t$$

where:

- X_t is the time series data,
- $\Delta X_t = X_t - X_{t-1}$ is the first difference of the series,
- α is a constant term,
- ρ is the coefficient tested for the presence of a unit root, and
- ϵ_t is the error term, which may exhibit autocorrelation and heteroskedasticity.

Note:

- *Autocorrelation or serial correlation occurs in regression analysis when the residuals or errors of a model are correlated with each other over time or across observations. This violates the OLS assumption that errors are uncorrelated.*
- *Heteroskedasticity refers to a situation in regression analysis where the variance of the error terms or residuals changes as the predictor variable changes.*

The key hypotheses tested in the PP test are as follows:

- **Null hypothesis**, meaning the series has a unit root (non-stationary).
- **Alternate hypothesis**, indicating stationarity (no unit root).

The Phillips-Perron test statistic is derived by adjusting the standard Dickey-Fuller statistic to account for autocorrelation and heteroscedasticity in residuals.

The PP test statistic is computed as:

$$PP = \frac{\hat{\rho}}{SE(\hat{\rho})} - \frac{(T \cdot s^2 \sigma_\epsilon^2)}{2SE(\hat{\rho}) \cdot s^2}$$

where:

$\hat{\rho}$ is the estimated regression coefficient from OLS regression,

$SE(\hat{\rho})$ is the standard error of ,

T is the sample size,

s^2 is the estimated variance of the residuals, and

σ_ϵ^2 is the long-run variance of the residuals.

The PP statistic follows similar critical values as the ADF statistic, allowing for straightforward interpretation.

Implementing the Math as a Python Function

In this section, let us write Python code to implement a simplified Phillips-Perron test.

To perform this, let us write functions to compute the mean and OLS for a time series dataset.

Code:

```
def mean(data):
    return sum(data) / len(data)
```

In the preceding code,

The function **mean** is defined to compute the average of a list of numbers.

Code:

```
def ols(y, x):
    n = len(y)
    x_mean = mean(x)
    y_mean = mean(y)
    numerator = sum([(x[i] - x_mean)*(y[i] - y_mean) for i in
range(n)])
    denominator = sum([(x[i] - x_mean)**2 for i in range(n)])
    b = numerator / denominator
    a = y_mean - b * x_mean
    residuals = [y[i] - (a + b * x[i]) for i in range(n)]
    return a, b, residuals
```

In the preceding code,

- The function **`ols`** performs linear regression using the Ordinary Least Squares method.
- It uncovers the hidden relationship between two variables by finding the best-fitting straight line through our data points.
- In the first step, the mean of the **x** and **y** values in the data is computed.
- **`numerator`** computes the covariance of **x** and **y**.
- **`denominator`** measures how **x** varies on its own by computing variance.
- **b** is calculated as the slope of the regression line.
- **a** is calculated as the intercept of the regression line.
- **`residuals`** capture the vertical distances between actual y values and our line's predictions.

Real-World Example

For this implementation, we will continue using synthetic data generation and generate data for electricity demand. This data usually exhibits daily, weekly, and annual cycles, trends due to growth, and occasional anomaly situations. Determining whether the electricity demand series is stationary is vital for selecting appropriate forecasting techniques.

The Phillips-Perron test helps us quickly assess the presence of unit roots in electricity demand data, guiding the decision to apply transformations such as differencing or detrending to obtain reliable forecasts. Such analysis improves grid management, economic planning, and investment decisions.

Python Implementation for the PP Test of the Electricity Demand Data

In this example, let us generate synthetic electricity demand data with realistic patterns and then analyze it using the PP test.

In the following code, we will create a synthetic dataset that mimics daily electricity usage data over 90 days.

Code:

```
def generate_electricity_demand(months=50):
    data = []
    base_demand = 1000
    for month in range(months):
        trend = month * 15
        seasonal = (-1)**month * 30
        data.append(base_demand + trend + seasonal)
    return data
electricity_demand = generate_electricity_demand()
electricity_demand[0:5]
```

In the preceding code,

- The **generate_electricity_demand** function is defined with a base demand level of 1000MW. This is considered the minimum expected demand regardless of other factors.
- The data is generated for 50 months.
- The demand increases by 15 MW every month.
- Seasonal fluctuations alternate between +30 and -30 MW each month.

The output of the generated data is displayed as follows:

```
[1030, 985, 1060, 1015, 1090]
```

The preceding output models gradual demand growth and captures predictable seasonal fluctuations.

Let us further perform a PP test on the generated synthetic demand data.

Code:

```
pp_stat = pp_test(electricity_demand)
print("Phillips-Perron Test for Electricity Demand Series:")
print(f"PP test statistic: {pp_stat:.4f}")
print(f"Critical value (5% significance): {pp_critical_
value_5pct}")
if pp_stat < pp_critical_value_5pct:
    print("Result: Reject null hypothesis (series is stationary).")
else:
    print("Result: Fail to reject null hypothesis (series is
non-stationary).")
```

In the preceding code,

- We have applied the Phillips-Perron test to our electricity demand time series.
- The **pp_test** function returns the test statistic **pp_stat**, which we will use to evaluate whether the series is stationary.
- We then display the test statistic and compare it to the 5% critical value, which serves as a benchmark.
- The null hypothesis of the Phillips-Perron test is that the series contains a unit root, which means it is non-stationary.
- If the test statistic is less than the critical value, we have enough evidence to reject the null hypothesis, concluding that the series is stationary.
- Otherwise, if the test statistic is greater than the critical value, we fail to reject the null, suggesting that the series is non-stationary and may require differencing or transformation before modeling.

Let us finally write code to plot the results of the PP test:

Code:

```
import matplotlib.pyplot as plt
test_name = "Phillips-Perron (PP)"
values = {"statistic": -0.9796, "critical_value": -2.86}
fig, ax = plt.subplots(figsize=(6, 4))
bar = ax.bar([test_name], [values["statistic"]], color='steel-
blue')
ax.axhline(y=values["critical_value"], color='red', line-
style='--', label='Critical Value (5%)')

ax.text(0, values["statistic"] + 0.1, f"{values['statis-
tic']:.2f}", ha='center', fontsize=10)
ax.text(0, values["critical_value"] + 0.1, f"CV: {values
['critical_value']}",
```

```
            color='red', fontsize=9, ha='center')

ax.set_ylim(min(values["statistic"], values["critical_value"]) - 1,
            max(values["statistic"], values["critical_value"]) + 1)
ax.set_ylabel("Test Statistic")
ax.set_title(f"{test_name} Test Result")
ax.legend()
ax.grid(axis='y', linestyle='--', alpha=0.7)
plt.tight_layout()
```

In the preceding code,

- This script produces a simple bar chart that compares the observed Phillips–Perron test statistic against its 5% critical value.

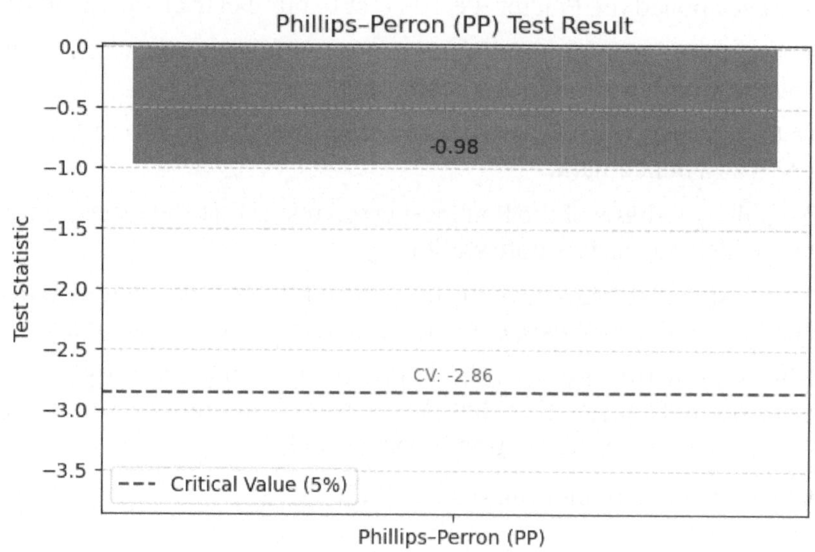

Figure 4.1: *Phillips-Perron Test Results*

Figure 4.1 helps in visually aligning the test statistic with the threshold to get an immediate sense of whether we would reject the null hypothesis (unit root) at the 5% level.

To summarize,

- This code generates synthetic electricity data with a seasonal pattern and checks for stationarity.
- It computes the mean and OLS on the data.
- It implements a simplified PP test to test the non-stationarity of the data.

The Phillips-Perron test remains a valuable statistical tool in time series analysis due to its robustness to autocorrelation and heteroskedasticity. Its flexibility and simplicity make it highly applicable in various fields, particularly energy management, economics, and environmental studies.

Kwiatkowski-Phillips-Schmidt-Shin (KPSS) Test

The Kwiatkowski-Phillips-Schmidt-Shin (KPSS) test is a widely utilized statistical method for testing the stationarity of a time series. Unlike other common stationarity tests, such as the Augmented Dickey-Fuller (ADF) and Phillips-Perron (PP) tests, which examine the presence of a unit root, the KPSS test assesses the stationarity of a time series directly by examining whether the series can be represented as stationary around a deterministic trend or mean.

In practical terms, the KPSS test is complementary to tests such as ADF and PP. We know that ADF and PP tests typically have a null hypothesis of non-stationarity or a unit root. However, the KPSS test reverses this hypothesis by providing a detailed cross-check for stationarity analysis. This makes the KPSS test particularly useful when interpreting ambiguous results from other tests. It is commonly applied in economics, finance, climatology, energy, and various domains where understanding and validating data stationarity is essential for accurate forecasting and modeling.

Mathematical Explanation

The KPSS test assumes a model of the following form:

$$X_t = \alpha + \beta t + r_t + \epsilon_t$$

where:

- X_t is the observed time series,
- α is a constant,
- βt represents a deterministic trend,
- r_t is a random walk component, and
- ϵ_t is a stationary error term with zero mean and constant variance.

The KPSS test hypotheses are formulated differently from most unit root tests:

- **Null Hypothesis** (H_0): The series is stationary (the variance of the random walk component r_t is zero).
- **Alternate Hypothesis** (H_a): The series is non-stationary (variance of r_t is greater than zero).

The random walk component is defined as follows:

$$r_t = r_{t-1} + u_t \text{ with } r_0 = 0$$

Or more explicitly:

$$r_t = \sum_{i=1}^{t} u_i$$

where:

- $u_t \sim N(0, \sigma_u^2)$ is a white noise process with mean zero and variance σ_u^2,
- r_t represents the accumulated effect of random shocks over time,
- If $\sigma_u^2 > 0$, then r_t is non-stationary, and consequently X_t is also non-stationary, and
- If $\sigma_u^2 = 0$, then $r_t = 0$ for all t, the series X_t is trend-stationary or level-stationary depending on β_t.

The KPSS test statistic is calculated as follows:

Estimate the residuals $(\hat{\epsilon}_t)$ from a regression of the series on a deterministic trend or mean.

Calculate the partial sum of these residuals:

$$S_t = \sum_{i=1}^{t} \hat{\epsilon}_t$$

Compute the test statistic:

$$KPSS = \frac{1}{T^2} \sum_{i=1}^{T} S_t^2 / \hat{\sigma}_\epsilon^2$$

where:

- T is the sample size, and
- $\hat{\sigma}_\epsilon^2$ is the estimated variance of residuals.

A high KPSS statistic indicates strong evidence against stationarity.

Critical values are provided by Kwiatkowski et al. (1992), allowing us to assess significance levels.

Implementing the Math as a Python Function

In this section, let us write Python code to implement a self-contained KPSS test from scratch.

To perform this, let us write functions to compute the mean, estimate residuals, cumulative sum, and variance for a time series dataset.

The following is the step-by-step implementation of the test:

Code:

```
def mean(series):
    return sum(series) / len(series)
```

In the preceding code,

- The function **mean** is defined to compute the average of a list of numbers.

Code:

```
def estimate_residuals(series):
    mu = mean(series)
    residuals = [x - mu for x in series]
    return residuals
```

In the preceding code,

- The **estimate_residuals** function calculates the residuals from the regression model by fitting a constant term (the mean) to a time series.
- These residuals represent the portion of the data unexplained by the average value.
- This is a critical first step in analyzing variability and model performance.

Code:

```
def cumulative_sum(residuals):
    cum_sum = []
    total = 0
    for r in residuals:
        total += r
        cum_sum.append(total)
    return cum_sum
```

In the preceding code,

- The **cumulative_sum** function computes the running total of residuals, the differences between observed and predicted values in the model.
- This helps detect systematic patterns in prediction errors that might otherwise go unnoticed.

Code:

```
def variance(series):
    mu = mean(series)
    var = sum([(x - mu)**2 for x in series]) / len(series)
    return var
```

In the preceding code,

- The **variance** function calculates the population variance of the time series dataset by measuring how far individual values deviate from the mean.
- This metric quantifies the spread or dispersion of the data.
- This is a critical step in understanding volatility, model performance, and inherent variability in time series.

Code:

```
def kpss_test(series):
    T = len(series)
    residuals = estimate_residuals(series)
    cum_sums = cumulative_sum(residuals)
    sigma_e2 = variance(residuals)

    numerator = sum([cs**2 for cs in cum_sums])
    kpss_stat = numerator / (T**2 * sigma_e2)

    return kpss_stat
```

In the preceding code,

- The **kpss_test** function implements a simplified version of the Kwiatkowski-Phillips-Schmidt-Shin (KPSS) test.
- This code covers the statistical procedure explained in the math above to determine whether a time series is stationary around a deterministic trend or contains a unit root (non-stationary).

Code:

```
kpss_critical_5pct = 0.463
```

In the preceding code,

- The KPSS critical value is set at the standard value at 5% significance.

Real-World Example

For this implementation, we will continue using synthetic data generation and generate data for electricity demand. This data usually exhibits daily, weekly, and annual cycles, trends due to growth, and occasional anomaly situations. Determining whether the electricity demand series is stationary and vital for selecting appropriate forecasting techniques.

The KPSS test helps energy utilities verify if electricity demand series are stationary or if transformations such as differencing or detrending are necessary for accurate modeling. This test is crucial to ensure that the forecasts used for grid management, energy trading, and infrastructure planning are reliable and consistent.

Python Implementation for the KPSS Test on Electricity Data

In this example, let us generate synthetic electricity demand data with realistic patterns and then analyze it using the KPSS test.

Code:

```
def generate_electricity_demand(months=48):
    data = []
    base_demand = 1000
    for t in range(months):
        trend = t * 20
        fluctuation = ((-1)**t) * 30
        demand = base_demand + trend + fluctuation
        data.append(demand)
    return data
electricity_demand = generate_electricity_demand()
electricity_demand[0:5]
```

In the preceding code,

- The **generate_electricity_demand** function is used to construct a synthetic time series that emulates key characteristics of real-world electricity consumption data.
- The base demand level has been set to 1000.
- This simulated series combines two critical components of non-stationary time series:
    - Deterministic Trend
    - Seasonal-Like Fluctuations

The output of the generated data is displayed as follows:

```
[1030, 990, 1070, 1030, 1110]
```

The preceding output models gradual demand growth and captures predictable seasonal fluctuations.

Let us further perform the KPSS test on the generated synthetic demand data.

Code:

```
kpss_stat = kpss_test(electricity_demand)
print("KPSS Test for Electricity Demand Series:")
print(f"KPSS test statistic: {kpss_stat:.4f}")
print(f"Critical value (5% significance): {kpss_critical_5pct}")
if kpss_stat > kpss_critical_5pct:
    print("Result: Reject null hypothesis (series is non-
stationary).")
else:
```

```
    print("Result: Fail to reject null hypothesis (series is
stationary).")
```

In the preceding code,

- We have applied the KPSS test to our electricity demand time series to determine whether the series is stationary around a deterministic trend or exhibits non-stationary behavior.
- The **kpss_test** function returns the test statistic **kpss_stat**, which we will use to evaluate whether the series is stationary.
- We then display the test statistic and compare it to the 5% critical value, which serves as a benchmark.
- The null hypothesis of the KPSS test is that the series is non-stationary.
- If the test statistic is less than the critical value, we have enough evidence to reject the null hypothesis, concluding that the series is stationary.
- Otherwise, if the test statistic is greater than the critical value, we fail to reject the null, suggesting that the series is non-stationary and may require differencing or transformation before modeling.

Let us finally write code to plot the results of the KPSS test.

Code:

```
import matplotlib.pyplot as plt
test_name = "KPSS Test"
values = {"statistic": 4.752, "critical_value": 0.463}
fig, ax = plt.subplots(figsize=(6, 4))
bar = ax.bar([test_name], [values["statistic"]],
color='steelblue')
ax.axhline(y=values["critical_value"], color='red', line-
style='--', label='Critical Value (5%)')

ax.text(0, values["statistic"] + 0.1, f"{values['statis-
tic']:.2f}", ha='center', fontsize=10)
ax.text(0, values["critical_value"] + 0.1, f"CV: {values
['critical_value']}",
        color='red', fontsize=9, ha='center')

ax.set_ylim(min(values["statistic"], values["critical_value"]) - 1,
            max(values["statistic"], values["critical_value"]) +
1)
ax.set_ylabel("Test Statistic")
ax.set_title(f"{test_name} Test Result")
ax.legend()
ax.grid(axis='y', linestyle='--', alpha=0.7)
plt.tight_layout()
```

In the preceding code,

- This script produces a simple bar chart that compares the observed KPSS test statistic against its 5% critical value.

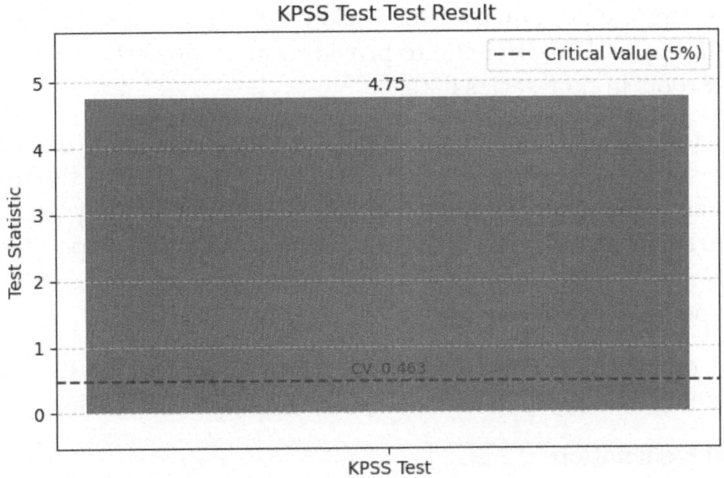

Figure 4.2: *KPSS Test Results*

Figure 4.2 helps in visually aligning the test statistic with the threshold to get an immediate sense of whether we would reject the null hypothesis (unit root) at the 5% level.

To summarize,

- This code generates synthetic electricity data with a seasonal pattern and checks for stationarity.
- It computes the mean, estimates residuals, and calculates the cumulative sum and variance on the data.
- It implements a simplified KPSS test to test the non-stationarity of the data.

The KPSS test is an indispensable method for determining the stationarity of time series data. Its distinctive approach of testing stationarity as the null hypothesis makes it a valuable complement to other stationarity tests, such as ADF or PP, ensuring comprehensive and reliable conclusions.

In real-world applications, particularly in energy management, finance, economics, and environmental studies, KPSS test results inform critical analytical decisions. This influences forecasting strategies and operational planning. It is recommended to employ KPSS in conjunction with other stationarity tests and domain knowledge to derive robust conclusions, thereby ensuring that their models and predictions remain valid and reliable.

Elliott-Rothenberg-Stock (DF-GLS) Test

The Elliott-Rothenberg-Stock (DF-GLS) test is also known as the Dickey-Fuller Generalized Least Squares (DF-GLS) test. It is an advanced stationarity test that improves upon the standard Augmented Dickey-Fuller (ADF) test. It was developed by Elliott, Rothenberg, and Stock (1996) to provide a more powerful and reliable test for detecting unit roots in time series data.

Like the ADF test, the DF-GLS test checks for the presence of a unit root, which indicates non-stationarity. However, instead of using raw data for the test regression, DF-GLS applies a Generalized Least Squares (GLS) detrending procedure before testing. This transformation makes the test more robust. This is powerful, especially for small samples. It helps reduce size distortions and improve power against the alternative hypothesis of stationarity.

In real-world practice, the DF-GLS test is highly regarded for its ability to more accurately detect stationarity in economics and financial time series.

Mathematical Explanation

The DF-GLS test can be mathematically explained as follows. The DF-GLS test is also mathematically based on a regression model and can be defined as:

$$\Delta X_t = \alpha + \beta t + \gamma X_{t-1} + \sum_{i=1}^{p} \delta_i \Delta X_{t-1} + \in_t$$

The DF-GLS test improves on this by **GLS-detrending** the data before estimating the regression. There are two detrending methods, depending on whether we include a constant or a constant plus a trend. We will focus on the constant-only method for simplicity.

GLS Detrending

For the constant-only case, the detrended series is obtained from:

$$\tilde{X}_t = X_t - \phi X_t$$

where:

- $\tilde{X}_t = \sum_{t=1}^{t} \rho^{t-i} X_i$, and
- $\rho = 1 + \frac{c}{T}, and\ c = -7$ is a recommended constant detrending.

This GLS-detrended series is then used in the ADF-type regression:

$$\Delta\tilde{X}_t = \gamma \tilde{X}_{t-1} + \in_t$$

where:

- $\Delta\tilde{X}_t = \tilde{X}_t - \tilde{X}_{t-1}$.

Hypothesis testing for the DF-GLS test is defined as follows:

Null Hypothesis: Series has a unit root (non-stationary).

Alternate Hypothesis: Series is stationary (after GLD detrending).

The test statistic is the t-statistic on, and critical values are provided in Elliot et al. (1996).

Implementing the Math as a Python Function

As we have seen earlier in this section, testing for stationarity can be performed on time series by testing if it contains a unit root, which indicates non-stationarity in the data. This can also be done by performing a DF-GLS test on the data.

Let us start by writing the code of the arithmetic mean as covered in many sections of this book.

Code:

```
def mean(series):
    return sum(series) / len(series)
```

In the preceding code,

- We have defined the function to calculate **mean** for a series of numbers.

In the next steps, let us define the function to calculate variance.

Code:

```
def variance(series):
    mu = mean(series)
    return sum((x - mu) ** 2 for x in series) / (len(series) - 1)
```

In the preceding code,

- The **variance** function calculates the sample variance of the time series dataset.
- This quantifies how much individual data points deviate from the mean.
- Variance provides critical insights into the spread and variability of data.
- This is key for diagnosing model performance, understanding uncertainty, and identifying outliers.

Let us now implement the GLS-detrending for the constant-only model.

Code:

```
def gls_detrend(series, c=-7):
```

```
    T = len(series)
    rho = 1 + c / T
    y = [0] * T
    for t in range(1, T):
        y[t] = series[t] - rho * series[t - 1]
    return y[1:]
```

In the preceding code,

- The **gls_detrend** function implements a Generalized Least Squares (GLS)-based detrending method to remove stochastic trends from the time series.
- This approach is particularly useful for testing stationarity or preparing data for models that assume no underlying trend.
- The input for this function is the time series to detrend.
- c is the tuning parameter influencing the detrending strength.
- We have provided the default value as 7, which aligns with critical values for unit root tests.
- We have defined the operations for this function as per the math explained earlier in this section.

Let us further define the first difference for the series.

Code:

```
def first_difference(series):
    return [series[i] - series[i - 1] for i in range(1,
len(series))]
```

In the preceding code,

- The **first_difference** function transforms the time series by computing the first differences between consecutive observations.
- This operation is fundamental in the DF-GLS test as part of pre-processing, for mitigating trends and achieving stationarity.

Let us next define the OLS regression to compute the test statistic.

Code:

```
def ols_regression(y, x):
    x_mean = mean(x)
    y_mean = mean(y)
    num = sum((x[i] - x_mean) * (y[i] - y_mean) for i in
range(len(y)))
    den = sum((x[i] - x_mean) ** 2 for i in range(len(y)))
    beta = num / den
    residuals = [y[i] - beta * x[i] for i in range(len(y))]
    s2 = sum(r ** 2 for r in residuals) / (len(y) - 1)
```

```
        se_beta = (s2 / den) ** 0.5
        t_stat = beta / se_beta
        return beta, t_stat
```

In the preceding code,

- The **ols_regression** function implements Ordinary Least Squares (OLS) regression.
- This method estimates the linear relationship between the dependent variable y and the independent variable x.
- This method provides both the slope of the relationship and a hypothesis test for its significance.
- The inputs for this function are the dependent variable y and the independent variable x.
- The outputs for this function are the estimated slope coefficient (**beta**) and t-statistic.

Let us now define the DF-GLS test function.

Code:

```
def df_gls_test(series):
    detrended = gls_detrend(series)
    diff = first_difference(detrended)
    lagged = detrended[:-1]
    y = diff[1:]
    x = lagged[:-1]
    beta, t_stat = ols_regression(y, x)
    return t_stat
```

In the preceding code,

- The **df_gls_test** function implements the Dickey-Fuller Generalized Least Squares (DF-GLS) test.
- This test, as explained in this section, is a powerful unit root test.
- It improves upon the traditional Dickey-Fuller test by first detrending the data using GLS.
- This enhances the test's ability to distinguish between true stochastic trends and deterministic patterns.

Real-World Example

For this implementation, we will continue using synthetic data generation and generate data for electricity demand. Electricity demand tends to grow over time due to increasing population, economic development, and industrial activity. However, this growth could be either a deterministic trend (linear and predictable) or a stochastic trend (random and unpredictable). If the latter, we must difference or transform the data before forecasting.

Using the DF-GLS test, we can test for unit roots more accurately than with ADF, especially in short samples. This helps identify whether electricity demand should be modeled using stationary methods or non-stationary approaches.

Python Implementation for the DF Test on Electricity Data

In this section, let us implement the DF-GLS test on synthetically generated electricity demand data to mimic the real-world application.

In the first step, let us start by generating synthetic electricity demand data with a stochastic trend.

Code:

```
def generate_electricity_demand(n=50):
    import random
    random.seed(42)
    series = [1000]
    for _ in range(1, n):
        noise = random.gauss(0, 10)
        series.append(series[-1] + noise + 5)
    return series
electricity_demand = generate_electricity_demand()
electricity_demand[0:5]
```

In the preceding code,

- The **generate_electricity_demand** function creates synthetic electricity demand data that mimics real-world behavior characterized by a stochastic trend.
- This is generated in a pattern where demand evolves unpredictably over time due to random shocks, while also exhibiting a persistent upward drift.
- This type of series is common in energy systems experiencing gradual load growth from population or economic expansion, combined with short-term volatility from external factors such as weather or market dynamics.
- By simulating stochastic trends, we can stress-test models against realistic scenarios where historical patterns only partially predict future behavior, preparing them for the challenges of real-world energy analytics.

Output:

```
[1000,
 1003.5590967042207,
 1006.8300607009055,
 1010.7169020852289,
```

```
 1022.7367393362175]
```

The preceding output models electricity demand data, which we stress-test models against realistic scenarios.

Code:

```
t_statistic = df_gls_test(electricity_demand)
critical_value_5pct = -1.95
print("Elliott-Rothenberg-Stock DF-GLS Test for Electricity
Demand:")
print(f"Test statistic: {t_statistic:.4f}")
print(f"Critical value at 5% significance: {critical_value_5pct}")
if t_statistic < critical_value_5pct:
    print("Result: Reject null hypothesis (series is stationary).")
else:
    print("Result: Fail to reject null hypothesis (series has
unit root).")
```

In the preceding code,

- It performs the Elliott-Rothenberg-Stock (DF-GLS) test to determine whether the electricity demand series exhibits a unit root (non-stationary behavior) or is stationary around a deterministic trend.
- This test is critical for validating assumptions in time series modeling and forecasting.
- We have set the critical value for this test at a 5% significance level of -1.95.

Output:

```
Elliott-Rothenberg-Stock DF-GLS Test for Electricity Demand:
Test statistic: -0.3410
Critical value at 5% significance: -1.95
Result: Fail to reject null hypothesis (series has unit root).
```

This output indicates that the series may be non-stationary and may require differencing.

Let us finally write code to plot the results of the DF-GLS test.

Code:

```
import matplotlib.pyplot as plt
test_name = "Elliott-Rothenberg-Stock DF-GLS Test"
values = {"statistic": -0.3410, "critical_value": -1.95}
fig, ax = plt.subplots(figsize=(6, 4))
bar = ax.bar([test_name], [values["statistic"]],
color='steelblue')
ax.axhline(y=values["critical_value"], color='red', linestyle='--',
label='Critical Value (5%)')
```

```
ax.text(0, values["statistic"] + 0.1, f"{values['statistic']
:.2f}", ha='center', fontsize=10)
ax.text(0, values["critical_value"] + 0.1, f"CV: {values
['critical_value']}",
        color='red', fontsize=9, ha='center')

ax.set_ylim(min(values["statistic"], values["critical_value"]) -
1,
            max(values["statistic"], values["critical_value"]) +
1)
ax.set_ylabel("Test Statistic")
ax.set_title(f"{test_name} Test Result")
ax.legend()
ax.grid(axis='y', linestyle='--', alpha=0.7)
plt.tight_layout()
```

In the preceding code,

- This script produces a simple bar chart that compares the observed KPSS test statistic against its 5% critical value.

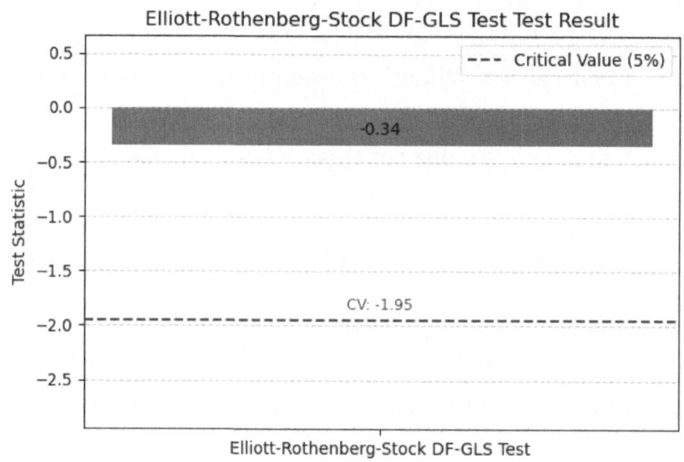

Figure 4.3: *DF-GLS Test Result*

Figure 4.3 helps in visually aligning the test statistic with the threshold to get an immediate sense of whether we would reject the null hypothesis (unit root) at the 5% level.

The Elliott-Rothenberg-Stock (DF-GLS) test provides a powerful and more efficient alternative to traditional unit root tests such as ADF. This is particularly useful in small samples or mildly persistent processes.

By using a GLS-based detrending method, the DF-GLS test increases power and reduces size distortions. This enables more accurate identification of stationarity.

In domains such as energy forecasting, economics, and finance, where time series data often include deterministic trends or drift, the DF-GLS test offers a reliable foundation for validating assumptions, choosing appropriate models, and enhancing forecast accuracy.

However, as with all statistical tools, the DF-GLS test should be applied thoughtfully, ideally in conjunction with visual inspection and other complementary tests (such as KPSS, ADF, or PP) to ensure robust and reliable conclusions.

Ng-Perron Test

The Ng-Perron Test is an advanced statistical approach developed by Serena Ng and Pierre Perron to detect the presence of a unit root in time series data, thus assessing stationarity. Unlike other unit root tests, such as the Augmented Dickey-Fuller (ADF) or Phillips-Perron (PP) tests, the Ng-Perron test combines multiple unit-root tests and significantly improves their performance. This is useful especially in small samples or series exhibiting complex autocorrelation structures.

The motivation behind the Ng-Perron test was to overcome limitations in standard tests. Other tests might often suffer from size distortions, leading to incorrect rejection rates under the null hypothesis. Some tests have low power in testing finite samples and might fail to detect stationarity.

Ng-Perron addresses these problems by employing sophisticated methods such as:

- The Modified Information Criteria to select lag lengths, and
- Using improved modified test statistics.

It provides more accurate and robust results, making it particularly useful in economics, finance, and energy-related domains, where precision in unit-root detection is crucial.

Mathematical Explanation

The Ng-Perron test is mathematically based on an autoregressive (AR) process and can be defined as follows:

$$X_t = \rho X_{t-1} + u_t$$

This equation represents a stochastic process, where:

- The value of time t, denoted X_t, depends on its own previous value X_{t-1},
- ρ is the coefficient that scales X_{t-1}, and
- u_t is a random shock or error term.

Hypothesis testing for Ng-Perron is defined as follows:

- **Null Hypothesis** (H_0): ρ=1, the series is non-stationary.
- **Alternate Hypothesis** (H_α): $\rho < 1$, the series is stationary.

The Ng-Perron test has four modified test statistics derived from previous tests, and they are denoted by MZ_α, MZ_t, MZ_B, and MZ_T.

Among these, the most frequently cited and used statistics are MZ_α and MZ_T. These tests are modifications of the Philips-Perron Z_α and Z_t statistics, respectively.

The Ng-Perron MZ_α statistic is given by:

$$MZ_\alpha = \frac{(T^{-1} X_T^2 - \hat{\sigma}_u^2)}{2T^{-2} \sum_{t=1}^{T-1} X_t^2}$$

The Ng-Perron MZ_t statistic is given by:

$$MZ_t = \frac{(T^{-1} X_T^2 - \hat{\sigma}_u^2)}{[4\hat{\sigma}_u^2 T^{-2} \sum_{t=1}^{T-1} X_t^2]^{\frac{1}{2}}}$$

where:

- T is the sample size,
- $\hat{\sigma}_u^2$ is the long-run variance estimator of the residuals, and
- X_t are detrended observations.

Critical values of these statistics are provided by Ng and Perron (2001). If the computed MZ_α and MZ_t statistics are more negative than critical values, the null hypothesis (unit root) is rejected, suggesting stationarity.

Implementing the Math as a Python Function

As we have seen earlier in this section, testing for stationarity can be performed on time series by testing if it contains a unit root, which indicates non-stationarity in the data. This can be done by performing the Ng-Perron test on the data.

In this section, let us write a simplified yet comprehensive Python implementation of the Ng-Perron test using MZ_α statistic.

Let us begin our journey with the simplest yet most powerful statistical tool, the arithmetic mean.

```
Code:
# Mean calculation
def mean(series):
    return sum(series) / len(series)
```

In the preceding code,

- The **mean** function captures the central tendency of data by summing all values and dividing by their count.

Let us further proceed with implementing MZ_{α} statistic Ng-Perron test.

```
Code:
def ng_perron_mza(series):
    T = len(series)
    mu = mean(series)
    series_demeaned = [x - mu for x in series]
    numerator = sum(series_demeaned[t] * series_demeaned[t-1] for
t in range(1, T))
    denominator = sum(series_demeaned[t-1]**2 for t in range(1, T))
    rho_hat = numerator / denominator
    residuals = [series_demeaned[t] - rho_hat*series_de-
meaned[t-1] for t in range(1,T)]
    sigma_u2 = variance(residuals)
    term1 = (series_demeaned[-1]**2 / T) - sigma_u2
    term2 = 2 * (sum(x**2 for x in series_demeaned[:-1]) / T**2)
    mza = term1 / term2
    return mza
```

In the preceding code,

The **ng_perron_mza** function computes the Ng-Perron statistic to evaluate whether a time series exhibits non-stationarity.

The following is a step-by-step breakdown of the code and its alignment with the theoretical framework of the Ng-Perron test:

1. The function removes the **mean** of the series to center it around zero.
2. It then implements Ordinary Least Squares (OLS) to estimate the autoregressive coefficient in the model explained in the math of this test.
3. It then calculates the variance of residuals from the AR(1) regression.
4. Then the formula for is defined as per the mathematical explanation in this section.

Real-World Example

Let us continue with the Electricity demand example to perform the Ng-Perron test as well. As already reviewed in this chapter and in previous chapters, Electricity demand patterns often exhibit non-stationary behavior due to trends of increasing usage over the years, seasonal patterns of high demand during summer/winter, and structural changes such as economic or demographic shifts. Determining whether electricity demand is stationary or not is critical, as non-stationary series require specific transformations before forecasting.

The Ng-Perron test, with its superior small-sample accuracy and robustness to autocorrelation, provides an ideal analytical tool for assessing the stationarity of electricity demand data.

Python Implementation for the Ng-Perron Test on Electricity Data

The first step for this application is to generate synthetic data to perform the Ng-Perron test.

```
Code:
def generate_electricity_demand(T=100):
    demand = []
    base_demand = 1000
    for t in range(T):
        if t == 0:
            demand.append(base_demand)
        else:
            demand.append(demand[-1] + 10 + ((-1)**t)*5)
    return demand
```

In the preceding code, like some of the previous examples discussed,

- The function **generate_electricity_demand** is defined to generate synthetic electricity demand time series data that emulates the electricity consumption patterns of a growing urban center.
- The series begins at 1000 MW, representing the baseline electricity demand of a mid-sized city.
- This initial value anchors the simulation, reflecting typical residential, commercial, and industrial power needs.
- Each subsequent month, demand increases by 10 MW, capturing the city's expansion.
- The term **((-1)**t)*5** introduces alternating monthly variations of ±5 MW, capturing cyclical fluctuations.

Let us further generate the data and call **ng_perron_mza** to calculate the statistic.

```
Code:
electricity_demand = generate_electricity_demand()
mza_statistic = ng_perron_mza(electricity_demand)
electricity_demand[0:5]
Output:
[1000, 1005, 1020, 1025, 1040]
```

In the preceding code,

- 100 months of electricity demand data are generated to run the Ng-Perron test.

Let us further call the function to run the Ng-Perron test.

```
Code:
mza_critical_5pct = -8.10
print("Ng-Perron MZa Test for Electricity Demand Series:")
print(f"MZa Statistic: {mza_statistic:.4f}")
print(f"Critical value at 5% significance: {mza_critical_5pct}")

if mza_statistic < mza_critical_5pct:
    print("Reject null hypothesis (series is stationary).")
else:
    print("Fail to reject null hypothesis (series has a unit 
root/non-stationary).")
```

In the preceding code,

The **ng_perron_mza** function computes the following:

- The statistic to quantify the evidence against non-stationarity.
- If the statistic plunges below the critical value -8.1 at 5% significance, we declare the series stationary.
- Otherwise, we acknowledge its non-stationary nature.

```
Output:
Ng-Perron MZa Test for Electricity Demand Series:
MZa Statistic: 1.3814
Critical value at 5% significance: -8.1
Fail to reject null hypothesis (series has a unit root/non-sta-
tionary).
```

The preceding output clarifies that the generated synthetic data has a unit root and is non-stationary in nature, and there is a need for transformations such as differencing.

Let us finally write the code to plot the results of the Ng-Perron test.

```
Code:
import matplotlib.pyplot as plt
test_name = "Ng-Perron MZa Test"
values = {"statistic": 1.3814, "critical_value": -1.95}
fig, ax = plt.subplots(figsize=(6, 4))
bar = ax.bar([test_name], [values["statistic"]], color='steel-
blue')
ax.axhline(y=values["critical_value"], color='red', 
linestyle='--', label='Critical Value (5%)')
ax.text(0, values["statistic"] + 0.1, f"{values['statis-
tic']:.2f}", ha='center', fontsize=10)
ax.text(0, values["critical_value"] + 0.1, f"CV: 
{values['critical_value']}",
        color='red', fontsize=9, ha='center')
ax.set_ylim(min(values["statistic"], values["critical_value"]) - 1,
```

```
                max(values["statistic"], values["critical_value"]) +
1)
ax.set_ylabel("Test Statistic")
ax.set_title(f"{test_name} Test Result")
ax.legend()
ax.grid(axis='y', linestyle='--', alpha=0.7)
plt.tight_layout()
```

In the preceding code,

This script produces a simple bar chart that compares the observed KPSS test statistic against its 5% critical value.

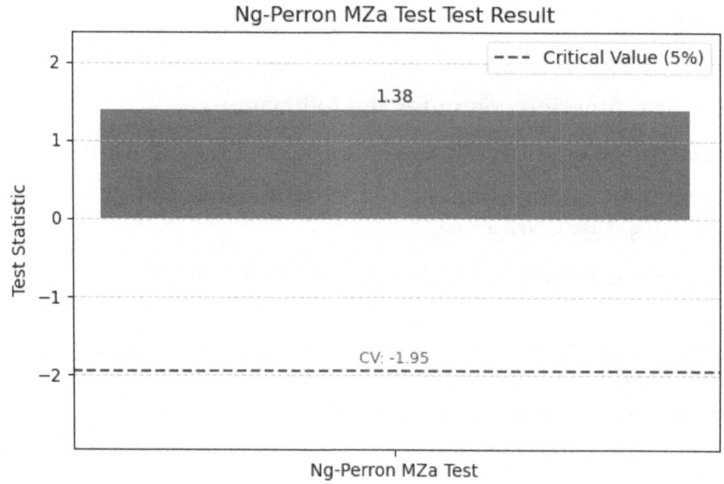

Figure 4.4: *Ng-Perron Test*

Figure 4.4 helps in visually aligning the test statistic with the threshold to get an immediate sense of whether we would reject the null hypothesis (unit root) at the 5% level.

This example demonstrates how to:

- Simulate realistic time series datasets for electricity demand analysis.
- Define functions needed to perform the Ng-Perron test for stationarity.
- Calculate the coefficients needed to perform the test.
- Define and test the null and alternative hypotheses.

This is a practical way to understand and prepare time series data for modeling, especially when dealing with stationary data.

To summarize,

- This code generates synthetic datasets that mirror real-world electricity
- demand.

- Defines all the functions needed to perform the Ng-Perron test on the simulated data.
- Performs the test and interprets the results.

The Ng-Perron test provides substantial improvements over traditional unit-root tests through its robustness to small samples and strong autocorrelation.

It addresses key limitations inherent in other tests. This includes size distortions and power issues. This is what makes it highly suitable for critical applications such as energy forecasting, financial modeling, and economic analysis.

Thus, by applying the Ng-Perron test, we can obtain clearer insights into the underlying properties of the time series data. However, it is recommended to use the Ng-Perron test in conjunction with other complementary methods to achieve comprehensive and reliable conclusions.

Conclusion

In this chapter, we covered a comprehensive exploration of advanced stationarity tests that serve as critical tools for analyzing and modeling time series data. Building upon the foundational methods introduced in the previous chapter, we delved into four powerful and complementary statistical tests: the Phillips–Perron (PP) Test, Kwiatkowski–Phillips–Schmidt–Shin (KPSS) Test, Elliott–Rothenberg–Stock (DF-GLS) Test, and Ng–Perron Test. Each of these tests addresses specific limitations of classical approaches, offering improved reliability, robustness, and diagnostic flexibility.

The **Phillips–Perron Test** extends the Augmented Dickey-Fuller framework by correcting for serial correlation and heteroscedasticity in the error terms without requiring explicit lag augmentation. This makes it particularly useful in analyzing macroeconomic and financial time series where such features are common. However, like ADF, it retains the unit root as the null hypothesis, making it susceptible to size distortions.

In contrast, the **KPSS Test** reverses the testing logic by positing stationarity as the null hypothesis and treating the presence of a unit root as the alternative. This fundamental difference allows KPSS to act as a diagnostic complement to ADF and PP. The ability to approach the stationarity question from both perspectives (null of stationarity versus null of non-stationarity) enables a more well-rounded and confident conclusion about the true nature of the data.

The **Elliott–Rothenberg–Stock (DF-GLS) Test** improves the statistical power of unit root detection by using Generalized Least Squares (GLS) detrending procedure before performing the test. Particularly effective in smaller samples and near-stationary cases, DF-GLS offers a more refined approach than traditional ADF or PP tests. This is especially useful when precise detection is essential for modeling.

The **Ng–Perron Test** is one of the most advanced tests in this group. This further enhances testing by incorporating improved lag-length selection and modified test statistics that correct for size and power problems found in ADF and PP. It combines features from previous tests into a robust package and is particularly recommended for empirical applications where sample size and serial dependence complicate analysis.

Collectively, these tests provide a multi-dimensional framework for evaluating stationarity. By using them in tandem, particularly by comparing results from tests with opposite null hypotheses such as PP and KPSS, we can mitigate the risk of misclassification and gain a deeper understanding of the underlying data dynamics. Moreover, these tools are not only diagnostic but also prescriptive, informing crucial decisions about model transformation, differencing, or the need for structural adjustments.

In the next chapter, we will extend this analytical toolkit further by examining advanced stationarity tests that incorporate structural breaks and variance shifts. These are scenarios frequently encountered in real-world time series where conventional assumptions do not hold.

References

- Shumway, R.H. and Stoffer, D.S. (2017) *Time Series Analysis and Its Applications: With R Examples*. 4th edn. *Springer*.
- Hamilton, J.D. (1994) *Time Series Analysis*. *Princeton University Press*.
- Enders, W. (2014) *Applied Econometric Time Series*. 4th edn. *Wiley*.
- Maddala, G.S. and Kim, I.-M. (1998) *Unit Roots, Cointegration, and Structural Change*. Cambridge: *Cambridge University Press*.
- Phillips, P. C. B. and Perron, P. (1988). Testing for a Unit Root in Time Series Regression. *Biometrika*, 75(2), pp. 335–346. https://doi.org/10.1093/biomet/75.2.335
- Kwiatkowski, D., Phillips, P. C. B., Schmidt, P. and Shin, Y. (1992). Testing the Null Hypothesis of Stationarity Against the Alternative of a Unit Root: How Sure Are We That Economic Time Series Have a Unit Root? *Journal of Econometrics*, 54(1–3), pp. 159–178. https://doi.org/10.1016/0304-4076(92)90104-Y
- Elliott, G., Rothenberg, T. J. and Stock, J. H. (1996). Efficient Tests for an Autoregressive Unit Root. *Econometrica*, 64(4), pp. 813–836. https://doi.org/10.2307/2171846
- Ng, S. and Perron, P. (2001). Lag Length Selection and the Construction of Unit Root Tests with Good Size and Power. *Econometrica*, 69(6), pp. 1519–1554. https://doi.org/10.1111/1468-0262.00256

CHAPTER 5
Tests for Stationarity – Part 3

Introduction

In the analysis of time series data, distinguishing between stationary and non-stationary processes is foundational for effective modeling and forecasting. Classical unit root tests such as the Augmented Dickey-Fuller (ADF) and Phillips-Perron tests offer a baseline framework. However, they often fall short in more complex or nuanced situations, such as the presence of structural breaks, trend stationarity, or stochastic components in finite samples.

This chapter introduces a suite of advanced econometric tools designed to address these limitations and enhance the robustness of time series inference. We will begin this chapter with the Schmidt-Phillips Test, which modifies the traditional unit root testing approach by incorporating deterministic trends and improving the handling of serial correlation, especially in the presence of long-term deterministic components.

We will then explore the Variance Ratio Tests, offering a non-parametric framework to assess whether a series follows a random walk. This is commonly used in the domain of capital markets to analyze market efficiency and asset pricing.

The third test in this chapter is the Zivot-Andrews Test, which extends unit root testing by allowing for one endogenous structural break in the data, thus overcoming the limitations of traditional tests that assume a fixed, known breakpoint.

Finally, we will cover the Leybourne-McCabe Test that targets the detection of stationarity versus non-stationarity, which is more useful when traditional tests exhibit low power.

By the end of this chapter, readers will be able to identify limitations of classical unit root tests (for example, ADF, Phillips-Perron) in real-world time series with structural breaks, stochastic components, or deterministic trends, and understand why advanced methods are needed for reliable inference.

Structure

In this chapter, the following topics will be covered under tests for stationarity:

- Test for Stationarity:
  - Schmidt-Phillips Test
  - Variance Ratio Tests
  - Zivot-Andrews Test
  - Leybourne–McCabe Test

Test for Stationarity

As discussed in earlier chapters, stationarity is one of the most important concepts in time series analysis. It plays a key role in helping us understand and model data that evolves over time. This section covers some more complementary tests of stationarity that can be performed on time series data.

Schmidt-Phillips Test

The Schmidt-Phillips (SP) test is a statistical test designed to determine whether a given time series is stationary around a deterministic trend, also known as trend stationarity, or non-stationary due to a unit root. It is particularly suitable when assessing, if observed trends are deterministic or stochastic. Deterministic trends are predictable and stable, whereas stochastic trends are random and unpredictable.

Unlike tests such as the Augmented Dickey-Fuller (ADF) or Phillips-Perron (PP), which primarily test for the presence of unit roots, the Schmidt-Phillips test explicitly evaluates whether the data can be modeled as stationary around a deterministic linear trend.

Identifying trend stationarity accurately is crucial for modeling and forecasting time series data, as it affects the choice of methods for detrending, differencing, or applying statistical models.

This test is valuable in economics, finance, environmental sciences, and energy markets, where distinguishing deterministic trends from stochastic ones significantly impacts forecasting accuracy and decision-making.

Mathematical Explanation

The Schmidt-Phillips test is based on estimating the following regression model:

$$X_t = \alpha + \beta t + \rho X_{t-1} + u_t$$

where:

- X_t is the time series,
- *a* is an intercept term,
- βt is a deterministic linear trend component,
- ρX_{t-1} represents the autoregressive component, and
- u_t is the error term, typically assumed to be independently and identically distributed with mean zero and constant variance.

The test hypotheses for the Schmidt-Phillips test are formulated as follows:

- **Null Hypothesis (H_0):** The series has a unit root (ρ-1), indicating non-stationarity.
- **Alternative Hypothesis (H_a):** The series is stationary around a deterministic trend ($\rho<1$).

To test these hypotheses, the Schmidt-Phillips test uses the estimated coefficient $\hat{p}$. The test statistic is:

$$SP = \frac{\hat{\rho} - 1}{SE(\hat{\rho})}$$

where:

- $\hat{p}$ is the estimated autoregressive parameter, and
- $SE(\hat{p})$ is the standard error of the estimate.

If the calculated SP statistic is more negative than the critical value at the chosen significance level, we reject the null hypothesis, concluding the series is trend-stationary.

Implementing the Math as a Python Function

In this section, let us write Python code to implement a simplified Schmidt-Phillips Test.

To perform this, let us write functions to compute the mean and OLS for a time series dataset.

Code:

```
def mean(series):
    return sum(series) / len(series)
```

In the preceding code,

The function **mean** is defined to compute the average of a list of numbers.

Code:

```
def sp_ols(y, t, x_lag):
    n = len(y)
    X = [[1, t[i], x_lag[i]] for i in range(n)]
    XtX = [[0]*3 for _ in range(3)]
    Xty = [0]*3

    for i in range(n):
        for j in range(3):
            Xty[j] += X[i][j] * y[i]
            for k in range(3):
                XtX[j][k] += X[i][j] * X[i][k]

    def determinant(m):
        return (m[0][0]*(m[1][1]*m[2][2]-m[1][2]*m[2][1])
                -m[0][1]*(m[1][0]*m[2][2]-m[1][2]*m[2][0])
                +m[0][2]*(m[1][0]*m[2][1]-m[1][1]*m[2][0]))

    det_XtX = determinant(XtX)
    epsilon = 1e-10
    if abs(det_XtX) < epsilon:
        raise ValueError("Singular matrix encountered in OLS
estimation.")

    def replace_col(matrix, col_index, new_col):
        replaced = [row[:] for row in matrix]
        for i in range(len(matrix)):
            replaced[i][col_index] = new_col[i]
        return replaced

    beta = [determinant(replace_col(XtX, i, Xty)) / det_XtX for i in
range(3)]

    residuals = [y[i] - sum(X[i][j]*beta[j] for j in range(3)) for i in
range(n)]
    residual_var = sum(e**2 for e in residuals) / (n - 3)

    numerator = residual_var * XtX[2][2]
    if abs(numerator) < epsilon:
        raise ValueError("Standard error of rho (se_rho) is zero or
nearly zero.")

    se_rho = (numerator / det_XtX)**0.5
    rho = beta[2]

    return rho, se_rho
```

In the preceding code,

- The function **sp_ols**, performs linear regression using the Ordinary Least Squares method specific to the Schmidt-Phillips test.
- It constructs the design matrix (X) with columns for:
    - Intercept (1),
    - Time trend (t), and
    - Lagged dependent variable (**x_lag**).
- It computes the cross product of the design matrix (X' X).
- It also computes X' *y* vector.
- It solves the normal equations by calculating determinants for matrix inversion.
- It also estimates the regression coefficients (beta), residual variance, and standard error of ρ.

In the next step, let us calculate the Schmidt-Phillips test statistic.

Code:

```
def schmidt_phillips_test(series):
    n = len(series)
    y = series[1:]
    t = list(range(2, n+1))
    x_lag = series[:-1]

    rho, se_rho = sp_ols(y, t, x_lag)
    if abs(se_rho) < 1e-10:
        raise ValueError("Standard error of rho is effectively zero.")
    sp_statistic = (rho - 1) / se_rho
    return sp_statistic
```

In the preceding code,

- The **schmidt_phillips_test** function implements the Schmidt-Phillips (SP) unit root test to detect non-stationarity in time series data.
- This test is particularly valuable when analyzing economic or energy time series that may contain both stochastic trends and deterministic time trends.
- We have created the following necessary components for regression in this function:
    - **y** - Dependent variable,
    - **t** - Time trend, and
    - **x_lag** - Lagged dependent variable.

- We have computed the following:
    - **rho**: Coefficient on the lagged term, and
    - **se_rho:** Standard error of rho.

These values are used to calculate the test statistic that is returned by the function.

Real-World Example

For this implementation, we will continue using synthetic data generation and generate data for electricity demand. As already seen, energy utilities often observe electricity demand series with pronounced upward trends due to economic and population growth. An important question is whether these trends are deterministic, implying predictable long-term growth, or stochastic, meaning unpredictable and potentially unstable. This distinction affects forecasting methods, capacity planning, and investment decisions.

The Schmidt-Phillips test helps distinguish deterministic trends from stochastic unit-root processes in electricity demand data. This ensures accurate forecasts, reliable infrastructure planning, and effective energy market strategies.

Python Implementation for the SP Test of Electricity Demand Data

In this example, let us generate synthetic electricity demand data with realistic patterns and then analyze it using the SP test.

In the following code, we will create a synthetic dataset that mimics monthly electricity usage data over 48 months.

Code:

```
def generate_electricity_demand(months=48):
    import random
    demand = []
    base = 1000
    for month in range(months):
        trend = month * 20
        fluctuation = (-1)**month * 25
        noise = random.gauss(0, 5)
        demand.append(base + trend + fluctuation + noise)
    return demand
electricity_demand = generate_electricity_demand()
electricity_demand[0:5]
```

In the preceding code,

- The **generate_electricity_demand** function is defined with a base demand level of 1000MW. This is considered the minimum expected demand regardless of other factors.

- The data is generated for 48 months.
- A random noise is added to the data.

The output of the generated data is displayed as follows:

Output:

```
[1024.2987886322137,
 999.022956437759,
 1068.4854517550373,
 1031.5085857788772,
 1107.7279023861488]
```

The preceding output models gradual demand growth and captures predictable seasonal fluctuations.

Let us further perform the SP test on the generated synthetic demand data.

Code:

```
sp_critical_value_5pct = -2.89
sp_statistic = schmidt_phillips_test(electricity_demand)
print("Schmidt-Phillips Test for Electricity Demand Series:")
print(f"SP Test Statistic: {sp_statistic:.4f}")
print(f"Critical Value at 5% significance: {sp_critical_value_5pct}")

if sp_statistic < sp_critical_value_5pct:
    print("Result: Reject null hypothesis (series is trend stationary).")
else:
    print("Result: Fail to reject null hypothesis (series has unit root/
non-stationary).")
```

In the preceding code,

- We have applied the Schmidt-Phillips test to our electricity demand time series.
- The **schmidt_phillips_test** function returns the test statistic **sp_statistic**, which we will use to evaluate whether the series is stationary.
- We then display the test statistic and compare it to the 5% critical value, which serves as a benchmark.
- The null hypothesis of the Schmidt-Phillips test is that the series contains a unit root, which means it is non-stationary.
- If the test statistic is less than the critical value, we have enough evidence to reject the null hypothesis, concluding that the series is stationary.

- Otherwise, if the test statistic is greater than the critical value, we fail to reject the null, suggesting that the series is non-stationary and may require differencing or transformation before modeling.

Let us finally write code to plot the results of the SP test:

Code:

```
import matplotlib.pyplot as plt

def plot_sp_test_result(statistic, critical_value, title="Schmidt-
Phillips Test Result"):
    fig, ax = plt.subplots(figsize=(6, 4))

    bar = ax.bar(["SP Statistic"], [statistic], color='steelblue')

    ax.axhline(y=critical_value, color='red', linestyle='--',
label='Critical Value (5%)')

    ax.text(0, statistic + 0.1, f"{statistic:.2f}", ha='center',
fontsize=10)
    ax.text(0, critical_value + 0.1, f"CV: {critical_value}",
            color='red', fontsize=9, ha='center')

    buffer = 1
    ax.set_ylim(min(statistic, critical_value) - buffer, max(statistic,
critical_value) + buffer)

    ax.set_ylabel("Test Statistic")
    ax.set_title(title)
    ax.legend()
    ax.grid(axis='y', linestyle='--', alpha=0.7)
    plt.tight_layout()
    plt.show()

plot_sp_test_result(sp_statistic, sp_critical_value_5pct)
```

In the preceding code,

This script produces a simple bar chart that compares the observed Schmidt-Phillips test statistic against its 5% critical value.

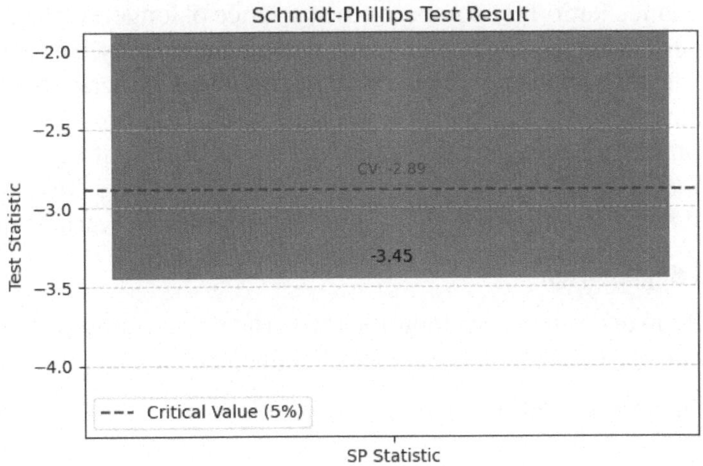

***Figure* 5.1:** *Schmidt-Phillips Test Results*

Figure 5.1 helps in visually aligning the test statistic with the threshold to get an immediate sense of whether we would reject the null hypothesis (unit root) at the 5% level.

To summarize,

- This code generates synthetic electricity data with a seasonal pattern and checks for stationarity.
- It computes the mean and OLS on the data.
- It implements a simplified SP test to test the non-stationarity of the data.

The Schmidt-Phillips test provides valuable insights into whether observed trends in the time series data are deterministic or stochastic, directly affecting modeling approaches and forecasting accuracy. By clearly identifying trend stationarity, we can choose appropriate methods for detrending, forecasting, and policy-making. In electricity demand forecasting and related fields, accurately distinguishing deterministic from stochastic trends using the Schmidt-Phillips test helps companies develop robust, accurate, and economically sound strategies. It remains essential, however, to complement this test with other stationarity analyses, visual inspection, and domain expertise for comprehensive data understanding.

Variance Ratio Test

The Variance Ratio Test is a statistical method primarily used to detect whether a time series follows a random walk or exhibits mean-reverting or stationary behavior. It is widely employed to analyze the properties of financial, economic, and energy-related time series data. This is used particularly to test market efficiency or determine whether changes in a series are random or predictable.

Overall, the Variance Ratio Test compares the variance of longer-term intervals of data with the variance of shorter-term intervals scaled proportionally. Under the hypothesis of a random walk, the variance of the increments of the series scales linearly with time. Deviations from this scaling suggest non-randomness or predictability, indicating possible stationarity or autocorrelation in the data. Due to its simplicity, intuitive interpretation, and minimal assumptions, the Variance Ratio Test is an essential diagnostic tool for analyzing stationarity and random walks in various domains.

Mathematical Explanation

The Variance Ratio test relies on comparing the variances computed from observations at different intervals. Consider a time series X_t in which:

Increments of length q is defined as:

$$X_t - X_{t-q}$$

The variance ratio VR(q) is defined as:

$$VR(q) = \frac{\frac{1}{q}\sigma^2(q)}{\sigma^2(1)}$$

where:

- σ^2 (q) is the variance of the q-period differences, and
- σ^2 (1) is the variance of single-period differences.

If the series follows a pure random walk, the variance scales linearly, and VR(q) should be approximately 1. Note that a pure random walk denotes non-stationarity with no autocorrelation.

The hypotheses tested by the Variance Ratio Test are defined as follows:

- Null Hypothesis (H_0): The series follows a random walk (*variance ratio* ≈1).
- Alternate Hypothesis (H_a): The series is stationary or mean-reverting (variance ratio ≠ 1).

Under the null hypothesis, significant deviation from 1 in either direction suggests predictability or non-randomness, implying stationarity or other structural properties.

Implementing the Math as a Python Function

In this section, let us write Python code to implement the Variance Ratio test from scratch.

To perform this, let us write functions to compute the mean, variance, and variance ratio test for a time series dataset.

The following is the step-by-step implementation of the test:

Code:

```
def mean(series):
    return sum(series) / len(series)
```

In the preceding code,

- The function **mean** is defined to compute the average of a list of numbers.

Code:

```
def variance(series):
    mu = mean(series)
    return sum([(x - mu)**2 for x in series]) / (len(series) - 1)
```

In the preceding code,

- The **variance** function calculates the sample variance of the time series dataset, providing a fundamental measure of how individual data points deviate from the mean.
- This metric is essential for understanding the spread and volatility in time series data.

Code:

```
def variance_ratio_test(series, q=2):
    n = len(series)
    increments_single = [series[i] - series[i-1] for i in range(1, n)]
    increments_q = [series[i] - series[i-q] for i in range(q, n)]

    var_single = variance(increments_single)
    var_q = variance(increments_q)

    vr = (var_q / (q * var_single))

    return vr
```

In the preceding code,

- The **variance_ratio_test** function calculates the variance ratio of the time series data.
- The goal of this function is to check if the series follows a random walk.
- It compares the variability of returns over different time horizons to detect trends or mean reversion.
- This function first computes the **single-step** increments, which provide the differences between consecutive values.

- Next, it calculates **q-step** increments, which provide the differences between values q steps apart.
- It then calculates the single increment variance and q-increment variance using the **variance** function.
- Finally, it calculates the variance ratio.

Real-World Example

For this implementation, we will continue using synthetic data generation and generate data for electricity demand. An essential question in electricity markets is whether demand increments follow random walks or exhibit predictable or stationary behavior, crucial for forecasting and decision-making.

For example, if daily electricity demand follows a random walk, future changes would be unpredictable. Conversely, a significant deviation from a variance ratio of 1 could indicate systematic patterns, seasonality, or stationarity. This will help in applying forecasting models confidently to manage supply, procurement, and trading strategies effectively.

Python Implementation for the Variance Ratio Test on Electricity Data

In this example, let us generate synthetic electricity demand data with realistic patterns and then analyze it using the Variance Ratio test.

Code:

```
import random
def generate_electricity_demand(days=100):
    demand = []
    base_demand = 1000
    trend = 2
    noise_level = 15

    for day in range(days):
        if day == 0:
            demand.append(base_demand)
        else:
            cyclical_change = 20 if day % 2 == 0 else -20
            noise = random.gauss(0, noise_level)
            trend_component = trend * day

              new_value = demand[-1] + cyclical_change + noise + trend_
component
            demand.append(new_value)
    return demand
electricity_demand = generate_electricity_demand()
electricity_demand[0:5]
```

In the preceding code,

- In the **generate_electricity_demand** function, we have constructed a synthetic time series that emulates the key characteristics of real-world electricity consumption data.
- The base demand level has been set to 1000.
- This function simulates daily electricity demand over the specified number of days.
- The generated demand includes cyclical patterns, random noise, and a long-term upward trend—making it a realistic time series data often seen in real-world data.

The output of the generated data is displayed as follows:

```
[1000,
979.0182782661414,
1009.1235100305771,
975.5198388194292,
996.5791498963569]
```

The preceding output models slight randomness in the electricity demand, but at the same time, with minor variations.

Let us further perform the Variance Ratio test on the generated synthetic demand data.

```
Code:
q = 2
vr_result = variance_ratio_test(electricity_demand, q)
print("Variance Ratio Test for Electricity Demand Series:")
print(f"Variance Ratio (VR): {vr_result:.4f}")
print("Expected VR under random walk ≈ 1")

if abs(vr_result - 1) > 0.1:
    print("Result: Series is likely stationary or exhibits predictable 
behavior.")
else:
    print("Result: Series likely follows a random walk (non-
stationary).")
```

In the preceding code,

- We have set the aggregation interval q to 2. This is to make the variance ratio test compare the variability of increments over 1-step versus 2-step periods.
- In the next step, the function **variance_ratio_test** is called with the synthetic electricity demand series we generated and with lag q=2.

- The function returns the Variance Ratio (VR), quantifying how the variance of 2-step increments compares to twice the variance of 1-step increments.
- We then printed the heading and the calculated VR value, formatted to four decimal places. It also reminds us that under the assumption of a random walk or non-stationarity, the VR should be close to 1.
- Finally, we have checked how far the VR deviates from 1 by more than 0.1. 0.1 is an arbitrary threshold for this example.
- If the VR differs significantly from 1, it suggests the series is not a random walk, indicating stationarity or predictable patterns such as mean reversion or trend persistence.
- If the VR is close to 1 (within ±0.1), it implies the series behaves like a random walk, typical of non-stationary processes with no predictable short-term structure.

Output:

```
Variance Ratio Test for Electricity Demand Series:
Variance Ratio (VR): 1.7068
Expected VR under random walk ≈ 1
Result: Series is likely stationary or exhibits predictable behavior.
```

From the preceding output, it is evident that the time series data exhibits stationarity.

Let us finally write code to plot the results of the Variance Ratio test.

Code:

```
import matplotlib.pyplot as plt
def plot_variance_ratio(vr_result, q=2):
    test_name = f"Variance Ratio Test (q={q})"
    critical_value = 1
    fig, ax = plt.subplots(figsize=(6, 4))
    bar = ax.bar([test_name], [vr_result], color='steelblue')
            ax.axhline(y=critical_value,   color='red',   linestyle='--',
label='Expected VR (Random Walk)')
       ax.text(0,  vr_result  +  0.02,  f"{vr_result:.4f}",  ha='center',
fontsize=12)
   ax.text(0, critical_value + 0.02, f"VR = {critical_value}", color='red',
ha='center', fontsize=10)
      ax.set_ylim(min(vr_result,  critical_value)  -  0.2,  max(vr_result,
critical_value) + 0.2)
    ax.set_ylabel("Variance Ratio (VR)")
    ax.set_title("Variance Ratio Test Result")
    ax.legend()
```

```
    ax.grid(axis='y', linestyle='--', alpha=0.7)
    plt.show()
plot_variance_ratio(vr_result, q)
```

In the preceding code,

This script produces a simple bar chart showing the variance ratio from the test alongside the expected value under the random walk hypothesis.

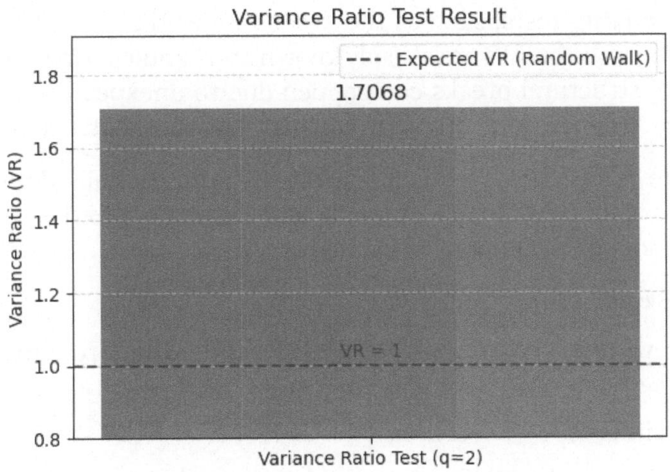

Figure 5.2: *Variance Ratio Test Results*

Figure 5.2 helps in visually aligning the test statistic with the threshold to get an immediate sense of whether we would reject the null hypothesis.

To summarize,

- This code generates synthetic electricity data with randomness and checks for stationarity.
- It computes the mean and variance, and calculates the variance ratio test on the data.
- It implements a simplified Variance Ratio test to test the non-stationarity of the data.

The Variance Ratio Test is a valuable tool for evaluating the randomness or stationarity of a time series. Its simplicity, intuitive interpretation, and minimal assumptions make it particularly effective for initial data diagnostics. This is especially useful when evaluating market efficiency, detecting predictability, and confirming the suitability of forecasting models.

In practice, especially in electricity demand analysis, accurate detection of non-randomness and stationarity allows for effective modeling strategies and better forecasting for strategic decision-making. Like other tests, while powerful, the

Variance Ratio Test also should be combined with other stationarity tests (ADF, PP, KPSS) and visual inspections for comprehensive analysis and robust conclusions.

Zivot-Andrews Test

The next test in our chapter is the Zivot-Andrews Test. This test is specifically designed to detect stationarity in the presence of structural breaks within a time series data. Traditional stationarity tests, such as the ADF assumes that the series either has no structural breaks or the breaks are already known and handled. However, in real-world time series data, structural breaks can happen due to unexpected scenarios such as economic crises, technological breakthroughs, or environmental changes.

The Zivot-Andrews test helps in handling this by automatically detecting the most likely break date within the data. This test then determines whether the series can be classified as stationary around this identified break.

Mathematical Explanation

The Zivot-Andrews test is based on a modified form of the unit-root testing procedure. It allows for three types of structural breaks:

- Break in intercept - Level break
- Break in slope - Trend break
- Break in both Level and Trend

The Zivot-Andrews regression can be mathematically defined as follows:

$$\Delta X_t = \alpha + \beta t + \gamma DU_t(\lambda) + \theta DT_t(\lambda) + \rho X_{t-1} + \sum_{i=1}^{k} \delta_i \Delta X_{t-i} + \epsilon_t$$

where:

- X_t is the time series.
- $DU_t(\lambda)$ is an indicator for the structural break in the intercept. This is equal to 1 if $t > \lambda T$, 0 otherwise.
- $DT_t(\lambda)$ is an indicator of the structural break in the trend. This is equal to $t-\lambda T$ if $t>\lambda T$, 0 otherwise.
- λ represents the relative position of the structural break in the sample period.
- ρ, γ, θ, and δ_i are parameters to estimate.
- ΔX_t is the first difference ($X_t - X_{t-1}$).

The hypotheses for the Zivot-Andrews Test are defined as follows:

Null Hypothesis (H_0): The series has a unit root or has non-stationarity with structural breaks.

Alternate Hypothesis (H_a): The series exhibits stationarity with a one-time structural break at an unknown point.

The test statistic is the minimum t-statistic for testing ρ=0, obtained by scanning over potential break points.

Implementing the Math as a Python Function

In this section, let us write a simplified implementation of the Zivot-Andrews Test from scratch.

Let us start by writing the code of the arithmetic mean as covered in many sections of this book.

Code:

```
def mean(series):
    return sum(series) / len(series)
```

In the preceding code,

- We have defined the function to calculate **mean** for a series of numbers.

In the next steps, let us define the function to compute OLS coefficients and residuals for the Zivot-Andrews regression.

Code:

```
def za_ols(y, X):
    XtX = [[sum(X[i][j]*X[i][k] for i in range(len(X))) for k in
range(len(X[0]))] for j in range(len(X[0]))]
    XtY = [sum(y[i]*X[i][j] for i in range(len(X))) for j in
range(len(X[0]))]

    def det3(m):
        return (m[0][0]*(m[1][1]*m[2][2]-m[1][2]*m[2][1])
                -m[0][1]*(m[1][0]*m[2][2]-m[1][2]*m[2][0])
                +m[0][2]*(m[1][0]*m[2][1]-m[1][1]*m[2][0]))
    det_XtX = det3(XtX)
    def replace(matrix, col, newcol):
        return [[newcol[i] if j==col else matrix[i][j] for j in
range(3)] for i in range(3)]
    betas = [det3(replace(XtX,j,XtY))/det_XtX for j in range(3)]
    residuals = [y[i] - sum(X[i][j]*betas[j] for j in range(3)) for i in
range(len(y))]
    s2 = sum(e**2 for e in residuals)/(len(y)-3)
    se_beta2 = (s2*XtX[2][2]/det_XtX)**0.5
    t_stat = betas[2]/se_beta2
    return t_stat
```

In the preceding code,

- The function **za_ols** performs an Ordinary Least Squares (OLS) regression on the time series dataset with 3 predictors and returns the t-statistic for the third regression coefficient (**beta**).
- This method is used in the ZA test to estimate linear relationships and assess the statistical significance of coefficients.
- We have defined inputs for this function as y (target variable) and x (dependent variables).
- This function then calculates a 3x3 matrix product $X^T X$ by summing products of predictor columns over all observations.
- It also computes the vector $X^T y$, summing products of each predictor column with the dependent variable.
- The helper function **det3** calculates the determinant of a 3x3 matrix using the rule of Sarrus. Sarrus' Rule is a simple, visual technique to compute the determinant of a 3×3 matrix without using cofactor expansion. It works only for 3×3 matrices and provides an easy shortcut.
- The determinant of $X^T X$ is used for solving the linear system via Cramer's rule. Cramer's Rule is a mathematical method for solving systems of linear equations using determinants.
- The other helper function, **replace**, creates a new matrix by replacing one column with a new column vector for applying Cramer's rule for each beta coefficient.
- The OLS estimates (**betas**) are then computed by calculating beta coefficients using Cramer's rule.
- Then the **residuals** are calculated.
- In the next step, the estimated variance of residuals s^2 are computed.
- Then the standard error of the third beta (index 2) is computed using the formula derived from the variance-covariance matrix of the estimator.
- Then the t-statistic is computed to measure how many standard errors the beta is away from zero. It is then used to test the null hypothesis that the coefficient equals to zero.
- The function returns the computed t-statistic for the third beta coefficient, which will be used for hypothesis testing.

Let us now implement the function for the Zivot-Andrews test.

Code:

```
def zivot_andrews(series):
```

```
    T = len(series)
    min_t_stat = float('inf')
    best_break = None
    for break_point in range(int(0.15*T), int(0.85*T)):
        DU = [1 if t > break_point else 0 for t in range(T)]
       DT = [t - break_point if t > break_point else 0 for t in range(T)]
        y = [series[t] - series[t-1] for t in range(1,T)]
        X_lag = series[:-1]
        DU = DU[1:]
        DT = DT[1:]
        X = [[1, DU[i], X_lag[i]] for i in range(T-1)]
        t_stat = za_ols(y,X)
        if t_stat < min_t_stat:
            min_t_stat = t_stat
            best_break = break_point
    return min_t_stat, best_break
```

In the preceding code,

- The **`zivot_andrews`** function implements the Zivot-Andrews test.
- It tries to identify whether the series is stationary or contains a unit root while accounting for a potential break in the intercept or trend at an unknown point.
- The function analyzes the length T of this series to determine break candidates.
- **`min_t_stat`** is initialized to infinity, to keep track of the minimum (most negative) test statistic.
- Lower t-statistics indicate stronger evidence against the null hypothesis of a unit root.
- **`best_break`** will store the time index of the detected structural break, giving the strongest evidence.
- The test scans all possible break points between 15% and 85% of the sample to avoid breaks too close to the start or end of the series.
- The **`DU`** variable models a potential sudden level shift (intercept change) after the break.
- The **`DT`** variable models a change in slope (trend) after the break.
- This function also runs the custom OLS function **`za_ols`** regression that returns the t-statistic of the lagged level coefficient, which tests the presence of a unit root.
- It finally returns the minimum t-statistic and the best break.

Real-World Example

For this implementation, we will continue using synthetic data generation and generate data for electricity demand. Electricity demand patterns frequently exhibit structural breaks due to economic shocks, policy interventions, energy efficiency measures, or sudden changes in consumer behavior (like during a pandemic).

Applying the Zivot-Andrews test enables utilities and grid operators to accurately assess whether electricity demand is stationary after accounting for structural changes. This informs decisions on forecasting models, infrastructure investments, and policy planning.

Python Implementation for the ZA Test on Electricity Data

In this section, let us implement the ZA test on synthetically generated electricity demand data to mimic the real-world application.

In the first step, let us start by generating synthetic electricity demand data with a structural break.

Code:

```
def generate_electricity_demand(n=100):
    demand = []
    for t in range(n):
        if t < 50:
            val = 1000 + t*5
        else:
            val = 1300 + t*2
        demand.append(val)
    return demand
electricity_demand = generate_electricity_demand()
electricity_demand[0:5]
```

In the preceding code,

- The **generate_electricity_demand** function creates synthetic electricity demand data that mimics real-world behavior characterized by a structural break.

Output:

```
[1000, 1005, 1010, 1015, 1020]
```

The preceding output models electricity demand data, which we stress-test models against realistic scenarios.

Code:

```
t_stat, break_point = zivot_andrews(electricity_demand)
critical_value_5pct = -4.80
```

```
print("Zivot-Andrews Test for Electricity Demand:")
print(f"Minimum t-statistic: {t_stat:.4f}")
print(f"Identified structural break at observation: {break_point}")
print(f"Critical value (5% significance): {critical_value_5pct}")
if t_stat < critical_value_5pct:
    print("Reject null hypothesis: Stationary with structural break.")
else:
    print("Fail to reject null hypothesis: Non-stationary (unit root).")
```

In the preceding code,

- It performs the Zivot-Andrews test to determine whether the electricity demand series exhibits a unit root (non-stationary behavior) or is stationary, along with a structural break.
- This test is critical for validating assumptions in time series modeling and forecasting.
- We have set the critical value for this test at a 5% significance level of -4.80.

Output:

```
Zivot-Andrews Test for Electricity Demand:
Minimum t-statistic: -0.0142
Identified structural break at observation: 49
Critical value (5% significance): -4.8
Fail to reject null hypothesis: Non-stationary (unit root).
```

This output indicates that the series may be non-stationary and may require differencing even though a structural break is identified at observation 49.

Let us finally write code to plot the results of the ZA test.

Code:

```
import matplotlib.pyplot as plt

def plot_za_test(series, break_point):
    T = len(series)
    time = list(range(T))

    plt.figure(figsize=(10, 5))
    plt.plot(time, series, label='Time Series', color='blue')

    if break_point is not None:
        plt.axvline(x=break_point, color='red', linestyle='--',
label=f'Estimated Break Point (t={break_point})')

    plt.title("Zivot-Andrews Test: Time Series with Estimated Structural
Break")
```

```
    plt.xlabel("Time")
    plt.ylabel("Series Value")
    plt.legend()
    plt.grid(True)
    plt.show()

plot_za_test(electricity_demand, break_point)
```

In the preceding code,

- The **plot_za_test** function visualizes the time series and marks the structural break point estimated by the Zivot-Andrews (ZA) test.

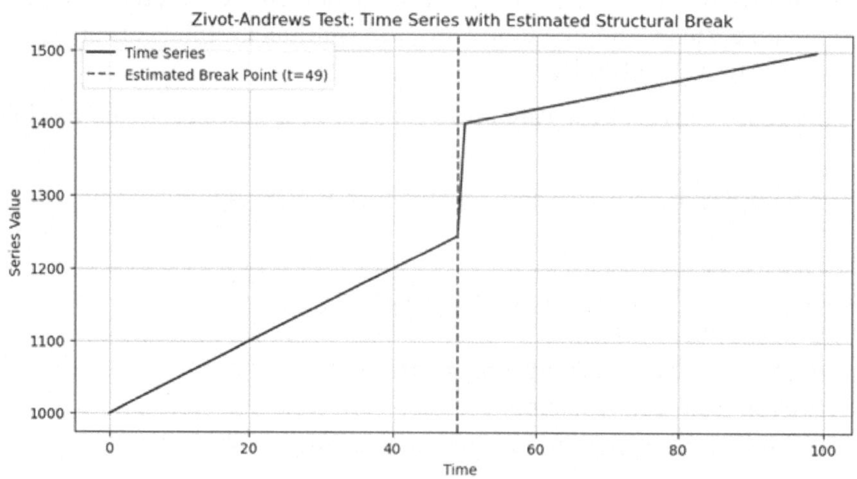

Figure 5.3: *ZA Test Result*

Figure 5.3 helps us to see where the test detects a regime change or structural break.

The Zivot-Andrews test is a highly effective method for identifying stationarity in the presence of structural breaks. It provides a critical advantage over standard stationarity tests by automatically pinpointing structural breaks, resulting in more accurate diagnostics and robust modeling. Its application is particularly beneficial in real-world scenarios, such as electricity markets, economics, finance, and environmental sciences, where sudden structural shifts are common.

However, to maximize the reliability of stationarity analysis, the Zivot-Andrews test should be complemented by visual diagnostics, additional statistical tests, and domain expertise, ensuring well-rounded and robust conclusions.

Leybourne-McCabe Test

The Leybourne-McCabe Test, introduced by Leybourne and McCabe (1994), is a statistical test specifically designed to assess the stationarity of a time series by examining potential changes in its variance over time. Unlike conventional unit root tests such as Dickey-Fuller or Phillips-Perron, which focus on detecting changes in the mean level or deterministic trends, the Leybourne-McCabe test explicitly addresses variance shifts or heteroscedasticity in the data.

In practical terms, many real-world time series such as financial market returns, energy prices, and climate data often display shifts or volatility clustering, indicating non-constant variance. Identifying these variance shifts is crucial because heteroscedasticity affects the reliability of traditional stationarity tests, forecasting accuracy, and model selection. The Leybourne-McCabe test addresses this issue by directly checking for the stability of variance, making it an essential tool in financial, economic, and environmental data analysis.

Mathematical Explanation

The Leybourne-McCabe test specifically evaluates the null hypothesis of variance stability or homoscedasticity against the alternative hypothesis of a single variance break at an unknown time point.

Consider a time series $\{X_t\}$, which is assumed to have zero mean (demeaned series) for simplicity. The variance stability hypothesis is stated as follows:

- **Null Hypothesis** (H_0)

  $Var(X_t) = \sigma^2$, constant for all t

- **Alternate Hypothesis** (H_a)

$$Var(X_t) = \{\sigma_1^2 \qquad t \le t^* \, \sigma_2^2 \quad t > t^*, \;\; \sigma_1^2 \neq \sigma_2^2$$

The Leybourne-McCabe test statistic is based on the ratio of cumulative sums of squared observations before and after each possible break point. Formally, for each possible breakpoint k, it is defined as follows:

$$LM(k) = \frac{\frac{1}{k}\sum_{t=1}^{k} X_t^2}{\frac{1}{T-k}\sum_{t=k+1}^{T} X_t^2}$$

where:

- T is the sample size,
- k is the breakpoint, and
- X_t^2 are squared observations.

Critical values provided by the Leybourne-McCabe test help to assess significance. The rejection of the null hypothesis indicates variance stability.

Implementing the Math as a Python Function

In this section, let us write a simplified yet comprehensive Python implementation of the Leybourne-McCabe test.

Let us begin our journey with the simplest yet most powerful statistical tool, the arithmetic mean.

Code:

```
# Mean calculation
def mean(series):
    return sum(series) / len(series)
```

In the preceding code,

- The **mean** function captures the central tendency of data by summing all values and dividing by their count.

Let us further proceed with implementing the Leybourne-McCabe test.

Code:

```
def leybourne_mccabe_test(series):
    T = len(series)
    LM_values = []
    for k in range(2, T-2):
        first_segment = series[:k]
        second_segment = series[k:]
        var_first = sum(x**2 for x in first_segment)/k
        var_second = sum(x**2 for x in second_segment)/(T - k)
        LM_k = abs((var_first/var_second) - 1)
        LM_values.append(LM_k)
    LM_statistic = max(LM_values)
    breakpoint = LM_values.index(LM_statistic) + 2
    return LM_statistic, breakpoint
```

In the preceding code,

- The function **leybourne_mccabe_test** implements the Leybourne-McCabe (LM) test, which detects a structural break in the variance of a time series.
- It tests whether the variance changes at some unknown point by comparing variance estimates before and after potential break points.
- **T** is the total number of observations in the series.
- **LM_values** is initialized as an empty list to store the test statistics calculated for each possible break point.
- This function evaluates each possible break point k from the 3rd observation to the $(T-3)^{th}$ observation, avoiding breaks too close to the edges to ensure meaningful segment sizes.

- For each candidate break **k**, the time series is split into two parts:
  - **first_segment** containing observations before **k**,
  - **second_segment** containing observations from **k** onward.
- It then computes the mean-squared values for each segment, assuming zero mean or detrended data.
- The test statistic **LM_k** at break point **k** measures the absolute relative difference between the two segment variances.
- Larger values suggest a more significant variance change at **k**.
- The maximum value in LM_values is chosen as the test statistic, indicating the most likely variance break.
- This function returns the maximum LM statistic found and the estimated breakpoint location where the variance likely changes.

Real-World Example

In the energy sector, electricity prices and demand often exhibit abrupt volatility changes due to regulatory shifts, sudden market shocks such as price spikes, or disruptive events such as pandemics. Utility companies must reliably assess whether electricity price volatility remains stable or changes over time.

The Leybourne-McCabe test provides a robust method to detect significant volatility shifts, crucial for accurate forecasting, risk management, and strategic planning.

Python Implementation for the Leybourne-McCabe Test on Electricity Data

The first step for this application is to generate synthetic data to perform Leybourne-McCabe test.

Code:

```
def generate_electricity_price_volatility(T=100):
    series = []
    for t in range(T):
        if t < 50:
            volatility = 5
        else:
            volatility = 15
        observation = ((-1)**t)*volatility
        series.append(observation)
    return series
```

In the preceding code, like some of the previous examples discussed,

- The function **generate_electricity_price_volatility** generates a synthetic time series simulating electricity price volatility over **T** time periods.

- This series is designed to have two distinct volatility regimes: low volatility initially and then higher volatility after a break point.
- This function simulates a volatility time series with a clear, abrupt change at the midpoint (**`t=50`**), transitioning from low amplitude oscillations to higher amplitude oscillations.
- The alternating sign pattern models fluctuations around zero, while the step increase in magnitude models a structural break in volatility level.

Let us further generate the data and call **`leybourne_mccabe_test`** to calculate the test statistic and breakpoint.

Code:

```
price_volatility = generate_electricity_price_volatility()
price_volatility[0:5]
Output:
[5, -5, 5, -5, 5]
```

In the preceding code,

- 100 months of electricity demand data are generated to run the LM test.

Let us further call the function to run the LM test.

Code:

```
LM_stat, breakpoint = leybourne_mccabe_test(price_volatility)
LM_critical_5pct = 1.358
print("Leybourne-McCabe Test for Electricity Price Volatility:")
print(f"LM Statistic: {LM_stat:.4f}")
print(f"Critical Value (5% significance): {LM_critical_5pct}")
print(f"Identified breakpoint at observation: {breakpoint}")
if LM_stat > LM_critical_5pct:
    print("Reject null hypothesis: Variance instability detected.")
else:
    print("Fail to reject null hypothesis: Variance stable.")
```

In the preceding code,

- We have computed the LM test statistic and breakpoint.
- This value, 1.358, is set as the critical threshold for the test statistic at a 5% significance level.
- It represents the cutoff above which we reject the null hypothesis of stable variance.
- If the LM test statistic exceeds the critical value, the null hypothesis of constant variance is rejected, indicating evidence of a structural break or instability in variance in the series.

- Otherwise, there is insufficient evidence to reject constant variance, so the variance is considered stable.

Output:

```
Leybourne-McCabe Test for Electricity Price Volatility:
LM Statistic: 0.8889
Critical Value (5% significance): 1.358
Identified breakpoint at observation: 50
Fail to reject null hypothesis: Variance stable.
```

The preceding output clarifies that the generated synthetic data has stable variance, and the LM test failed to reject the null hypothesis.

Let us finally write the code to plot the results of the LM test.

Code:

```
import matplotlib.pyplot as plt
def plot_leybourne_mccabe_result(series, breakpoint):
    T = len(series)
    time = list(range(T))

    plt.figure(figsize=(10, 5))
    plt.plot(time, series, label='Electricity Price Volatility',
color='blue')

    if breakpoint is not None:
        plt.axvline(x=breakpoint, color='red', linestyle='--',
label=f'Estimated Variance Break (t={breakpoint})')

    plt.title("Leybourne-McCabe Test: Electricity Price Volatility with
Detected Break")
    plt.xlabel("Time")
    plt.ylabel("Volatility")
    plt.legend()
    plt.grid(True)
    plt.show()

plot_leybourne_mccabe_result(price_volatility, breakpoint)
```

In the preceding code,

- The blue line plots the values of the electricity price volatility over time. It shows how volatility evolves across the observed period. Using this line, we can see fluctuations or patterns indicating changes in variance behavior.
- The red dashed vertical line marks the estimated break point identified by the Leybourne-McCabe test. This is the time index where the test detects the most significant change in variance, indicating a structural break in volatility.

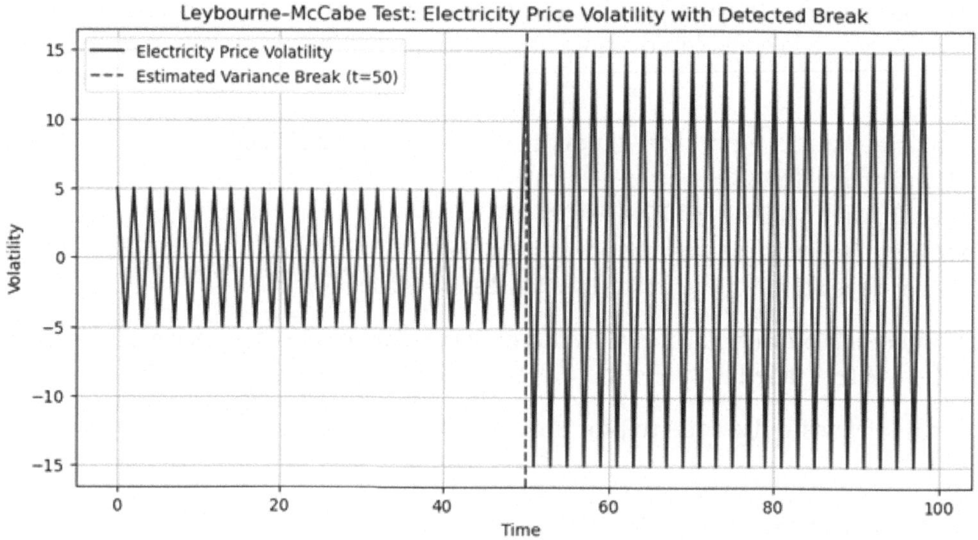

Figure 5.4: *Leybourne–McCabe Test*

Figure 5.4 provides an intuitive visualization of the variance stability test result by highlighting where the volatility shifts structurally. It helps us to quickly assess the timing and impact of variance changes in electricity price volatility data.

This example demonstrates how to:

- Simulate realistic time series datasets for electricity demand analysis.
- Define functions needed to perform the LM test for stationarity.
- Calculate the coefficients needed to perform the test.
- Define and test the null and alternative hypotheses.

This is another practical way to understand and prepare time series data for modeling, especially when dealing with the stationary data.

To summarize,

- This code generates synthetic datasets that mirror real-world electricity
- demand.
- Defines all the functions needed to perform the LM test on the simulated data.
- Performs the test and interprets the results.

The Leybourne–McCabe test provides a valuable and specialized diagnostic tool for detecting variance shifts. This is crucial in time series where volatility and stability assumptions are questionable. Its simplicity, intuitive interpretation, and ability to identify exact breakpoints make it particularly useful in real-world scenarios involving financial markets, energy prices, and environmental data.

However, while effective, the Leybourne–McCabe test specifically assesses variance stability. This test should be complemented with mean-level stationarity tests (such as ADF or KPSS) and visual inspections. Employing the Leybourne–McCabe test alongside traditional stationarity assessments ensures a robust, holistic analysis of time series behavior.

Conclusion

In this chapter, we explored a range of advanced methodologies designed to rigorously test for unit roots and stationarity in time series data. These tools extend far beyond the capabilities of conventional tests. Each test examined serves a unique purpose in addressing specific limitations often encountered in empirical research.

The Schmidt-Phillips Test enhances traditional unit root testing by effectively accounting for deterministic trends, providing a more reliable framework when long-run deterministic components are present. The Variance Ratio Tests offer a non-parametric alternative for assessing the random walk hypothesis, making them particularly valuable in financial time series analysis.

With the Zivot-Andrews Test, we addressed a critical shortcoming of standard unit root tests, their inability to accommodate structural breaks. By allowing the break point to be determined endogenously, this test provides more realistic and accurate inference in the presence of sudden economic shifts. Lastly, the Leybourne-McCabe Test offers a robust approach for testing stationarity against non-stationarity, especially in borderline or near-integrated cases where conventional tests may lack power.

Collectively, these tools will help us with a more nuanced understanding of the dynamic properties of time series data. Applying them appropriately enhances the reliability of model specification, forecasting accuracy, and policy interpretation. As time series analysis continues to evolve, mastering these advanced techniques remains essential for robust empirical work.

In the next chapter, we will extend this analytical toolkit further to look at various aspects of data preparation and visualization of time series.

References

- Shumway, R.H. and Stoffer, D.S. (2017) *Time Series Analysis and Its Applications: With R Examples*. 4th edn. *Springer*.
- Hamilton, J.D. (1994) *Time Series Analysis*. *Princeton University Press*.
- Enders, W. (2014) *Applied Econometric Time Series*. 4th edn. *Wiley*.

- Schmidt, P. and Phillips, P. C. B. (1992). LM Tests for a Unit Root in the Presence of Deterministic Trends. *Oxford Bulletin of Economics and Statistics*, 54(3), pp. 257–287.
- Lo, A. W. and MacKinlay, A. C. (1988). Stock Market Prices Do Not Follow Random Walks: Evidence from a Simple Specification Test. *Review of Financial Studies*, 1(1), pp. 41–66.
- Campbell, J. Y., Lo, A. W. and MacKinlay, A. C. (1997). *The Econometrics of Financial Markets. Princeton University Press.*
- Box, G. E. P., Jenkins, G. M., Reinsel, G. C. and Ljung, G. M. (2015). *Time Series Analysis: Forecasting and Control*. 5th edn. *Wiley*.
- Zivot, E. and Andrews, D. W. K. (1992). Further Evidence on the Great Crash, the Oil-Price Shock, and the Unit-Root Hypothesis. *Journal of Business & Economic Statistics*, 10(3), pp. 251-270.
- Leybourne, S. and McCabe, B. P. M. (1994). A Consistent Test for a Unit Root. *Journal of Business & Economic Statistics*, 12(2), pp. 157–166.
- Leybourne, S., McCabe, B. P. M. and Tremayne, A. R. (1996). Can Economic Time Series be Differenced to Stationarity? *Journal of Business & Economic Statistics*, 14(4), pp. 435–446.

CHAPTER 6

Foundations of Time Series Preparation

Introduction

Time series forecasting is only as powerful as the quality of its inputs. Before models can uncover patterns or make predictions, the underlying data must be carefully curated, understood, and transformed. This chapter provides a comprehensive foundation for preparing and exploring time series data. Preparing and exploring data is a critical phase that directly impacts the accuracy, interpretability, and performance of forecasting models.

We will begin this chapter with practical steps for loading and parsing time-indexed datasets, followed by establishing a consistent time series structure and index that supports temporal operations. Real-world time series data is often impacted by missing entries, irregular intervals, and non-stationary behavior. Techniques such as resampling, interpolation, and detrending are introduced to handle these issues and to create uniformity in the data.

Finally, we will delve into transformation strategies such as logarithmic scaling and differencing to stabilize variance and make trends and seasonality more interpretable.

By the end of this chapter, readers will learn:

- How to load and parse time-indexed datasets, including converting date-time strings and ensuring correct frequency recognition.
- Establishing a robust time series index, which enables efficient temporal operations such as slicing, lag creation, and rolling computations.
- Transformation techniques to transform various time series variables efficiently.

Structure

In this chapter, the following topics will be covered:

- Data Loading and Parsing
- Time Series Structure and Indexing
- Time Series Indexing and Resampling
- Handling Missing and Irregular Data
- Detrending and Deseasonalizing
- Transformation Techniques

Data Loading and Parsing

Before any meaningful analysis or modeling can be conducted on time series data, the data must be loaded correctly and parsed into a time-aware format. This process transforms raw data into a structured time-indexed dataset that preserves the temporal ordering essential for time series analysis.

In time series data, while loading and parsing it, we might encounter the following types of challenges:

- Converting date strings to datetime objects
- Setting the datetime column as the index
- Handling different time formats (for example, "2025-04-23", "23-Apr-2025", timestamps)
- Dealing with missing or duplicated timestamps
- Ensuring the correct frequency (daily, monthly, and so on)

Effective time parsing ensures that all future operations, such as resampling, lagging, and rolling windows, work as intended.

Mathematical Explanation

Though data loading and parsing are primarily implementation tasks, they are mathematically framed around injective mappings and indexing.

Let:

$$D=\{d_1,d_2,\ldots d_n\}: \textit{a set of datetime values}$$

$$X=\{x_1,x_2,\ldots x_n\}: \textit{a set of observed values}$$

We map each datetime to a corresponding value:

$$f: D \rightarrow X \textit{ such that } f(d_i) = x_i$$

Once indexed, a time series is typically modeled as a function:

$$X{:}t \rightarrow x_t \qquad \textit{where } t \in T$$

where T represents time intervals (for example, Z for discrete time, such as daily/monthly).

Implementing CSV Parser as a Python Function

In this section, let us create a simple CSV parser that:

- Accepts a file path
- Parses the datetime column
- Sets it as the index
- Sorts by date

Code:

```
def load_time_series(file_path, date_col, delimiter=','):
    with open(file_path, 'r') as file:
        lines = file.readlines()

    header = lines[0].strip().split(delimiter)

    if date_col not in header:
        raise ValueError(f"Date column '{date_col}' not found in header:
{header}")

    date_idx = header.index(date_col)
    data = []

    for line in lines[1:]:
        parts = line.strip().split(delimiter)
        date = parts[date_idx]
        try:
            year, month, day = [int(x) for x in date.split('-')]
        except:
            raise ValueError("Date must be in YYYY-MM-DD format")

        timestamp = (year, month, day)
        values = parts[:date_idx] + parts[date_idx+1:]
        data.append((timestamp, values))

    data.sort(key=lambda x: x[0])

    return data
```

In the preceding code,

- The **load_time_series** function is implemented to parse time-indexed data from a structured text file, such as CSV.

- The input parameters of this function are the path to the time series file, the name of the column containing the date, and the character used to separate fields in the file, defaulting to a comma for CSVs.
- It then opens the file in read mode and reads all its lines into a list. Each element in lines represents one row of the file as a string.
- The first line of the file, typically the header row, is then processed. It is stripped of whitespace and split into individual column names based on the specified delimiter.
- A validation check is then performed to ensure that the specified date column exists in the file. If not, the function raises an informative error.
- We determine the index of the date column to extract it easily from each row later. We also initialize an empty list to store our processed rows.
- We then iterate over all data rows (skipping the header). Each line is stripped and split into individual fields, and the date field is extracted using its column index.
- We then parse the date by splitting it on dashes and converting the components to integers.
- The parsed date is converted into a tuple, which is used as a sortable proxy for datetime values. All non-date columns are combined into a list called values, and each row is appended as a tuple (timestamp, values).
- To ensure the time series is chronologically ordered, we sort the list of tuples based on their timestamp key.
- The function returns the final, chronologically sorted list of timestamped data rows.

Real-World Example

To look at this example, let us continue with our electricity demand use case. An energy company receives electricity usage logs in CSV format. Each row has the date and the units consumed. To build consumption forecasts or detect anomalies, they must parse the CSV file into a time-indexed series.

Code:

```
parsed_data = load_time_series('electricity_usage.csv', date_col='Date')
for timestamp, values in parsed_data:
    print(f"Date: {timestamp}, Usage: {values[0]}")
```

In the preceding code,

- The **load_time_series** function is called to load and parse the electricity usage time series data.

Output:

```
Date: (2025, 4, 19), Usage: 130
Date: (2025, 4, 20), Usage: 120
Date: (2025, 4, 21), Usage: 118
```

The output is a list of tuples, where each tuple contains:

- A date represented as (year, month, day).
- A list of string values corresponding to the remaining columns.
- In the next step, let us calculate the Schmidt-Phillips test statistic.

This custom loader function is useful for:

- Learning the mechanics of parsing and validating time series formats.
- Preparing raw logs or delimited files for further processing of time series data.

The process of loading and parsing time series data is the first and most critical step in time series analysis. Without a properly indexed datetime column, even the best forecasting models will yield invalid results. While tools such as pandas in Python simplify this process, understanding the logic behind parsing and ordering prepares us to troubleshoot and adapt to real-world datasets with inconsistencies, unusual formats, or missing data.

This foundational understanding also reinforces the mathematical concept of time-indexed functions, which is central to time series modeling and forecasting.

Time Series Structure and Indexing

Once time series data is parsed correctly, the next critical step is structuring and indexing the data. This involves setting the time component as the index and understanding the granularity and frequency of the observations (for example, hourly, daily, or monthly).

Indexing allows for time-aware operations such as:

- **Slicing ranges: `df['2024-01':'2024-03']`**
- **Resampling: `df.resample('M').mean()`**
- **Rolling windows: `df.rolling(window=7).mean()`**

Indexing is what differentiates time series from other tabular data. A properly indexed time series enables seamless application of techniques such as lag creation, differencing, or autocorrelation.

Mathematical Explanation

At its core, time series indexing is about associating each observation in the data with a time point $t_i \in T$. The set of all time points is the index:

$$T=\{t_1,t_2,...t_n\}$$

Each t_i corresponds to an observation X_i, forming the set:

$$\{(t_1,X_1),(t_2,X_2),...,(t_n,X_n)\}$$

This mapping is fundamental in defining the domain of a time series function. In discrete time, $t_i \in Z$ (integers), often evenly spaced. In an irregular series, t_i can belong to arbitrary subsets of R.

Frequency

If $\Delta t= t_i-t_{i-1}$ is constant, the time series is regular. Otherwise, it is irregular and requires special handling during analysis.

Implementing the Math as a Python Function

In this section, let us write a function that creates an indexed time series from raw data using pure Python.

Code:

```
class IndexedTimeSeries:
    def __init__(self, timestamps, values):
        if len(timestamps) != len(values):
            raise ValueError("Timestamps and values must be the same
length")
        data = sorted(zip(timestamps, values), key=lambda x: x[0])
        self.index = [ts for ts, _ in data]
        self.values = [v for _, v in data]
    def show_range(self, start, end):
        for t, v in zip(self.index, self.values):
            if start <= t <= end:
                print(f"Time: {t}, Value: {v}")
```

In the preceding code,

- In time series analysis, maintaining a reliable index-to-value mapping is crucial. The IndexedTimeSeries class is a lightweight implementation designed to represent and query ordered time series data. This class mimics foundational behavior of more complex time series structures (such as **pandas.Series**) in a minimalist way.
- This class encapsulates two aligned lists:

  - **index** defines the list of timestamps (for example, dates or time tuples).
  - **values** define the corresponding observations (for example, sensor readings, stock prices).
- It ensures chronological ordering and provides a basic method to inspect a specific range of data.
- The **__init__** method initializes the time series object.
  - It first checks if the input lists are aligned. Each timestamp must correspond to exactly one value.
  - If they differ in length, a **ValueError** is raised, preventing data mismatch errors later.
- The timestamps and values are zipped together into pairs such as (timestamp, value).
- These pairs are then sorted chronologically using the timestamp as the key. This guarantees that the time series is ordered, even if the inputs were not.
- After sorting, the timestamp-value pairs are unpacked into two separate aligned lists:
  - **self.index** stores a list of sorted timestamps.
  - **self.values** stores the values aligned with the corresponding timestamps.

This ensures that the data is ready for time-aware queries and slicing.

Real-World Example

Assuming a scenario where a bank logs the daily total number of ATM withdrawals. We must structure this data with the date as an index to compute moving averages and analyze trends.

Python Implementation on the Bank Example

In this section, we will look at a practical example of how to use the custom **IndexedTimeSeries** class to store and query daily ATM withdrawals.

Code:

```
dates = [(2025, 4, 19), (2025, 4, 20), (2025, 4, 21), (2025, 4, 22)]
withdrawals = [150, 172, 180, 145]
atm_series = IndexedTimeSeries(dates, withdrawals)
atm_series.show_range((2025, 4, 20), (2025, 4, 22))
```

In the preceding code,

After defining a minimalist time series class (IndexedTimeSeries), this example demonstrates how it can be used to create and explore a simple financial time series: daily ATM cash withdrawals over a few consecutive days.

- **`dates`** define a list of 4 daily timestamps in tuple form **`(YYYY, M, D)`**.
- **`withdrawals`** define a corresponding list of ATM cash withdrawal amounts, one for each date.
- Each withdrawal value is implicitly associated with its corresponding date through positional alignment.

We have then instantiated the **`IndexedTimeSeries`** class with the dates and withdrawals lists.

Internally, this class will:

- Validate that both lists are of equal length.
- Sort the data chronologically.
- Store the dates and values in aligned internal lists: **`self.index`** and **`self.values`**.

This step is analogous to creating a **`pandas.Series`** or **`DataFrame`**, but in a manually controlled, class-based structure.

- The **`show_range`** method call displays the ATM withdrawals for April 20, 21, and 22, 2025.
- It checks each timestamp in the time series to see if it falls within the specified range.

The output of the generated data is displayed as follows:

```
Time: (2025, 4, 20), Value: 172
Time: (2025, 4, 21), Value: 180
Time: (2025, 4, 22), Value: 145
```

The preceding output prints the matching entries in the format:

"**`Time: (YYYY, M, D), Value: amount`**"

Time-based indexing is the cornerstone of time series manipulation. Whether we are forecasting stock prices or tracking climate trends, everything relies on properly structuring the data along a reliable and interpretable timeline.

A well-indexed time series simplifies:

- Time window selection
- Rolling calculations

- Seasonal aggregations
- Forecast horizon setup

Indexing turns the dataset from a raw sequence into a structured, analyzable time series.

Time Series Indexing and Resampling

Resampling is the process of converting a time series from one frequency to another. This is essential when:

- We want to aggregate high-frequency data (for example, hourly to daily).
- We need to interpolate lower-frequency data to higher frequency (for example, monthly to daily).
- We are aligning data sources with different frequencies.

Resampling is divided into two types:

- **Downsampling:** Reducing frequency (for example, minute to hour). This requires aggregation (for example, mean, sum).
- **Upsampling:** Increasing frequency (for example, day to minute). This requires interpolation to fill gaps.

Indexing ensures that these operations happen relative to a time-aware structure, not arbitrary row numbers.

Mathematical Explanation

Let $\{X\_t\}^{n}_{t=1}$ be a time series indexed by discrete time points $t \in T$, where $T=\{t_1,t_2,\dots t_n\}$

Downsampling:

Given a lower frequency interval Δ, we group all values X_t such that:

$$Group_i = \{X_t : t \in [t_i, t_i + \Delta]\}$$

Then apply an aggregation function f (for example, mean, sum):

$$X_i^{(\Delta)} = f\,(Group_i)$$

Upsampling:

Given missing values for time points between known intervals, we interpolate:

$$X_t = X_{t_i} + \frac{(X_{t_{i+1}} - X_{t_i})}{t_{i+1} - t_i} \cdot (t - t_i), \qquad for\; t_i < t < t_{i+1}$$

This maintains continuity or creates estimates for missing values.

Implementing the Math as a Python Function

In this section, let us write two functions for downsampling and upsampling.

The following pair of functions, **downsample_time_series** and **upsample_time_series**, illustrates two essential techniques in time series processing.

- Downsampling is used for temporal aggregation, and
- Upsampling is used for temporal interpolation.

These are fundamental operations used in data preprocessing for smoothing, memory reduction, or preparing data for modeling.

Code:

```
def downsample_time_series(data, interval_size):
    n = len(data)
    downsampled = []
    for i in range(0, n, interval_size):
        group = data[i:i+interval_size]
        timestamps = [t for t, _ in group]
        values = [v for _, v in group]
        avg_value = sum(values) / len(values)
        downsampled.append((timestamps[0], avg_value))
    return downsampled
```

In the preceding code,

- Downsampling is done by the **downsample_time_series** function to reduce the frequency of a time series by grouping data points into fixed-size intervals and computing the average value for each group. This is useful to smooth short-term noise.
- This will help the downstream model to benefit from lower-frequency data (for example, weekly or monthly instead of daily).
- The input variable **data** defines a list of (timestamp, value) tuples.
- The input **interval_size** defines the number of data points to group together.
- The variable **n** defines the total number of data points.
- The return value **downsampled** provides the output list that will contain reduced entries.

Code:

```
def upsample_time_series(data, steps_between):
    upsampled = []
    for i in range(len(data) - 1):
        t1, v1 = data[i]
        t2, v2 = data[i+1]
```

```
        step = (v2 - v1) / (steps_between + 1)
        for j in range(steps_between + 2):
            interpolated_value = v1 + step * j
            upsampled.append((t1 + j, interpolated_value))
    return upsampled
```

In the preceding code,

- Upsampling is done by the **upsample_time_series** function to increase the frequency of the time series by interpolating new points between existing values. This is useful when we need finer granularity (for example, minute-level from hourly data).
- This will help us align irregular data to a regular grid for model input.
- This will also help us prepare data for visualization with smooth transitions.
- The input variable **data** defines the list of (timestamp, value) pairs.
- The variable **steps_between** defines the number of interpolated steps to add between existing points.
- The variables **t1** and **t2** are timestamps.
- The variables **v1** and **v2** are values to interpolate between.
- The variable **upsampled** returns the new, higher-frequency time series.

Real-World Example

For this implementation, let us consider the following real-world scenario.

In a smart building, temperature sensors record indoor temperature every 2 minutes to track and optimize HVAC (Heating, Ventilation, and Air Conditioning) usage. However:

- Downsampling is needed when generating hourly reports for building management. They only care about the average temperature every few minutes or hours, and not fine-grained noise.
- Upsampling is essential for modeling or visualization since:
    - o A forecasting algorithm may require minute-level granularity.
    - o Interpolated points help generate smooth plots for dashboard visualizations.

Python Implementation for Resampling

In this section, let us create a synthetic dataset for temperature readings taken every 2 minutes and apply upsampling and downsampling on the same.

Code:

```
temperature_data = [(0, 22.5), (2, 22.7), (4, 23.1), (6, 22.9)]
downsampled = downsample_time_series(temperature_data, interval_size=2)
```

```
print("Downsampled (4-minute):")
for t, v in downsampled:
    print(f"Time: {t}, Temp: {v:.2f}°C")
upsampled = upsample_time_series(temperature_data, steps_between=1)
print("\nUpsampled (1-minute):")
for t, v in upsampled:
    print(f"Time: {t}, Temp: {v:.2f}°C")
```

In the preceding code,

- **`temperature_data`** is a synthetic dataset of temperature readings, taken every 2 minutes.
- Each tuple consists of:
    - A timestamp in minutes since the start (0, 2, 4, 6)
    - A temperature reading in degrees Celsius
- **`downsampled`** groups every 2 consecutive readings (spanning 4 minutes) into a single interval.
    - The **`downsample_time_series`** function computes the average temperature for each interval.
    - The timestamp used is the first in each group.
- **`upsampled`** interpolates one extra point between each pair of existing readings.
    - Linear interpolation is used between each pair.
    - It returns both the original and interpolated values.

Output:

```
Downsampled (4-minute):
Time: 0, Temp: 22.60°C
Time: 4, Temp: 23.00°C
Upsampled (1-minute):
Time: 0, Temp: 22.50°C
Time: 1, Temp: 22.60°C
Time: 2, Temp: 22.70°C
Time: 2, Temp: 22.70°C
Time: 3, Temp: 22.90°C
Time: 4, Temp: 23.10°C
Time: 4, Temp: 23.10°C
Time: 5, Temp: 23.00°C
Time: 6, Temp: 22.90°C
```

The preceding output provides the downsampled and upsampled data.

Indexing and resampling unlock the flexibility to view the data at various temporal scales, such as daily trends, hourly spikes, or quarterly aggregates. These operations are essential before modeling because models often expect data in regular, complete intervals. Resampling also facilitates feature extraction (for example, moving averages on downsampled data), temporal alignment across different datasets (for example, matching weather and sales), simulation, and data augmentation through upsampling. Understanding the math and logic behind resampling helps prevent misinterpretation, especially when handling missing timestamps or uneven intervals of data.

Handling Missing and Irregular Data

Missing and irregular data are one of the most common and challenging issues in time series analysis. It occurs when:

- Sensors fail to record values,
- Data is lost during collection or transmission, and
- Observations are recorded at inconsistent intervals.

Before performing analysis, forecasting, or modeling, we must handle these inconsistencies to maintain the temporal integrity of the series.

Missing data refers to gaps where no value is present at an expected timestamp.

Irregular data refers to data points that are not recorded at a consistent frequency.

Common strategies to handle them are:

- Forward fill (ffill) – fill using the last known value.
- Backward fill (bfill) – fill using the next known value.
- Interpolation – estimate using mathematical methods.
- Deletion – drop missing rows when justifiable.

Mathematical Explanation

Let $T=\{t_1, t_2,\ldots t_n\}$ be a set of regular time intervals.

Let $\{(t_i, x_i)\}$ be observed values, but for some $t_j \in T$, xj is missing.

Forward Fill:

$$\hat{x}_t = x_{t-k}, where\ k = max\ \{k: t - k < t \wedge x_{t-k} \neq null\}$$

Linear Interpolation:

Given two valid points (t_a, x_a) and (t_b, x_b), for a missing t_m in between:

$$\hat{x}_{t_m} = x_a + \frac{(x_b - x_a)}{t_b - t_a}.(t_m - t_a)$$

Interpolation assumes a linear change between points and is best for smooth, continuous variables such as temperature, price, and so on.

Implementing the Math as a Python Function

In this section, let us write a basic linear interpolation method that handles missing values in a time series list.

Code:

```
def linear_interpolation(time_series):
    filled_series = time_series.copy()
    n = len(filled_series)
    for i in range(n):
        if filled_series[i] is None:
            prev_idx = i - 1
            while prev_idx >= 0 and filled_series[prev_idx] is None:
                prev_idx -= 1
            next_idx = i + 1
            while next_idx < n and filled_series[next_idx] is None:
                next_idx += 1
            if prev_idx >= 0 and next_idx < n:
                x0, x1 = filled_series[prev_idx], filled_series[next_idx]
                filled_series[i] = x0 + (x1 - x0) * ((i - prev_idx) / 
(next_idx - prev_idx))
    return filled_series
```

In the preceding code,

- The **`linear_interpolation`** function is designed to fill in missing values within the time series data by using linear interpolation.
- It assumes the time series is sampled at regular intervals, such as hourly or minute-by-minute, so each index corresponds to a consistent time step.
- This function creates a copy of the original series to preserve the input and then iterates through each element to identify missing entries.
- For every gap encountered, it searches both backward and forward in the series to locate the nearest known values on either side.
- Once a valid previous and next value is found, the function computes the interpolated value using the standard linear interpolation formula.
- This calculation treats the missing point as lying on a straight line between the surrounding values, assigning it a value proportional to its position between them.
- If either a previous or a next value is missing, the function skips interpolation, and the gaps at the very beginning or end of the series remain unfilled.

Real-World Example

Assume a scenario where a weather station records hourly temperatures. Due to a transmission failure, 3 readings are missing. Before using this data for forecasting or calculating rolling averages, the missing values need to be estimated.

Python Implementation

In this section, let us create synthetic temperature data and perform linear interpolation on the missing values.

Code:

```
temperature_readings = [22.1, 22.3, None, None, 23.0, 23.2, None, 23.8]
filled_temperatures = linear_interpolation(temperature_readings)
print("Original Readings: ", temperature_readings)
print("Filled Readings:   ", [round(x, 2) if x is not None else None for
x in filled_temperatures])
```

Output:

```
Original Readings:  [22.1, 22.3, None, None, 23.0, 23.2, None, 23.8]
Filled Readings:    [22.1, 22.3, 22.53, 22.77, 23.0, 23.2, 23.5, 23.8]
```

The preceding output demonstrates the concept of handling missing data through linear interpolation.

Handling missing or irregular data is central to the integrity of any time series analysis. Overlooking such gaps can distort trends, bias models, and lead to unreliable forecasts. Effective imputation strategies do more than fill nulls; they preserve the underlying signal while minimizing the risk of introducing misleading patterns.

For continuous variables such as temperature, stock prices, or energy consumption, interpolation techniques provide smooth, context-aware estimates that maintain continuity. In contrast, for discrete or categorical data such as status updates or event logs, forward and backward filling are more appropriate, ensuring logical consistency without implying intermediate states that never existed.

Visual inspection remains an essential step before any imputation. It helps determine whether missing values occur randomly, follow a systematic pattern, or signal something meaningful, such as sensor failure or behavioral anomalies. Understanding the nature of missingness guides the selection of the most appropriate strategy.

Detrending and Deseasonalizing in Time Series Analysis

Detrending and deseasonalizing are foundational preprocessing techniques in time series analysis, particularly when preparing data for modeling and forecasting. These methods are designed to isolate the core stochastic or stationary component of a time series by removing systematic, persistent patterns that can obscure the true behavior of the underlying process.

Trends represent long-term directional movements in the data, either upward or downward. It is often driven by factors such as economic growth, technological adoption, or structural shifts. Seasonality, on the other hand, reflects short-term, recurring cycles that occur at regular intervals, such as daily traffic patterns, weekly sales peaks, or quarterly revenue fluctuations.

Eliminating these components offers several advantages. It simplifies the data structure, making patterns easier to detect and interpret. More importantly, it helps satisfy the stationarity assumptions required by many classical forecasting models, such as ARIMA, which assume constant mean and variance over time. Additionally, by removing trend and seasonality, residual anomalies or abrupt structural changes become more visible. This offers valuable insights for diagnostics, model refinement, or business intervention.

In essence, detrending and deseasonalizing do not discard information; they uncover it. Thus, by separating predictable structure from randomness, these techniques empower us to build more accurate, reliable, and interpretable time series models.

Mathematical Explanation

Time series data that exposes trend, seasonality, and residual noise can often be decomposed into these components using additive and multiplicative techniques. The choice between these two techniques depends on the nature of the relationships between the components. If the relationship is linear and independent, the additive technique will be used. If it is proportional and dependent, the multiplicative technique will be used.

An additive model can be defined as follows:

$$X_t = T_t + S_t + R_t$$

where:

X_t is the observed time series,

T_t is the trend component,

S_t is the seasonal component, and

R_t is the residual or irregular component, which denotes random noise.

A multiplicative model can be defined as follows:

$$X_t = T_t \cdot S_t \cdot R_t$$

where:

X_t is the observed time series,

T_t is the trend component,

S_t is the seasonal component, and

R_t is the residual or irregular component, which denotes random noise.

Detrending is the removal of T_t from the time series data.

Deseasonalizing is the removal of S_t from the time series data.

In the additive model, detrending and deseasonalizing are achieved by obtaining:

$$R_t = X_t - T_t - S_t$$

In the multiplicative model, detrending and deseasonalizing are achieved by obtaining:

$$R_t = \frac{X_t}{T_t \cdot S_t}$$

Implementing the Math as a Python Function

Let us write a simple Python implementation of detrending using a moving average and deseasonalizing using seasonal index estimation. The following set of functions implements a manual decomposition and transformation pipeline for time series analysis. It covers trend estimation via moving average, detrending, seasonality estimation, and deseasonalization.

Code:

```
def moving_average(series, window):
    return [None if i < window - 1 else sum(series[i-window+1:i+1]) / 
window for i in range(len(series))]
```

In the preceding code,

- The function **moving_average** estimates the trend by smoothing the original series over a sliding window of fixed size.
- This smoothed series serves as a baseline, capturing the long-term direction of the data while filtering out short-term fluctuations.

Code:

```
def detrend(series, trend):
    return [x - t if x is not None and t is not None else None for x, t 
in zip(series, trend)]
```

In the preceding code,

- The **detrend** function subtracts the estimated trend from the original series, yielding a detrended series.
- This series ideally reflects the short-term variations, especially seasonal cycles and random noise, by removing the overarching movement.

Code:

```
def estimate_seasonality(detrended, period):
    season_sums = [0.0] * period
    season_counts = [0] * period
    for i in range(len(detrended)):
        if detrended[i] is not None:
            idx = i % period
            season_sums[idx] += detrended[i]
            season_counts[idx] += 1
    return [season_sums[i] / season_counts[i] if season_counts[i] > 0
else None for i in range(period)]
```

In the preceding code:

- To isolate the seasonal component, **estimate_seasonality** analyzes the detrended series by grouping values based on their position within the seasonal cycle.
- For example, in a weekly cycle (period = 7), all Mondays, Tuesdays, and so on, are grouped together.
- The average of each group is computed, forming a sequence of seasonal indices that capture recurring patterns at each position in the cycle.

Code:

```
def deseasonalize(detrended, period, seasonal_indices):
    return [detrended[i] - seasonal_indices[i % period] if detrended[i]
is not None else None for i in range(len(detrended))]
```

In the preceding code,

- The **deseasonalize** function removes this repeating seasonal pattern from the detrended series.
- By subtracting the appropriate seasonal index from each point using modular arithmetic to align it within the cycle, the function produces a fully deseasonalized series.
- It leaves behind the irregular or residual component. This residual component is closer to a stationary process and is often the input to forecasting models such as ARIMA.

Together, these functions exemplify the additive decomposition model and form a complete pipeline for preparing a time series for advanced modeling or anomaly detection.

Real-World Example

Let us assume a scenario where a retail chain wants to analyze weekly sales for trend and seasonality. Sales usually spike on weekends and rise steadily near holidays. To build a reliable model, the data must be detrended and deseasonalized.

Python Implementation of Retail Example

In this section, let us write code to demonstrate a complete additive decomposition of the retail time series data into its core components: trend, seasonality, and residual.

This example will manually apply the decomposition process step by step, using the functions explained earlier. The time series in this example will represent daily sales data over a two-week period, with observable patterns influenced by weekly shopping behavior. The goal is to break this series down into interpretable components to better understand the underlying structure before applying techniques such as forecasting or anomaly detection.

Let us start by defining synthetic sales data for this example.

Code:

```
sales = [100, 120, 130, 140, 180, 200, 250, 110, 125, 135, 145, 190, 210,
260]
```

In the next step, let us estimate the trend by calling the **`moving_average`** function.

Code:

```
trend = moving_average(sales, window=3)
```

In the preceding code,

- We have estimated the trend component using a moving average with a window size of 3.
- This smoothing technique reduces the influence of short-term fluctuations and highlights the long-term direction of sales, providing a clearer sense of gradual increases or decreases over time.

Code:

```
detrended = detrend(sales, trend)
```

In the preceding code,

- Once the trend is obtained, the **`detrend`** function computes the detrended series by subtracting the trend from the original sales values.
- This isolates the faster-changing components of the series, specifically the cyclical or irregular parts, by removing the long-term movement.

Code:

```
seasonal_indices = estimate_seasonality(detrended, period=7)
```

In the preceding code,

- The function **estimate_seasonality** estimates the seasonal pattern using a cycle length of 7, corresponding to a weekly pattern.
- It groups the values from the detrended series by their position in the week (for example, all Mondays, Tuesdays, and so on), and then computes the average for each group.

Code:

```
residual = deseasonalize(detrended, period=7, seasonal_indices=seasonal_
indices)
```

In the preceding code,

- The function **deseasonalize** deseasonalizes the detrended series by subtracting the seasonal indices based on their position within the weekly cycle.
- This removes both the long-term trend and the weekly seasonal effect, leaving behind the residual component.
- This residual denotes the random noise or unstructured variation that might reflect anomalies in the data.

Code:

```
print("Original:     ", sales)
print("Trend:        ", [round(t, 2) if t else None for t in trend])
print("Detrended:    ", [round(d, 2) if d else None for d in detrended])
print("Seasonality:  ", [round(s, 2) if s else None for s in seasonal_
indices])
print("Residual:     ", [round(r, 2) if r else None for r in residual])
```

The preceding code prints the following output.

```
Original:      [100, 120, 130, 140, 180, 200, 250, 110, 125, 135, 145,
190, 210, 260]
Trend:         [None, None, 116.67, 130.0, 150.0, 173.33, 210.0, 186.67,
161.67, 123.33, 135.0, 156.67, 181.67, 220.0]
Detrended:     [None, None, 13.33, 10.0, 30.0, 26.67, 40.0, -76.67,
-36.67, 11.67, 10.0, 33.33, 28.33, 40.0]
Seasonality:   [-76.67, -36.67, 12.5, 10.0, 31.67, 27.5, 40.0]
Residual:      [None, None, 0.83, None, -1.67, -0.83, None, None, None,
-0.83, None, 1.67, 0.83, None]
```

The output displays the evolution of the data at each stage, from the original series to the trend, detrended values, estimated seasonality, and final residuals.

- As the moving average cannot be calculated for the first few values due to insufficient prior data, the trend list begins with None placeholders for alignment.
- The seasonality output is a list of seasonal indices that capture the repeating structure within each week, such as consistently higher sales on weekends.
- This step-by-step decomposition is fundamental for preparing time series data for forecasting models such as ARIMA or for conducting diagnostics such as outlier detection and change point analysis.

Detrending and deseasonalizing are essential steps in time series preprocessing. They remove dominant patterns that often obscure the true dynamics of the data. Left unaddressed, trend and seasonality can distort forecasts, mask subtle signals, and lead to misleading statistical inferences or spurious regressions.

By systematically removing these components, we can prepare the data for models that require stationarity, such as ARIMA and SARIMA. These techniques help us uncover residuals that may contain valuable insights, including structural changes or anomalies. This not only improves the interpretability of the series but also enhances the accuracy and reliability of predictive models.

Importantly, even simple techniques such as moving averages for trend estimation and seasonal means for cycle detection can yield significant benefits. These foundational methods provide a robust starting point for deeper analysis and ensure that the time series is model-ready and insight-rich.

Transformation Techniques

As we have seen earlier, time series data frequently displays heteroscedasticity, a condition where the variance of observations changes over time. This non-constant variance, often visible as increasing or decreasing amplitude in fluctuations, can compromise the performance of statistical models by violating key assumptions such as homoscedasticity or constant variance, stationarity, and normality. If left untreated, heteroscedasticity may lead to biased parameter estimates, inefficient forecasts, and misleading inferences.

To address this issue, transformation techniques are applied as a crucial step in time series preprocessing. These methods aim to stabilize the variance, normalize the distribution, and often linearize nonlinear relationships within the data. By doing so, it helps in preparing the series for accurate modeling and valid statistical inference, particularly in models that assume a stable variance structure over time.

The following are the widely used transformation methods:

Log Transformation:

- This method compresses the scale of data, especially effective for series with exponential growth or multiplicative seasonality.
- It reduces the impact of large values and helps normalize skewed distributions.

Square Root Transformation:

- This method is a gentler alternative to the log transformation, particularly useful for count data or series with moderate right skew.
- It reduces the influence of extreme values while preserving interpretability.

Box-Cox Transformation:

- This method is a flexible, parameterized power transformation that stabilizes variance and improves normality.
- By tuning the parameter, it generalizes several standard transformations (for example, log, square root) into a single framework.

Yeo-Johnson Transformation:

- This method is an extension of Box-Cox that supports zero and negative values, making it more versatile for datasets that span both positive and negative domains.

Incorporating these transformations is often a prerequisite for time series modeling, particularly when using classical techniques such as ARIMA, where stationarity and normality of residuals are key. Ultimately, transformation techniques are not only mathematical tools but also are essential for revealing the true structure of the data and ensuring the validity of downstream analyses.

Mathematical Explanation

Time series transformations are performed to alter the functional form of the data such that:

- Variance becomes constant over time, which means homoscedasticity.
- The distribution of values becomes approximately normal, which means Gaussian.
- Relationships become linear to simplify modeling.

Log Transformation

The log transformation is the method that applies the natural logarithm to the data to transform each value in the series.

$$y_t^{(log)} = log\,(y_t)$$

This is useful mainly when the data exhibits exponential growth or multiplicative seasonality.

Square Root Transformation

The square root transformation is the method that applies the square root to the data to transform each value in the series.

$$y_t^{(\sqrt{})}=\sqrt{y_t}$$

This method is appropriate when the variance increases linearly with the mean.

Box-Cox Transformation

The Box-Cox transformation is the technique used to handle the variance and make the distribution of a time series dataset more normal or Gaussian.

It is defined as follows:

For a given time series y_t with only positive values (y_t>0), the Box-Cox transformation is defined as:

$$y_t^{(\lambda)} = \{\frac{y_t^{\lambda} - 1}{\lambda}, \ if\ \lambda \neq 0\ log\ (y_t), \qquad if\ \lambda = 0$$

y_t – original value at time t

λ – is the transformation parameter

$y_t^{(\lambda)}$- is the transformed value

Yeo-Johnson Transformation

The Yeo-Johnson transformation is a powerful and flexible technique used to stabilize variance, normalize data, and linearize relationships, much like the Box-Cox transformation, but with a key advantage. It works with both positive and negative values. This makes it especially valuable for datasets that contain zeros or negative numbers, which are common in real-world datasets.

Let $y_t \in R$ be any real-valued data point at time t, and let $\lambda \in R$ be the transformation parameter. The Yeo-Johnson transformation is defined as:

$$y_t^{(\lambda)} = \{\frac{(y_t + 1)^{\lambda} - 1}{\lambda}, \ if\ y_t \geq 0\ and\ \lambda \neq 0\ \ log\ log\ (y_t + 1)\ , \ \ if\ y_t \geq 0\ and\ \lambda$$
$$= 0\ \ - \frac{(-y_t + 1)^{2-\lambda} - 1}{2 - \lambda}, if\ y_t < 0\ and\ \lambda \neq 2\ \ -log\ log\ (-y_t + 1)\ , if\ y_t$$
$$< 0\ and\ \lambda = 2$$

The Yeo-Johnson transformation extends the Box-Cox transformation to the entire real line.

Python Implementation of the Math

In this section, let us implement the functions for log, square root, Box-Cox, and Yeo-Johnson techniques.

Code:

```
import math
def log_transform(series):
    return [math.log(x) if x > 0 else None for x in series]
```

In the preceding code,

- The **log_transform** function takes in a list of numerical values and applies the natural logarithm to each value.
- Log transformation is particularly useful when the variance increases with the level of the data.

Code:

```
def sqrt_transform(series):
    return [math.sqrt(x) if x >= 0 else None for x in series]
```

In the preceding code,

- The **sqrt_transform** function applies the square root transformation to a sequence of numerical values in the time series.

Code:

```
def boxcox_transform(series, lam):
    transformed = []
    for x in series:
        if x <= 0:
            transformed.append(None)
        elif lam == 0:
            transformed.append(math.log(x))
        else:
            transformed.append((x ** lam - 1) / lam)
    return transformed
```

In the preceding code,

- The function accepts two inputs: a list of numerical values and a transformation parameter (lambda), which controls the shape and intensity of the transformation.
- The Box-Cox method is particularly powerful because it generalizes many standard transformations, including the log and square root, into a single framework.

- It dynamically adjusts how much the data is compressed or expanded depending on the value of lambda.

Code:

```
def yeojohnson_transform(series, lam):
    transformed = []
    for x in series:
        if x >= 0:
            if lam == 0:
                transformed.append(math.log(x + 1))
            else:
                transformed.append(((x + 1) ** lam - 1) / lam)
        else:
            if lam == 2:
                transformed.append(-math.log(-x + 1))
            else:
             transformed.append(-(((-x + 1) ** (2 - lam) - 1) / (2 - lam)))
    return transformed
```

In the preceding code,

- The function accepts two inputs: a list of numerical values (series) and a transformation parameter (lambda), which controls the shape and intensity of the transformation.
- The Box-Cox method is particularly powerful because it generalizes many standard transformations, including the log and square root, into a single framework. It dynamically adjusts how much the data is compressed or expanded depending on the value of lambda.
- Inside this function, a new list called transformed is initialized to store the output values.
- The function then iterates over each value, x in the input series.
- For every element, it first checks whether the value is strictly positive, as the Box-Cox transformation is only defined for positive numbers.
- If a value is zero or negative, the function appends None to the result, signaling that the transformation is not applicable to that entry.
- This is important because applying the transformation to invalid inputs would result in a mathematical error.
- For values greater than zero, the function distinguishes two cases. If the lambda parameter is exactly zero, it applies the natural logarithm to the value.
- Once all elements have been processed, the function returns the transformed series.

Code:

```
def yeojohnson_transform(series, lam):
    transformed = []
    for x in series:
        if x >= 0:
            if lam == 0:
                transformed.append(math.log(x + 1))
            else:
                transformed.append(((x + 1) ** lam - 1) / lam)
        else:
            if lam == 2:
                transformed.append(-math.log(-x + 1))
            else:
                transformed.append(-(((-x + 1) ** (2 - lam) - 1) / (2 -
lam)))
    return transformed
```

In the preceding code,

- The **yeojohnson_transform** function is a practical implementation of the Yeo-Johnson transformation.
- It is a versatile and robust method used to stabilize variance and normalize data distributions in datasets containing both positive and negative values.
- This function is particularly useful in data preprocessing, especially when preparing real-world time series or regression inputs for models that assume homoscedasticity and normality, two key properties often violated in raw data.
- The function takes in a time series and lambda as input.
- The Yeo-Johnson transformation logic is applied for four different lambda values as explained in the equation in this section.

Real-World Example

Let us assume that an analyst is modeling monthly sales revenue for a startup that has seen exponential growth. As time progresses, the sales variance increases dramatically, violating key assumptions of stationarity. Transformation techniques are applied to stabilize the variance before modeling.

Python Implementation of Sales Example

In this section, let us write the code to demonstrate how different transformation techniques can be applied to a time series exhibiting exponential growth, specifically, monthly revenue figures that rise sharply over time. Such growth leads to heteroscedasticity, where the variance increases as the values grow, making it difficult for many time series models to produce reliable forecasts. To address this, this code applies four common transformations: logarithmic, square root, Box-Cox, and Yeo-Johnson.

Code:

```
monthly_revenue = [10000, 12000, 16000, 25000, 40000, 60000, 90000, 
130000]
log_rev = log_transform(monthly_revenue)
sqrt_rev = sqrt_transform(monthly_revenue)
boxcox_rev = boxcox_transform(monthly_revenue, lam=0.3)
lam = 0.5
yeo_data = yeojohnson_transform(monthly_revenue, lam)
print("Original:    ", monthly_revenue)
print("Log:         ", [round(x, 2) if x else None for x in log_rev])
print("Sqrt:        ", [round(x, 2) if x else None for x in sqrt_rev])
print("Box-Cox:     ", [round(x, 2) if x else None for x in boxcox_rev])
print("Yeo-Johnson: ", [round(x, 2) if x else None for x in yeo_data])
```

In the preceding code,

- The original data consists of monthly revenue values ranging from 10,000 to 130,000.
- As is typical with business metrics such as revenue or sales, the increases from month to month are not constant but accelerate, suggesting an underlying multiplicative process. This is where transformations become essential by reducing the scale of large values and stabilizing variance. They make the data more suitable for modeling techniques that assume homoscedasticity or normally distributed residuals.
- The log transformation is applied first. It compresses the range of the data significantly, especially for larger values.
- Next, the square root transformation is applied. It works well when the variance grows moderately with the level of the data.
- The Box-Cox transformation follows, with a lambda value of 0.3. Box-Cox is a flexible power transformation that generalizes several common techniques, including the log transformation and the square root.
- Finally, the Yeo-Johnson transformation is applied using a lambda of 0.5. Unlike Box-Cox, which is limited to positive values, Yeo-Johnson extends the approach to include zero and negative numbers, making it more broadly applicable in this dataset.

Output:

```
Original:    [10000, 12000, 16000, 25000, 40000, 60000, 90000, 130000]
Log:         [9.21, 9.39, 9.68, 10.13, 10.6, 11.0, 11.41, 11.78]
Sqrt:        [100.0, 109.54, 126.49, 158.11, 200.0, 244.95, 300.0, 360.56]
```

```
Box-Cox:      [49.5, 52.47, 57.5, 66.21, 76.74, 87.1, 98.8, 110.71]
Yeo-Johnson:  [198.01, 217.1, 250.99, 314.23, 398.0, 487.9, 598.0, 719.11]
```

The preceding output helps to compare each transformation.

Transformation techniques play a vital role in preparing time series data for accurate and reliable analysis. When a dataset exhibits characteristics such as increasing variance, skewed distributions, or nonlinear patterns, applying the right transformation can significantly improve the performance and interpretability of forecasting models.

Conclusion

In this chapter, we began with data loading and parsing, highlighting the importance of correctly interpreting temporal formats and ensuring clean ingestion of date-indexed observations. This was followed by a detailed look at time series structure and indexing, where we established how temporal data can be aligned, sorted, and enriched through custom indexing to support time-aware computations.

From there, we explored resampling techniques, a vital operation for aligning data to consistent intervals, whether through aggregation (downsampling) or interpolation (upsampling). These resampling strategies enable us to match data to the granularity required by the problem at hand while preserving temporal coherence.

Real-world data is rarely perfect, and our focus on handling missing and irregular data offered practical approaches to bridging gaps and addressing data irregularities. The next foundational layer covered detrending and deseasonalizing, techniques that remove long-term patterns and cyclical behavior. These operations are essential for exposing the stationary, core dynamics of a time series, making it suitable for classical modeling techniques such as ARIMA or exponential smoothing.

Finally, we examined transformation techniques, which serve to stabilize variance, normalize distributions, and linearize nonlinear relationships. By applying tools such as the logarithmic, square root, Box-Cox, and Yeo-Johnson transformations, we can reshape raw data into forms that better conform to modeling assumptions and enhance interpretability.

In the next chapter, we will cover statistical models for time series forecasting, beginning with foundational approaches such as Autoregressive (AR), Moving Average (MA), and their combination in ARMA and ARIMA models. These models bridge the gap between stochastic theory and practical forecasting, enabling analysts to model temporal dependencies, trends, and noise with mathematical precision. This sets the stage for more complex machine learning and deep learning models in subsequent chapters.

References

- McKinney, W. (2022) *Python for Data Analysis*. 3rd edn. O'Reilly Media.
- Hyndman, R. J. and Athanasopoulos, G. (2021). *Forecasting: Principles and Practice*. 3rd edn. https://otexts.com/fpp3/
- Hamilton, J. D. (1994). *Time Series Analysis. Princeton University Press.*
- pandas Time Series Documentation: https://pandas.pydata.org/pandas-docs/stable/user_guide/timeseries.html
- Shumway, R. H. and Stoffer, D. S. (2017). *Time Series Analysis and Its Applications. Springer.*
- Little, R. J., & Rubin, D. B. (2019). *Statistical Analysis with Missing Data.* 3rd edn. *Wiley.*
- Box, G. E. P., Jenkins, G. M., Reinsel, G. C. and Ljung, G. M. (2015). *Time Series Analysis: Forecasting and Control. Wiley.*
- Chatfield, C. (2003). *The Analysis of Time Series: An Introduction. Chapman & Hall.*
- Statsmodels seasonal decomposition: https://www.statsmodels.org/stable/generated/statsmodels.tsa.seasonal.seasonal_decompose.html
- Box, G. E. P. and Cox, D. R. (1964). An Analysis of Transformations. *Journal of the Royal Statistical Society: Series B.*
- scipy.stats.boxcox documentation: https://docs.scipy.org/doc/scipy/reference/generated/scipy.stats.boxcox.html
- Official Python datetime documentation: https://docs.python.org/3/library/datetime.html
- Official pandas resample() documentation: https://pandas.pydata.org/pandas-docs/stable/user_guide/timeseries.html#dateoffset-objects
- pandas handling missing data: https://pandas.pydata.org/docs/user_guide/missing_data.html

CHAPTER 7
Statistical Models for Forecasting

Introduction

Forecasting time series data requires more than just intuition or trend observation. It demands structured, statistical models that can capture the underlying temporal dependencies and project them forward with precision. This chapter provides a comprehensive exploration of the foundational statistical models used in time series forecasting, guiding readers from the simplest autoregressive models to more advanced seasonal and hybrid formulations.

We will begin with Autoregressive (AR) models, which express current values as linear combinations of their past values, capturing momentum and lag effects inherent in many natural and economic processes. This is followed by Moving Average (MA) models, which model the current observation as a function of past forecast errors, providing a powerful framework for modeling shock and noise propagation in time series.

The combination of these two approaches gives rise to Autoregressive Moving Average (ARMA) models, which blend the memory of past values with the structure of past errors. However, real-world data often contain trends or non-stationarity, which is where Autoregressive Integrated Moving Average (ARIMA) models come in. By including differencing (I), ARIMA models handle evolving mean levels and long-term changes in data.

To handle recurring patterns such as quarterly sales or weekly demand, we extend ARIMA to Seasonal ARIMA (SARIMA) models, incorporating seasonal differencing and additional seasonal AR and MA terms to better model periodicity.

Parallel to these models, we will also explore the family of Exponential Smoothing techniques, which emphasize recent observations with exponentially decaying weights. From simple exponential smoothing to Holt-Winters methods, these models provide intuitive and flexible alternatives to ARIMA, especially for data with clear trends and seasonality.

While this chapter focuses on classical statistical techniques, it is important to note the growing intersection between these methods and modern machine learning. Hybrid models that blend statistical rigor with machine learning flexibility are increasingly used in production systems. A foundational understanding of statistical forecasting, therefore, is not just essential for traditional analysis but also serves as a springboard into advanced forecasting architectures such as Prophet, LSTMs, and transformer-based time series models.

By the end of this chapter, readers will be able to understand the building blocks of classical time series models used for forecasting, including their assumptions, components, and suitability. The readers will also gain exposure to hybrid modeling strategies, showing how statistical models can serve as a foundation for integrating machine learning and modern forecasting tools.

Structure

In this chapter, the following topics will be covered:

- Autoregressive (AR) Models
- Moving Average (MA) Models
- Autoregressive Moving Average (ARMA) Models
- Autoregressive Integrated Moving Average (ARIMA) Models
- Seasonal ARIMA (SARIMA) Models
- Exponential Smoothing Models

Autoregressive (AR) Models

Autoregressive (AR) models are among the most fundamental and widely used models in time series analysis. They are built on a simple but powerful idea: the future can be predicted from the past. Specifically, AR models assume that the current value of a time series can be explained by a linear combination of its own past values and a random error term.

Mathematical Explanation

Let X_t denote the value of the time series at time t. Then, an AR(p) process is defined as:

$$X_t = c + \phi_1 X_{t-1} + \phi_2 X_{t-2} + \cdots + \phi_p X_{t-p} + \varepsilon_t$$

Where:

- c is the intercept
- $\phi_1, \phi_2, \ldots, \phi_p$ are the AR coefficients
- $\varepsilon_t \sim N(0, \sigma^2)$ is a white noise error term
- *p* is the lag order

Stationarity

The AR model assumes weak stationarity, meaning:

- Constant mean $E[X_t]$
- Constant variance $Var(X_t)$
- Autocovariance $\gamma(h)=Cov(X_t, X_{t-h})$ depends only on lag *h*.

A key condition for stationarity of an AR model is that the roots of the characteristic polynomial must lie outside the unit circle.

For example, for AR(1):

$$X_t = \phi_1 X_{t-1} + \varepsilon_t$$

The process is stationary only if $|\phi_1|<1$.

If $\phi_1=1$, the process becomes a random walk (non-stationary).

Estimation of Parameters

We aim to estimate the coefficients ϕ_i by minimizing the sum of squared residuals as follows:

$$\frac{min}{\phi_1, \ldots, \phi_p} \sum_{t=p}^{T} \left(X_t - c - \sum_{i=1}^{p} \phi_i X_{t-i} \right)^2$$

This is a classic linear regression problem with lagged predictors:

$$X \cdot \beta = Y$$

Where:

- X is the lag matrix of the series
- $\beta = [intercept, \phi_1, \ldots \phi_p]$
- Y is the target vector

β can be solved via **Normal Equation** as follows:

$$\beta = (X^T X)^{-1} X^T Y$$

This is the closed-form solution to the Ordinary Least Squares (OLS) method used in linear regression to solve for β. This equation gives us the optimal vector of coefficients that best fits the model.

Implementing the AR model as a Python Function

In this section, let us implement the estimation of AR(*p*) parameters using raw matrix operations:

Code:

```
def fit_ar_model(time_series, p):
    n = len(time_series)
    if n <= p:
        raise ValueError("Time series too short for specified AR order.")
    X, Y = [], []
    for t in range(p, n):
        X.append([1] + [time_series[t - i - 1] for i in range(p)])
        Y.append(time_series[t])

    def transpose(matrix): return list(zip(*matrix))
    def matmul(A, B):
        return [[sum(a * b for a, b in zip(A_row, B_col)) for B_col in
zip(*B)] for A_row in A]
    def invert_2x2(matrix):
        det = matrix[0][0]*matrix[1][1] - matrix[0][1]*matrix[1][0]
        return [[matrix[1][1]/det, -matrix[0][1]/det],
                [-matrix[1][0]/det, matrix[0][0]/det]]
    XT = transpose(X)
    XTX = matmul(XT, X)
    XTY = [sum(xi * yi for xi, yi in zip(col, Y)) for col in XT]
    from numpy.linalg import inv
    beta = inv(XTX).dot(XTY)
    return beta
```

In the preceding code,

- The **fit_ar_model** function demonstrates how to estimate the parameters of an Autoregressive model of order p for AR(p), using the Ordinary Least Squares (OLS) method.
- The function takes in a univariate time series and the desired lag order p, and then returns the optimal model coefficients.
- At its core, an AR(p) model assumes the current value of a time series is linearly dependent on its past p values, along with a constant term (intercept) and a random error.

The function proceeds in the following key steps:

1. **Input Validation:** It first ensures that the length of the time series is greater than p, since we need at least p+1 data points to fit an AR(p) model.
2. **Design Matrix Construction:** It then constructs a design matrix X, where each row contains a 1 (for the intercept) followed by the previous p lagged values of the time series. Alongside, it builds a target vector Y, containing the current values corresponding to each lagged input row.
3. **Matrix Operations:** The function computes the required matrices for the OLS solution.
    a. X^TX is the matrix of feature covariances
    b. X^TY is the projection of the output onto the feature space
4. Finally, the beta, β, coefficient is calculated using the closed-form least squares equation and returned by this function.

Real-World Example

To look at this example, let us continue with our electricity demand use case. Imagine a utility provider collecting the monthly electricity usage of a city over the last two years. The aim is to predict next month's demand based on historical usage. The data exhibits seasonality, where hot months lead to higher consumption, and autocorrelation, where recent usage influences current usage. Given the consistency in consumer behavior and climate conditions, an AR(2) model can provide reliable forecasts. This model will use the last 2 months' consumption to estimate the current month's usage.

This is particularly useful in use cases involving:

- Grid load balancing
- Planning resource procurement for fuel for thermal plants
- Energy pricing strategies

Python Implementation of the Example

In this section, let us look at a practical example for predicting electricity usage for a city.

Code:

```
electricity_usage = [
    310, 295, 280, 275, 290, 305, 315, 330, 320, 310, 300, 290,
    295, 300, 310, 325, 340, 345, 350, 360, 355, 340, 330, 320
]
coeffs = fit_ar_model(electricity_usage, p=2)
print(f"Estimated coefficients (Intercept, phi1, phi2): {coeffs}")
```

In the preceding code,

- The **electricity_usage** list contains 24 observations representing monthly electricity consumption in kilowatt-hours (kWh). It spans two full years of usage data. The data has an upward trend and some seasonality, but the AR model will primarily capture short-term dependencies.
- The next step fits the AR(2) model, which assumes that the electricity usage for any given month depends on the values from the previous two months, plus a random error term.

Output:

```
Estimated coefficients (Intercept, phi1, phi2): [63.43240784  1.52958516
-0.7285916 ]
```

The preceding output prints the resulting vector of estimated parameters.

Code:

```
def predict_next_ar(series, coeffs):
    intercept, phi1, phi2 = coeffs
    return intercept + phi1 * series[-1] + phi2 * series[-2]
predicted_usage = predict_next_ar(electricity_usage, coeffs)
print(f"Forecasted usage for next month: {predicted_usage:.2f} kWh")
```

In the preceding code,

- The function **predict_next_ar** takes two inputs:
  - **series:** The original time series data of monthly electricity usage.
  - **coeffs:** The coefficients estimated from the AR(2) model, which includes the Intercept, Lag-1 coefficient, and Lag-2 coefficient.
- It then uses these to predict the next value in the sequence.

Output:

```
Forecasted usage for next month: 312.46 kWh
```

The preceding output is the demand predicted for next month.

Autoregressive models form the theoretical and practical foundation for numerous time series forecasting tasks. Their strengths lie in their simplicity, ease of interpretation, and effectiveness in capturing temporal dependence, especially when the series is stationary. While modern techniques such as LSTM and Prophet offer more flexibility, AR models remain indispensable for short-term operational forecasting.

They also serve as key components in more sophisticated frameworks such as ARIMA, which handles non-stationary data through differencing, SARIMA, which incorporates seasonality, and VAR, which handles multiple interrelated time series. Thus, understanding and implementing AR models from scratch deepens the grasp of the temporal structure in data.

Moving Average (MA) Models

A Moving Average (MA) model is another foundational approach in time series analysis, distinct from the Autoregressive (AR) model. While AR models regress current values on past observations, MA models regress the current value on past forecast errors, also known as shocks.

In other words, the MA model views today's outcome as a weighted sum of past unexpected deviations from the mean. The model is built on the idea that the effects of past random disturbances (for example, news, external shocks, market anomalies) fade over time.

The MA model of order q, denoted as MA(q), is especially effective in handling irregular fluctuations and capturing short-term dependencies in stationary time series. It is also a core component of the more general ARMA and ARIMA models.

Mathematical Explanation

At its core, a Moving Average model of order q is defined as:

$$X_t = \mu + \varepsilon_t + \theta_1\varepsilon_{t-1} + \theta_2\varepsilon_{t-2} + \cdots + \theta_q\varepsilon_{t-q}$$

Where:

- X_t is the observed value at time t
- μ is the mean of the series
- $\varepsilon_{t \sim N(0,\sigma^2)}$ is a white noise term
- $\theta_1, \theta_2, \ldots \theta_q$ are the MA coefficients
- q is the order of the model (i.e., how many past errors are used)

The MA model does not use lagged observations of X_t directly. Instead, it models the current value as a function of past shocks, making it useful when autocorrelation dies out quickly due to short memory processes.

Properties of MA Models

Always Stationary: MA models are stationary by construction as long as the white noise is stationary.

Invertibility: An MA process is invertible if it can be represented as an infinite-order AR model. Hence, invertibility ensures that model estimation is unique and stable.

Estimation

Unlike AR models, which can be estimated using least squares, MA models are harder to estimate directly because the lagged error terms ε_{t-1}, ε_{t-2}, ... are not observed. As a result, estimation typically requires:

- Maximum Likelihood Estimation (MLE)
- Iterative optimization methods, such as the Kalman filter

However, for this section, we will approximate the estimation by assuming residuals.

Implementing the Math as a Python Function

In this section, let us write a function that estimates the parameters of an MA(1) model by minimizing the sum of squared forecast errors through brute force grid search.

Code:

```
def fit_ma1_model(time_series, theta_range=(-0.99, 0.99), step=0.01):
    n = len(time_series)
    mean_val = sum(time_series) / n
    best_theta, min_error = None, float('inf')
    for theta in [round(i, 2) for i in list(frange(theta_range[0],
theta_range[1], step))]:
        errors = [0]
        predictions = []

        for t in range(1, n):
            pred = mean_val + theta * errors[-1]
            err = time_series[t] - pred
            errors.append(err)
            predictions.append(pred)
        sse = sum((time_series[t] - predictions[t - 1]) ** 2 for t in
range(1, n))
        if sse < min_error:
            min_error = sse
            best_theta = theta
    return mean_val, best_theta
```

In the preceding code,

The **`fit_ma1_model`** provides a foundational approach to estimate the parameters of the Moving Average model of order 1(MA(1)) using exhaustive search.

In the MA(1) model, future values are forecasted not from past values but from past forecast errors.

Since these errors cannot be observed in advance, the model is simulated recursively.

At each time step, the previous error is used to forecast the current value, and the current error is then computed from the difference between actual and predicted values.

This function systematically evaluates a range of θ values by simulating the MA(1) model of each data point.

It then evaluates the predictions using the sum of squared forecast errors.

The result is the best-fitting θ, along with the constant mean μ, and they together define the MA(1) process.

Code:

```
def frange(start, stop, step):
    while start < stop:
        yield start
        start += step
```

In the preceding code,

The **frange** function is defined to generate an iteration over floating-point values with a custom step size.

Real-World Example

In this section, let us look at an example of daily asset returns prediction using the MA(1) model. Daily returns of a stock often exhibit sudden, short-lived deviations that are not easily explained by trends or past values alone. A traditional Autoregressive (AR) model might not be beneficial in such situations because they rely solely on the past values of the returns. Since MA(1) explicitly incorporates prediction error, we will use it in this example to capture short-term shocks in the market.

Python Implementation on the Example

In this section, we will look at a practical example of how to use the MA(1) to forecast asset returns.

Let us start by defining a synthetic stock returns dataset with volatility bursts.

Code:

```
returns = [0.01, 0.03, -0.02, 0.04, -0.01, -0.03, 0.05, -0.04, 0.02, 0.00,
0.01, -0.02]
```

In the next step, let us call **fit_ma1_model** on the data set.

Code:

```
mu, theta = fit_ma1_model(returns)
print(f"Estimated mean: {mu:.4f}, Estimated theta1: {theta:.2f}")
```

The preceding code returns μ the θ values.

Output:

```
Estimated mean: 0.0033, Estimated theta1: -0.83
```

Using these values, let us further predict the next return.

Code:

```
last_error = returns[-1] - (mu + theta * 0)
next_return = mu + theta * last_error
print(f"Forecasted next return: {next_return:.4f}")
```

In the preceding code,

The last error is calculated as previous returns, μ *and* θ values.

The next return is then calculated from the last error and the μ *and* θ values.

Output:

```
Forecasted next return: 0.0227
```

The next return is the forecast in the preceding output.

Moving Average models, despite their conceptual simplicity, are powerful tools for modeling time series with irregular bursts and short-lived dependencies. MA models are useful in scenarios where data is influenced by past shocks, such as financial returns or event-driven series. Unlike AR models, which model memory of past values, MA models capture memory of past disturbances. This distinction is very helpful in handling time series data with sudden shocks or volatility.

Autoregressive Moving Average (ARMA) Model

In this section, we will look at the Autoregressive Moving Average (ARMA) model. This forecasting technique is designed to model stationary processes by combining both Autoregression (AR) and Moving Average (MA).

Autoregressive models leverage the predictive power of past observations, assuming that previous values can explain current behavior. Conversely, Moving Average models capture the impact of past forecast errors or shocks. By integrating both components, the ARMA model offers a unified framework that can model both persistent patterns and short-term disturbances, making it more expressive than either component alone.

An ARMA model is typically denoted as **ARMA(p,q)**, where:

- **p** is the number of autoregressive terms (lags of series).
- **q** is the number of moving average terms (lags of forecast errors).

This model is particularly well-suited when:

- The time series is stationary, showing constant mean and variance over time.
- The data exhibits both autocorrelation and short-lived irregularities.

Mathematical Explanation

The ARMA model combines both AR(*p*) and MA(*q*) processes:

$$X_t = c + \sum_{i=1}^{p} \phi_i X_{t-i} + \varepsilon_t + \sum_{j=1}^{q} \theta_j \varepsilon_{t-j}$$

Where:

- X_t: value of the time series at time t
- ϕ_i: autoregressive coefficients for lagged values
- θ_j: moving average coefficients for past errors
- ε_t: white noise error term
- c: constant term
- *p*: order of the AR component
- *q*: order of the MA component

As per this equation, the current value depends on:

- A linear combination of the past *p* values, which is the AR part.
- A linear combination of the past *q* error terms, which is the MA part.
- A constant drift and current error.

Stationarity and Invertibility

- The AR part must satisfy stationarity, which means that the roots of the characteristic equation $1-\sum\phi_i z^i=0$ must lie outside the unit circle.
- The MA part must be invertible, which ensures a unique model representation in terms of past observations.

Identification and Estimation

- Use ACF and PACF plots to select suitable values of *p* and *q*.
- Estimation is typically done via maximum likelihood, as the MA component involves unobserved errors.

Implementing the Math as a Python Function

In this section, let us implement the basic approximation of an ARMA(1,1) model fitting using brute force optimization over coefficient ranges.

Code:

```
def fit_arma11(time_series, phi_range=(-0.9, 0.9), theta_range=(-0.9, 
0.9), step=0.1):
    n = len(time_series)
    mu = sum(time_series) / n
    best_phi, best_theta, min_sse = None, None, float('inf')

    for phi in frange(phi_range[0], phi_range[1], step):
        for theta in frange(theta_range[0], theta_range[1], step):
            sse = 0
            prev_error = 0
            for t in range(1, n):
                pred = mu + phi * time_series[t - 1] + theta * prev_error
                error = time_series[t] - pred
                sse += error**2
                prev_error = error
            if sse < min_sse:
                min_sse = sse
                best_phi = phi
                best_theta = theta
    return mu, best_phi, best_theta
```

In the preceding code,

- The **fit_arma11** function provides a simple implementation of the ARMA(1,1) model fitting by exhaustively searching over a predefined grid of parameter values.
- By simulating the role of past values (AR) and past errors (MA), this function helps illustrate how ARMA models capture both memory and shocks in the data.

In the next step, let us write the function for **frange**.

Code:

```
def frange(start, stop, step):
    while start <= stop:
        yield round(start, 3)
        start += step
```

In the preceding code,

The **frange** function is defined to generate an iteration over floating-point values with a custom step size.

This simplified method scans possible ϕ and θ combinations and finds the best-fitting parameters by minimizing squared errors.

Real-World Example

In this section, let us look at an example of an ARMA model on a real-world scenario. Internet Service Providers (ISPs) rely on accurate traffic forecasting to maintain smooth and uninterrupted service across their networks. The key metrics that are impacted in this scenario includes number of active connections, data throughput, and packet counts per second. They exhibit both predictable patterns driven by user behavior and unpredictable fluctuations driven by software updates, outages, or viral events. To effectively capture this dual behavior, the ARMA(1,1) model will be very useful, since it incorporates both AR and MA models.

Python Implementation on the Example

In this section, we will look at a practical example of how to use the ARMA(1,1) to forecast network traffic.

Let us start by defining synthetic internet traffic data as packets per second.

Code:

```
traffic_data = [102, 107, 110, 105, 108, 111, 113, 112, 114, 115, 113, 110]
```

In the next step, let us call the **fit_arma11** function on the synthetic data.

Code:

```
mu, phi, theta = fit_arma11(traffic_data, step=0.05)
print(f"Estimated mean: {mu:.2f}, phi: {phi:.2f}, theta: {theta:.2f}")
```

The output is generated for the estimated mean, phi, and theta as follows.

```
Estimated mean: 110.00, phi: 0.00, theta: 0.40
```

In the next step, let us further forecast the next traffic load.

Code:

```
last_val = traffic_data[-1]
last_error = traffic_data[-1] - (mu + phi * traffic_data[-2] + theta * 0)
next_pred = mu + phi * last_val + theta * last_error
print(f"Forecasted next packet load: {next_pred:.2f} (k packets/sec)")
```

In the preceding code,

- The **last_val** fetches the most recent observation from the traffic data series.
- The **last_error** computes the last residual or forecast error ε_t using ARMA(1,1) equation.
- The **next_pred** captures the forecasted next traffic value computed using ARMA(1,1) formula.

The forecasted next packet load is generated as follows.

Output:

```
Forecasted next packet load: 110.00 (k packets/sec)
```

This model provides a robust prediction, balancing the effects of historical trends and recent anomalies in network traffic data.

The ARMA model is a versatile and interpretable method for modeling and forecasting stationary time series data. Its strength lies in combining memory of both past values (AR) and past shocks (MA), enabling it to handle a wide range of real-world time series scenarios.

Autoregressive Integrated Moving Average (ARIMA) Model

The Autoregressive Integrated Moving Average (ARIMA) model is one of the most robust and widely applied techniques in time series forecasting. Its strength lies in its ability to model both stationary and non-stationary time series by combining three essential components: Autoregression (AR), Integration (I), and Moving Average (MA). AR or MA models require the data to be stationary, which means the mean and variance of the time series are expected to be constant over time. On the other hand, ARIMA can handle non-stationarity in the time series data by transforming a non-stationary series into a stationary series through differencing. The term 'Integrated' (I) in ARIMA refers to this transformation. Once the series is made stationary, AR and MA terms are applied to model the linear temporal structure and random shocks in the data, respectively.

The ARIMA model is described using three parameters:

p – the number of Autoregressive (AR) terms. It captures the influence of past values on the current value.

d – the number of differences required to make the series stationary. It controls how many times we subtract previous observations to remove trends or seasonality.

q – the number of Moving Average (MA) terms. It models the influence of past forecast errors on the current value.

Mathematically, once the series has been differenced d times, the model fits an ARMA (p, q) model to the transformed series.

Conceptually, ARIMA can be understood as follows:

Autoregression (AR): Uses the past values of the series as predictors.

Integration (I): Applies differencing to eliminate trends or seasonality and achieve stationarity.

Moving Average (MA): Models the dependency between an observation and a residual error from a moving window of previous errors.

This blend allows ARIMA to handle a wide range of time series behaviors from gradual trends and sudden shocks to cyclical patterns with seasonal extensions such as SARIMA.

Mathematical Explanation

In this section, let us review the mathematical concept behind the ARIMA *(p,d,q)* Model structure.

An ARIMA model applies differencing *d times and then f its and* ARIMA *(p,d,q)* model on the differenced series.

Let X_t be the original time series.

Differencing it once can be defined as follows:

$$Y_t = X_t - X_{t-1}$$

Similarly, differencing it *d* times can be defined as follows:

$$Y_t = \nabla^d X_t$$

After differencing, apply ARMA:

$$Y_t = c + \sum_{i=1}^{p} \phi_i Y_{t-i} + \varepsilon_t + \sum_{j=1}^{q} \theta_j \varepsilon_{t-j}$$

Where:

- ϕ_i: AR coefficients
- θ_j: MA coefficients
- ε_t: white noise error

Implementing the Math as a Python Function

In this section, let us look at a simplified ARIMA(1,1,1) implementation with one round of differencing and brute-force parameter estimation.

Code:

```
def difference(series, d=1):
    for _ in range(d):
        series = [series[i] - series[i - 1] for i in range(1,
len(series))]
    return series
```

In the preceding code,

- The **difference** function is defined for preprocessing to transform the non-stationary time series into a stationary one by computing differences between consecutive observations.

- This transformation is fundamental in preparing the data for ARIMA modeling, where stationarity is a requirement for valid inference and prediction.
- This function supports recursive differencing, making it suitable for preparing time series data for ARIMA(p,d,q), where d is the number of times differencing is required to stabilize the series.

Code:

```
def fit_arima111(series, step=0.1):
    diff_series = difference(series, d=1)
    mu = sum(diff_series) / len(diff_series)
    best_phi, best_theta, min_sse = None, None, float('inf')
    for phi in frange(-0.9, 0.9, step):
        for theta in frange(-0.9, 0.9, step):
            sse, prev_error = 0, 0
            for t in range(1, len(diff_series)):
                pred = mu + phi * diff_series[t - 1] + theta * prev_error
                error = diff_series[t] - pred
                sse += error**2
                prev_error = error
            if sse < min_sse:
                min_sse = sse
                best_phi, best_theta = phi, theta
    return mu, best_phi, best_theta
```

In the preceding code,

- The function **`fit_arima111`** takes in the time series data and incremental step as input.
- It also applies first-order differencing to remove trends and produce a stationary series.
- It calculates the mean of the differenced series.
- It initializes variables to track the best-fitting parameters by minimizing the Sum of Squared Errors (SSE).
- It performs a grid search over combinations of ϕ *(autoregressive) and* θ (moving average) values, testing each one for fit.
- It then forecasts each point in the differenced series.
- It then stores the error between actual and predicted values, and accumulates squared errors (SSE) to evaluate model performance.
- It tracks **`prev_error`** for the moving average component.
- It keeps the ϕ and θ values that minimize the total forecasting error.

- It returns the estimated parameters for the ARIMA(1,1,1) model.

In the next step, let us write the function for **frange**.

Code:

```
def frange(start, stop, step):
    while start <= stop:
        yield round(start, 3)
        start += step
```

In the preceding code,

The **frange** function is defined to generate an iteration over floating-point values with a custom step size.

Real-World Example

A retail chain tracks monthly sales data across its outlets. Sales often exhibit trends due to seasonality, inflation, or growth. Assuming that the data is non-stationary, direct AR or MA modeling will not work on the data. Instead, we will apply the ARIMA(1,1,1) model on the sales data.

Python Implementation on the Example

In this section, let us look at the implementation of ARIMA(1,1,1) on the retail chain example.

Code:

```
sales = [120, 132, 143, 150, 165, 172, 180, 194, 205, 213, 225, 239]
```

In the preceding code,

- The monthly sales data (in thousands) is defined for the retail chain.
- The data exhibits a gradual upward trend, signaling non-stationarity.

Code:

```
mu, phi, theta = fit_arima111(sales)
print(f"Estimated mean: {mu:.2f}, phi: {phi:.2f}, theta: {theta:.2f}")
```

In the preceding code,

The example fits an ARIMA(1,1,1) model using the previously defined **fit_arima111** function. The output is displayed as follows.

Output:

```
Estimated mean: 10.82, phi: -0.00, theta: -0.60
```

Let us further forecast the next differenced value.

Code:

```
last_diff = sales[-1] - sales[-2]
next_diff_forecast = mu + phi * last_diff + theta * 0
next_value = sales[-1] + next_diff_forecast
print(f"Forecasted next month sales: {next_value:.2f}K")
```

In the preceding code,

- The last difference, which is the change from second-last to last month, is computed.
- The ARIMA(1,1,1) model is used to forecast the next differenced value, assuming no error term is available, as a common starting assumption.
- Since ARIMA(1,1,1) models differenced values, we must add the forecasted change to the last known actual value to get the next month's sales prediction on the original scale.

The following output displays the forecasted retail sales for the next month in thousands of units.

```
Forecasted next month sales: 249.82K
```

The ARIMA model forecasts a continued upward trend in sales, helping the company prepare resources in advance.

The ARIMA model remains one of the most powerful and widely adopted techniques in time series analysis. By seamlessly integrating Autoregression (AR), differencing (I) for non-stationarity, and Moving Average (MA) components, ARIMA provides a versatile framework for modeling time-dependent data with temporal structure and noise.

Seasonal ARIMA (SARIMA) Model

While ARIMA models effectively capture trends and noise in time series, they fall short in handling seasonal patterns. The recurring fluctuations at regular intervals in data are seasonal fluctuations (for example, monthly sales spikes, daily energy loads). To address this, the ARIMA model can be extended to SARIMA (Seasonal ARIMA), since it explicitly incorporates seasonal autoregressive and moving average terms, as well as seasonal differencing.

SARIMA is denoted as ARIMA(p,d,q) (P,D,Q,s), where:

- (p,d,q): Non-seasonal ARIMA terms
- (P,D,Q,): Seasonal ARIMA terms
- s: Seasonal period (for example, s = 12 for monthly data with annual seasonality)

This model is widely used in retail for seasonal demand, weather for temperature cycles, and finance for quarterly trends, offering robust forecasts when data exhibits both trend and seasonality.

Mathematical Explanation

SARIMA is defined mathematically as follows:

Non-seasonal ARIMA(*p,d,q*) **terms:**

$$\phi(B)(1-B)^d X_t = \theta(B)\varepsilon_t$$

Seasonal ARIMA(P,D,Q,s) **terms:**

$$\Phi(B^s)(1-B^s)^D X_t = \Theta(B^s)\varepsilon_t$$

Where:

- B: *Backshift operator,* $BX_t = X_{t-1}$,
- $\phi(B)$: *Non-seasonal* AR *polynomial of order p*
- $\theta(B)$: *Non-seasonal* MA *polynomial of order q*
- $\Phi(B^s)$, $\Theta(B^s)$: *Seasonal AR and MA polynomials*
- $(1-B)^d$: Differencing to remove trend
- $(1-B)^d$: Seasonal differencing

SARIMA is a multiplicative model, capturing both regular and seasonal behavior simultaneously.

$$\Phi_P(B^s)\phi_p(B)(1-B)^d(1-B^s)^D X_t = \Theta_Q(B^s)\theta_q(B)\varepsilon_t$$

Implementing the Math as a Python Function

In this section, let us define a simple implementation of the SARIMA(1,1,1)(1,1,1,12) simulation framework using seasonal differencing.

Let us start by defining seasonal differencing.

Code:

```
def seasonal_difference(series, lag):
    return [series[i] - series[i - lag] for i in range(lag, len(series))]
```

In the preceding code,

- The **seasonal_difference** function is a simple yet powerful preprocessing tool in time series analysis, particularly for handling seasonal non-stationarity.
- It operates by computing the difference between each observation and its counterpart from a previous season, defined by the lag.
- It can effectively remove recurring seasonal patterns from the data.

Code:

```
def difference(series):
    return [series[i] - series[i - 1] for i in range(1, len(series))]
```

In the preceding code,

- The **difference** function is a foundational tool in time series preprocessing, designed to transform a non-stationary series into a stationary one by removing trends or long-term structure.
- It works by computing the first-order difference, that is, the change between each value and its immediate predecessor.

Code:

```
def sarima_forecast(series, s=12):
    seasonally_diff = seasonal_difference(series, s)
    fully_diff = difference(seasonally_diff)

    if len(fully_diff) < 1:
        raise ValueError("Series too short to forecast after 
differencing.")

    phi, theta = 0.5, 0.4
    Phi, Theta = 0.3, 0.2
    mu = sum(fully_diff) / len(fully_diff)

    last = fully_diff[-1]
    seasonal_lag = fully_diff[-s] if len(fully_diff) >= s else 0
    error, error_s = 0, 0

    pred = mu + phi * last + Phi * seasonal_lag + theta * error + Theta 
* error_s

    base = series[-1] + (series[-s] if len(series) >= s else 0)
    return base + pred
```

In the preceding code,

- The **sarima_forecast** function encapsulates the logic of forecasting the next point in a seasonal time series using the core principles of the SARIMA model.
- This function models both short-term and seasonal dependencies while handling non-stationarity in the data.
- To begin, the function applies seasonal differencing with a lag of s to remove repetitive seasonal patterns.
- It then performs first-order differencing on this result to eliminate long-term trends.
- These two steps together transform the original time series into a stationary series, which is essential for SARIMA modeling.
- Next, the function estimates the **mean (mu)** of this fully differenced series, which serves as a constant drift term.

- It then defines fixed coefficients representing both non-seasonal **(AR: ϕ, MA: θ)** and seasonal **(AR: Φ, MA: Θ)** dynamics.
- These values are not estimated from data here but serve to demonstrate the forecasting logic.

The forecast is computed using a linear combination of:

- The most recent differenced value (**lag 1**),
- The corresponding seasonal lag (**lag s**),
- And two placeholder error terms, both initialized as 0, which stand in for residuals in a real model.
- Finally, to return the forecast on the original scale, the model reverses the differencing by adding back the last known value (**series[-1]**) and the seasonal component (**series[-s]**), along with the forecasted change (**pred**).

Real-World Example

Airline passenger data is a classic example of a time series that exhibits both trend and seasonality. Over time, global air travel tends to increase due to economic growth and rising mobility, reflecting a long-term upward trend. Simultaneously, the number of passengers fluctuates predictably each year, spiking during holiday seasons, summer vacations, and festive periods, which introduces strong annual seasonality into the data. To accurately model and forecast such patterns, a SARIMA(1,1,1)(1,1,1,12) model is well-suited.

Python Implementation on the Example

In this section, let us implement the SARIMA model on Airline passenger data.

Code:

```
passengers = [112, 118, 132, 129, 121, 135, 148, 148, 136, 119, 104, 118,
              115, 126, 141, 135, 125, 149, 170, 170, 158, 133, 114, 140]
forecast = sarima_forecast(passengers)
print(f"Forecasted passengers for next month: {forecast:.2f}")
```

In the preceding code,

The simplified SARIMA-based time series forecast is applied to simulated monthly airline passenger data, showcasing the use of seasonal modeling to anticipate future travel volumes.

Output:

```
Forecasted passengers for next month: 262.73
```

In the preceding output, the forecasted passenger count for the next month is printed.

SARIMA models are essential for forecasting time series with seasonality and trend. Their flexibility and interpretability make them a suitable choice in production forecasting pipelines.

Exponential Smoothing Models

Exponential Smoothing is a family of forecasting methods that are well-suited for time series data exhibiting trend and seasonality. Unlike ARIMA, which models the data in terms of autoregressive and moving average components, Exponential Smoothing directly uses weighted averages of past observations to make predictions. The weights decay exponentially, giving more importance to recent data.

Exponential Smoothing models are divided into:

- **Simple Exponential Smoothing (SES):** For stationary data without trend or seasonality.
- **Holt's Linear Trend Model:** For data with a trend and no seasonality.
- **Holt-Winters Seasonal Model:** For data with both trend and seasonality.

Mathematical Explanation

In this section, let us look at the simplified mathematical definitions of Exponential Smoothing models.

Simplified Exponential Smoothing (SES)

The Simple Exponential Smoothing is applicable when the time series data does not exhibit any trend or seasonality. The forecast is a weighted average of past observations, where more recent observations are given higher weight.

The formula for SES is defined as follows:

$$\hat{X}_{t+1} = \alpha X_t + (1 - \alpha)\hat{X}_t$$

Where:

- $\hat{X}_{t+1}$ is the forecast for the next time period
- X_t is the actual observation at time t
- $\hat{X}_t$ is the forecasted value at time t
- α is the smoothing constant between 0 and 1, which determines how much weight is placed on the most recent observation

Holt's Linear Trend Model

When the time series data exhibits a linear trend but no seasonality, we use Holt's Linear Trend Model. The model extends SES by introducing two equations: one for the level and one for the trend.

The formulas for Holt's method are:

$$\hat{X}_{t+1} = l_t + b_t$$

Where:

- l_t is the level of the time series at time t
- b_t is the trend at time t
- $\hat{X}_{t+1}$ is the forecast.

Level and trend equations:

$$l_t = \alpha X_t + (1-\alpha)(l_{t-1} + b_{t-1})$$

$$b_t = \beta(l_t - l_{t-1}) + (1-\beta)b_{t-1}$$

Where:

- α is the smoothing factor for the level
- β is the smoothing factor for the trend

Holt-Winters Seasonal Model

The Holt-Winters model incorporates both trend and seasonality in the forecast. It is widely used for time series data, seasonal patterns, such as monthly sales or energy consumption.

The model is defined by three components:

- **Level:** The smoothed value of the series.
- **Trend:** The rate of change in the level.
- **Seasonality:** The repeating pattern in the data.

The equations for Holt-Winters are:

$$\hat{X}_{t+1}=(l_t+b_t)\cdot s_{t+1}$$

Where:

- s_{t+1} is the seasonal component for the next period

Level equation:

$$l_t = \alpha\left(\frac{X_t}{s_{t-m}}\right) + (1-\alpha)(l_{t-1} + b_{t-1})$$

Trend equation:

$$b_t = \beta(l_t - l_{t-1}) + (1-\beta)b_{t-1}$$

Seasonal equation:

$$s_t = \gamma\left(\frac{X_t}{l_t + b_t}\right) + (1-\gamma)s_{t-m}$$

Where:

- α: Level smoothing factor
- β: Trend smoothing factor
- γ: Seasonal smoothing factor
- m: *Periodicity of the seasonality (for example,* m=12 for monthly data with yearly seasonality)

Python Implementation on the Example

In this section, let us look at a simplified implementation of Exponential Smoothing Models.

Simple Exponential Smoothing (SES)

Let us look at Simple Exponential Smoothing as the first implementation.

Code:

```
def simple_exponential_smoothing(series, alpha):
    if not 0 < alpha < 1:
        raise ValueError("Alpha must be between 0 and 1 (exclusive).")
    if len(series) == 0:
        return []
    smoothed = [series[0]]
    for t in range(1, len(series)):
        prev = smoothed[-1]
        new = alpha * series[t] + (1 - alpha) * prev
        smoothed.append(new)
    forecast = smoothed[-1]
    return smoothed, forecast
```

In the preceding code,

- The **simple_exponential_smoothing** function implements Simple Exponential Smoothing (SES) in time series analysis, which is used when the data shows no clear trend or seasonality.
- This method works by assigning exponentially decreasing weights to older observations.
- This is governed by the smoothing parameter alpha ($0 < \alpha < 1$), which controls how quickly the influence of older data decays.
- A higher alpha gives more weight to recent observations, making the model more responsive to changes; a lower alpha emphasizes longer-term history, leading to smoother outputs.
- The function begins by checking if alpha lies within a valid range and ensures the input series is not empty.

- It initializes the smoothed series with the first observed value. Then, for each time point, it computes the next smoothed value.
- This recursive update continues until the entire series is processed.
- The final smoothed value is returned as the forecast for the next period under the assumption that future values will continue at the current level.

Holt's Linear Trend Model

Let us look at Holt's Linear Trend Model as the next implementation of Exponential Smoothing models.

Code:

```
def holt_linear_trend(series, alpha, beta):
    if not 0 < alpha < 1 or not 0 < beta < 1:
        raise ValueError("Alpha and Beta must be between 0 and 1.")
    if len(series) < 2:
       raise ValueError("Series must contain at least two observations.")
    level = series[0]
    trend = series[1] - series[0]
    forecast_series = [level + trend]
    for t in range(1, len(series)):
        value = series[t]
        prev_level = level
        level = alpha * value + (1 - alpha) * (prev_level + trend)
        trend = beta * (level - prev_level) + (1 - beta) * trend
        forecast = level + trend
        forecast_series.append(forecast)
    next_forecast = level + trend
    return forecast_series, next_forecast
```

In the preceding code,

- The **holt_linear_trend** function implements Holt's Linear Trend Method, an extension of simple exponential smoothing designed to forecast time series data that exhibits a linear trend but no seasonality.
- The function begins by validating that both alpha and beta (smoothing parameters) fall within the (0, 1) interval.
- Alpha controls the smoothing of the level component, and beta adjusts the sensitivity of the trend.
- It then initializes the level to the first observation and estimates the initial trend as the difference between the first two data points.
- In each iteration, the model updates:

- The level using a weighted average of the current actual value and the previous level adjusted by the trend.
- The trend as a smoothed update of the change in level.

- The forecast for the next point is computed by summing the updated level and trend.
- The function returns two outputs:
  - A forecasted series that includes smoothed predictions for each time step.
  - A next-step forecast, which projects the value for the period immediately following the input data.

Holt-Winters Seasonal Model

Let us look at the Holt-Winters Seasonal Model as the next implementation of Exponential Smoothing models.

Code:

```
def holt_winters_additive(series, season_length, alpha, beta, gamma, 
n_preds=1):
    n = len(series)
    if n < 2 * season_length:
        raise ValueError("Series must have at least two full seasons of 
data.")
    seasonals = initial_seasonal_components(series, season_length)
    level = sum(series[:season_length]) / season_length
    trend = sum([(series[i + season_length] - series[i]) / season_length 
for i in range(season_length)]) / season_length
    result = []
    for t in range(n + n_preds):
        if t < n:
            value = series[t]
            last_level = level
            level = alpha * (value - seasonals[t % season_length]) + (1 
- alpha) * (level + trend)
            trend = beta * (level - last_level) + (1 - beta) * trend
            seasonals[t % season_length] = gamma * (value - level) + (1 
- gamma) * seasonals[t % season_length]
            result.append(level + trend + seasonals[t % season_length])
        else:
            m = t - n + 1
           result.append(level + m * trend + seasonals[t % season_length])
    return result
```

In the preceding code,

- The **`holt_winters_additive`** function implements the additive Holt-Winters seasonal method, a powerful forecasting technique for time series data exhibiting both trend and seasonality.
- Unlike simple or double exponential smoothing, this method incorporates a third component: seasonality, making it suitable for time series with repeating cycles.
- This model decomposes a time series into three components:
    - **Level:** The smoothed estimate of the baseline value of the series.
    - **Trend:** The direction and magnitude of the series' slope.
    - **Seasonality:** The recurring deviation from the level-trend curve based on season (for example, monthly or weekly).
- These components are updated at each time step.

Function Logic:

Input Validation:

- It ensures that there is enough data to compute at least two full seasonal cycles, the minimum required for stable seasonal component estimation.

Initialization:

- Seasonality is estimated using another function, **`initial_seasonal_components`**, a helper that extracts the baseline seasonality for each position in the seasonal cycle. This function will be explained next.
- Level is initialized as the average of the first season.
- Trend is initialized using the average difference between corresponding points in successive seasons.

Recursive Smoothing and Forecasting:

For each point in the series:

- The observed value is adjusted for seasonality to update the level.
- The change in level is used to refine the trend.
- The seasonality is updated based on how much the actual value deviates from the current level.
- The forecast is then recombined as level + trend + seasonality.

For future predictions beyond the input (**`n_preds`**), the model extrapolates using the last estimated level and trend, cycling through the seasonal components.

Return:

- The function returns a list of smoothed values and forecasts extending **n_preds** steps into the future.

Let us further define a function for initializing seasonality in the model.

Code:

```
def initial_seasonal_components(series, season_length):
    season_averages = []
    n_seasons = len(series) // season_length
    for j in range(n_seasons):
        start = season_length * j
        end = start + season_length
        season_avg = sum(series[start:end]) / season_length
        season_averages.append(season_avg)
    seasonals = [0] * season_length
    for i in range(season_length):
        sum_over_seasons = sum(series[j * season_length + i] - season_
averages[j] for j in range(n_seasons))
        seasonals[i] = sum_over_seasons / n_seasons
    return seasonals
```

In the preceding code,

The function **initial_seasonal_components** plays a critical foundational role in seasonal time series modeling.

Function Logic:

Compute Seasonal Averages:

The dataset is split into complete, non-overlapping seasons (for example, full years of monthly data).

For each season, the average of its values is computed. This represents the **level** of that specific season, effectively normalizing for trend or absolute scale.

Compute Seasonal Components:

For each position within a seasonal cycle (for example, all Januaries, all Februaries, and so on), the function:

- Computes how much each value at that position deviates from its season's average.
- Averages these deviations across all seasons.

This gives the initial estimate of the seasonal effect for each period in the cycle.

Return:

The function returns a list of length **season_length**, where each element corresponds to the average seasonal effect for that specific period in the cycle.

The **initial_seasonal_components** function is a preprocessing step that ensures a time series model starts with a reasonable understanding of seasonality. Without this, the forecasting algorithm would misinterpret structural seasonal patterns as noise or trend, leading to biased predictions.

Real-World Example

Imagine a company selling ice cream wanting to forecast its sales for the upcoming months. Their monthly sales data exhibit an increasing trend and seasonality in the summer months.

For such data, Exponential Smoothing models will be more suitable.

Python Implementation on the Example

Let us first start by defining synthetic ice cream sales data at a monthly level.

Code:

```
sales = [
    120, 135, 150, 160, 180, 195, 210, 220, 205, 180, 160, 140,
    130, 145, 160, 175, 190, 205, 220, 230, 215, 190, 170, 150
]
```

For the first example, let us implement Simple Exponential Smoothing.

Code:

```
alpha = 0.5
smoothed_values, forecast = simple_exponential_smoothing(sales, alpha)
print("Smoothed values:", [round(v, 2) for v in smoothed_values])
print(f"Forecast for next period: {forecast:.2f}")
```

In the preceding code,

- We have defined a value only for alpha since this model needs only alpha to be defined.
- We have then called the **simple_exponential_smoothing** function on the sales data and alpha.

The output for the preceding model is displayed as follows:

```
Smoothed values: [120, 127.5, 138.75, 149.38, 164.69, 179.84, 194.92,
207.46, 206.23, 193.12, 176.56, 158.28, 144.14, 144.57, 152.28, 163.64,
176.82, 190.91, 205.46, 217.73, 216.36, 203.18, 186.59, 168.3]
Forecast for next period: 168.30
```

For the next example, let us apply Holt's Linear Trend Model to the data.

Code:

```
alpha = 0.8
beta = 0.2
forecasts, next_value = holt_linear_trend(sales, alpha, beta)
print("In-sample forecasts:", [round(f, 2) for f in forecasts])
print(f"Forecast for next month: {next_value:.2f}")
```

In the preceding code,

- We have defined both alpha and beta parameters for the model.
- We have then called the **`holt_linear_trend`** on the sales data.

The output for the preceding model is displayed as follows:

Output:

```
In-sample forecasts: [135, 150.0, 165.0, 175.2, 194.01, 209.93, 225.12,
235.34, 220.53, 191.08, 164.22, 138.97, 124.49, 136.87, 155.05, 173.88,
192.22, 209.94, 227.09, 238.99, 225.53, 197.15, 171.13, 146.55]
Forecast for next month: 146.55
```

For the next example, let us apply Holt-Winters' Seasonal Model to the data.

Code:

```
forecast = holt_winters_additive(
    series=sales_data,
    season_length=12,
    alpha=0.5,
    beta=0.3,
    gamma=0.2,
    n_preds=6
)
print("Forecasted values:")
print([round(f, 2) for f in forecast[-6:]])
```

In the preceding code,

We have defined alpha, beta, and gamma since this model captures level, trend, and seasonality.

We have then called the **`holt_winters_additive`** on the sales data.

The output for the preceding model is displayed as follows:

```
Forecasted values:
[130.85, 145.06, 159.58, 171.84, 189.14, 204.1]
```

These models help the company prepare for peak sales seasons, allocate resources, and plan marketing strategies.

Exponential Smoothing models are highly efficient for forecasting time series data with trends and seasonality. The key strengths of these models include:

- **Simplicity:** Easy to implement and interpret.
- **Flexibility:** Suitable for different types of time series data (stationary, trend, seasonal).
- **Computational Efficiency:** Less resource-intensive compared to machine learning models.

The main drawback is that they assume linear relationships. Thus, if the time series has non-linear behavior or large irregularities, more complex models (for example, machine learning or deep learning models) may be needed.

The Holt-Winters seasonal method (with its level, trend, and seasonal components) is ideal for real-world forecasting, such as demand planning, financial forecasting, and inventory management.

Conclusion

In this chapter, we systematically explored the foundations, mathematical formulations, and practical applications of statistical models for time series forecasting. Beginning with basic building blocks such as Autoregressive (AR) and Moving Average (MA) models, we progressively developed an understanding of more powerful frameworks such as ARMA, ARIMA, SARIMA, and Exponential Smoothing techniques. Each of these models offers distinct strengths suited to different characteristics of time series data, from simple stationary processes to those exhibiting complex trends and seasonality.

A key insight is that model choice is rarely one-size-fits-all. AR models are ideal for data where current values are closely tied to past observations, while MA models perform well when shocks or unexpected changes dominate the structure. ARIMA models excel at forecasting when the series is non-stationary but can be made stationary through differencing. SARIMA models further extend this capability to seasonal data, making them indispensable for applications such as retail sales forecasting and energy demand planning.

Exponential Smoothing methods, on the other hand, provide a different perspective, forecasting future values as weighted averages of past observations without needing a heavy mathematical framework. They offer computational simplicity and quick responsiveness to changes in trends and seasonal patterns, making them highly practical for real-time forecasting.

Looking ahead, the next natural progression will involve delving into state space models, Kalman filters, and deep learning approaches such as LSTM networks for sequence prediction. However, regardless of technological evolution, the principles of structure, stationarity, seasonality, and residual diagnostics, as detailed in this chapter, will remain at the core of sound forecasting practice.

References

- Hyndman, R. J. and Athanasopoulos, G. (2021) *Forecasting: Principles and Practice*. 3rd edn. https://otexts.com/fpp3/.
- Hamilton, J. D. (1994) *Time Series Analysis. Princeton University Press.*
- pandas Time Series Documentation: https://pandas.pydata.org/pandas-docs/stable/user_guide/timeseries.html.
- Shumway, R. H. and Stoffer, D. S. (2017) *Time Series Analysis and* Its *Applications. Springer.*
- Box, G. E. P., Jenkins, G. M., Reinsel, G. C. and Ljung, G. M. (2015) *Time Series Analysis: Forecasting and Control. Wiley.*
- Chatfield, C. (2003) *The Analysis of Time Series: An Introduction. Chapman & Hall.*
- Enders, W. (2014) *Applied Econometric Time Series*. 4th edn. *Wiley.*
- Tsay, R. S. (2010) *Analysis of Financial Time Series*. 3rd edn. *Wiley.*
- Makridakis, S., Wheelwright, S. C. and Hyndman, R. J. (1998) *Forecasting: Methods and Applications*. 3rd edn. *Wiley.*
- Brown, R. G. (1963) *Smoothing, Forecasting, and Prediction of Time Series. Prentice-Hall.*
- Taylor, J. W. (2003) Exponential Smoothing with a State-Space Model: An Application to Short-Term Forecasting. *International Journal of Forecasting.*

CHAPTER 8
ML and DL for Timeseries

Introduction

In the evolving landscape of time series forecasting, **Machine Learning (ML)** and **Deep Learning (DL)** models have emerged as capable alternatives to classical statistical models. We covered traditional time series models such as ARIMA and SARIMA in the previous chapters. There are certain areas where these models might struggle, such as with non-linear patterns and complex and high-dimensional time series data.

The flexibility of machine learning models such as Decision Trees, Random Forests, and Gradient Boosting can be helpful in modeling complex and non-linear relationships in the data. These models can scale across large data sets.

A deep learning model, such as Long Short-Term Memory (LSTM) networks, is specifically designed to learn from sequences. It is particularly well-suited for capturing long-range dependencies, sequential patterns, and dynamic behaviors in time series.

However, it is important to note that the success of ML and DL in time series forecasting is contingent on correctly reframing the forecasting problem into a supervised learning format. This includes creating lagged features, rolling statistics, handling temporal ordering carefully, and validating models in a manner that respects the sequence of time. Additionally, ML and DL models require specialized training procedures, hyperparameter tuning, and often, significantly more data compared to classical models.

By the end of this chapter, readers will be able to understand how to transform time series data into a supervised learning format, apply and interpret tree-based models for time series regression tasks. The readers will also be able to design and train LSTM models for sequential forecasting problems and gain intuition about when to prefer machine learning, deep learning, or traditional models based on the nature of the data.

Structure

In this chapter, the following topics will be covered:

- Decision Tree Regressor
- Random Forest
- Gradient Boosted Trees (XGBoost)
- Long Short-Term Memory (LSTM)

Decision Tree Regressor

A Decision Tree Regressor is a supervised learning algorithm used for predicting continuous outcomes. In the context of time series forecasting, a Decision Tree can model the relationship between past values, such as lags, rolling averages, and so on, and future values.

Unlike linear models, which impose a specific parametric form such as a line or a curve, Decision Trees split the data into homogeneous regions based on feature thresholds. They are non-parametric and tree-structured, which means they can naturally model non-linear, discontinuous, and complex relationships without requiring manual transformation of the data.

Mathematical Explanation

The goal of a Decision Tree for regression is to partition the input space into regions $R_1, R_2, \ldots R_m$, and predict a constant value c_m for each region.

At each node of the tree, the algorithm chooses:

- A feature j
- A split point s

to solve:

$$min_{j,s}\left[min_{c_1}\sum_{x_i\in R_1(j,s)}(y_i-c_1)^2+min_{c_2}\sum_{x_i\in R_2(j,s)}(y_i-c_1)^2\right]$$

where:

- $R_1(j, s) = \{x|x_j \leq s\}$, and
- $R_2(j, s) = \{x|x_j > s\}$.

In words:

- For each feature and every possible split point, find the split that minimizes the Sum of Squared Errors (SSE) within each partition

The prediction at any leaf node is simply the average of the target values in that region:

$$\widehat{y}_{leaf} = \frac{1}{|R_m|} \sum_{i \in R_m} y_i$$

Key Concepts:

- **Recursive Binary Splitting:** At each node, a binary split divides the data.
- **Greedy Search:** The best split is chosen locally without considering future splits.
- **Stopping Criteria:**
    - Minimum samples per node
    - Maximum depth
    - Minimum decrease in error
- **Pruning:** Reducing the size of the tree to prevent overfitting.

Implementing the Math as a Python Function

In this section, let us implement a simple form of a Decision Tree Regressor for time series.

Let us start by creating a class to implement a Decision Tree Regressor and add the methods required.

Code:

```
import numpy as np
class DecisionTreeRegressorSimple:
```

Let us next implement the **init** method to initialize the parameters.

Code:

```
    def __init__(self, min_samples_split=2, max_depth=5):
        self.min_samples_split = min_samples_split
        self.max_depth = max_depth
        self.tree = None
```

In the preceding code,

- The parameter **min_samples_split** defines the minimum number of samples required to split an internal node.

- If the number of samples at a node falls below this threshold, the tree stops splitting and declares the node a leaf.
- This serves as a regularization mechanism to prevent the model from creating overly fine-grained partitions that capture noise rather than signal.

In the next step, let us create the method to fit the model.

The **fit** method initiates the training process by calling the **_build_tree** method, which recursively constructs the decision tree structure from the training data **X** (features) and **y** (target), starting at the root node with depth=0.

- **X** is a 2D list or array where each row is a training instance, and each column is a feature.
- **y** is a 1D list of continuous target values corresponding to each row in X.

Let us further define the **_build_tree** method.

Code:

```
    def _build_tree(self, X, y, depth):
        n_samples, n_features = len(X), len(X[0])
        if (n_samples < self.min_samples_split) or (depth >=
self.max_depth):
            return np.mean(y)

        best_split = self._best_split(X, y, n_features)
        if best_split is None:
            return np.mean(y)

        left_idxs, right_idxs, split_feature, split_value = best_
split
        left = self._build_tree([X[i] for i in left_idxs], [y[i]
for i in left_idxs], depth + 1)
        right = self._build_tree([X[i] for i in right_idxs],
[y[i] for i in right_idxs], depth + 1)
        return (split_feature, split_value, left, right)
```

In the preceding code,

The **_build_tree** method is the recursive constructor that builds the regression tree from top (root node) to bottom (leaf nodes).

It performs three main tasks:

- Check stopping criteria
- Find the best split based on Mean Squared Error (MSE)
- Recursively build left and right subtrees

If the number of samples is too small or the tree has reached its maximum allowed depth, it stops splitting and returns the **mean** of the **target values**; this becomes a **leaf node**.

It searches for the optimal feature and threshold that best splits the data into two groups with minimal combined variance in target values.

If no valid split exists (for example, all values are identical), the node again becomes a leaf.

Once a split is found, the data is partitioned into left and right subsets, and the **_build_tree** method is called recursively on each. This recursive expansion continues until the stopping criteria are met at all branches.

Each internal node of the tree returns a tuple:

- **split_feature**: Index of the feature to split on
- **split_value**: Threshold value to compare against
- **left**: Subtree for data <= threshold
- **right**: Subtree for data > threshold

This recursive nesting forms the entire decision tree, where leaves hold scalar predictions and branches hold split rules.

In the next step, let us define the method to compute the best split.

Code:

```
def _best_split(self, X, y, n_features):
    best_mse = float('inf')
    split_idx, split_val = None, None
    left_idxs, right_idxs = None, None
    for feature_idx in range(n_features):
        feature_values = [row[feature_idx] for row in X]
        thresholds = set(feature_values)
        for threshold in thresholds:
            left, right = [], []
            for i, value in enumerate(feature_values):
                if value <= threshold:
                    left.append(i)
                else:
                    right.append(i)
            if len(left) == 0 or len(right) == 0:
                continue
            left_mse = np.var([y[i] for i in left]) * len(left)
            right_mse = np.var([y[i] for i in right]) * len(right)
            mse = (left_mse + right_mse) / len(X)
```

```
                if mse < best_mse:
                    best_mse = mse
                    split_idx = feature_idx
                    split_val = threshold
                    left_idxs = left
                    right_idxs = right
        if split_idx is None:
            return None
        return left_idxs, right_idxs, split_idx, split_val
```

In the preceding code,

- The **_best_split** method is the optimization engine of the decision tree regressor.
- It determines the most effective way to partition the data at a given node by evaluating all possible splits and selecting the one that minimizes prediction error, measured by Mean Squared Error (MSE).
- This method is crucial to ensure the tree learns meaningful patterns from data.
- This method systematically searches for the best possible binary split across all features and candidate thresholds at a decision node.
- The goal is to identify the split that produces the lowest combined variance in the target values on either side of the threshold.
- The variables **split_idx** and **split_val** store the best split found so far, starting with no split and infinite MSE.
- For each feature in the time series data, all unique values are treated as potential thresholds to split the data. This creates a brute-force but exhaustive search over possible split points.
- The method splits the dataset into left and right subsets based on whether values fall below or above the threshold. It skips any split that would create an empty group.
- Each potential split is evaluated by computing the weighted variance of the target values in the left and right groups. The weighting ensures that larger subsets contribute more to the total error.
- If a candidate split results in a lower error than previously found, it is stored as the new best.
- After evaluating all possible splits, the method returns the indices for the left and right partitions, the best feature to split on, and the optimal threshold value.
- If no valid split exists (for example, all values are identical), it returns None.

In the next step, let us define a method to make a prediction on a single input observation.

Code:

```
def predict_one(self, x, tree):
    if not isinstance(tree, tuple):
        return tree
    feature_idx, threshold, left_subtree, right_subtree = tree
    if x[feature_idx] <= threshold:
        return self.predict_one(x, left_subtree)
    else:
        return self.predict_one(x, right_subtree)
```

In the preceding code,

The method **predict_one** is responsible for making a prediction on a single input observation x by walking through the trained decision tree in a depth-first, recursive fashion.

Code:

```
def predict(self, X):
    return [self.predict_one(x, self.tree) for x in X]
```

In the preceding code,

- While **predict_one** handles a single observation, **predict** generalizes this process to an entire dataset, enabling the model to make predictions for all input instances in one go.
- It is the final step in transforming a trained tree structure into actionable predictions.

Real-World Example

Let us consider the scenario of an electricity provider attempting to forecast the next day's power demand using consumption data from the previous three days. Electricity usage typically exhibits short-term dependencies. Yesterday's load significantly influences today's, along with occasional abrupt shifts due to external factors such as weather changes or public holidays. In such settings, a Decision Tree Regressor becomes a particularly effective tool. It learns by identifying critical thresholds in past consumption values and forms decision rules that account for nonlinear patterns and localized variations. This enables the model to produce interpretable, region-specific predictions that can adapt to both steady trends and sudden disruptions in electricity demand.

Python Implementation on the Example

In this section, let us look at the practical example of predicting electricity usage for an electricity provider. This example models short-term electricity demand forecasting by leveraging the intuition that today's demand is influenced by the preceding days. It uses a lag-based feature engineering strategy to convert time series data into a supervised learning format and then fits a **DecisionTreeRegressorSimple** model to learn predictive rules.

Code:

```
demand = [300, 310, 320, 330, 345, 360, 370, 380, 400, 420, 440, 460]
def create_supervised(data, lag=3):
    X, y = [], []
    for i in range(lag, len(data)):
        X.append([data[i-3], data[i-2], data[i-1]])
        y.append(data[i])
    return X, y
X, y = create_supervised(demand, lag=3)
```

In the preceding code,

- A sample demand data is created as a list.
- The function **create_supervised** performs a sliding window transformation of the time series data:
- Each row in X consists of the previous 3 days of electricity demand.
- The corresponding y value is the demand on the next day.
- This structure allows the model to learn how previous consumption patterns relate to future values, and this is ideal for short-term forecasting, where autocorrelation is strong.

Code:

```
tree_model = DecisionTreeRegressorSimple(min_samples_split=2, max_
depth=3)
tree_model.fit(X, y)
```

In the preceding code, the **DecisionTreeRegressorSimple** function is initialized with:

- **min_samples_split=2:** allowing splits as soon as 2 data points are available.
- **max_depth=3:** constraining the tree's depth to prevent overfitting on this small dataset.

The model learns split rules that segment the training examples based on key thresholds in the lagged demand values, allowing it to capture nonlinear relationships.

Code:

```
latest_input = [[demand[-3], demand[-2], demand[-1]]]
predicted_demand = tree_model.predict(latest_input)
print(f"Forecasted electricity demand for next day: {predicted_
demand[0]:.2f}")
```

In the preceding code,

- The latest three demand values are used as input to predict the next day's demand.
- The tree model applies its learned logic to this input path and returns a single forecasted value.

The results of the forecast are then printed as follows.

Output:

```
Forecasted electricity demand for next day: 460.00
```

The use of a decision tree makes the learned model structure easy to inspect, while the lagged inputs make it naturally suited for time series with short memory effects.

The Decision Tree Regressor offers a straightforward and interpretable approach to time series forecasting by learning decision rules that segment the input space based on meaningful thresholds in past observations. This makes it particularly effective in scenarios where relationships between input and output are non-linear, abrupt, or governed by discrete patterns, such as in cases of regime shifts or rule-based systems. However, decision trees are not without limitations. They can overfit the training data if the tree is allowed to grow too deep, capturing noise rather than signal. Additionally, they often struggle to model smooth, continuous trends and may underperform in comparison to more advanced ensemble-based approaches such as Random Forests or Gradient Boosted Trees, which offer better generalization. Despite these constraints, decision trees remain a valuable tool that is ideal for quick baseline models, applications where model interpretability is crucial, or problems where understanding the decision logic is just as important as making accurate predictions.

Random Forest

A Random Forest Regressor is a powerful ensemble learning technique that constructs multiple decision trees and aggregates their outputs to improve forecasting performance. In contrast to a single decision tree, which can be prone to overfitting, Random Forests leverage diversity and averaging to enhance generalization, reduce variance, and increase robustness. This makes them highly effective for modeling complex, non-linear patterns often present in time series data.

In the context of time series forecasting, Random Forests do not operate on raw sequential data. Instead, they require careful feature engineering, such as using lagged values, rolling window statistics such as moving averages or standard deviations, and external regressors to convert the sequential signal into a supervised learning problem. Each tree in the forest is trained on a random subset of the data and a random subset of features, promoting diversity and decorrelation among trees. The final prediction is obtained by averaging the predictions of all trees, which stabilizes the output and reduces the risk of overfitting to anomalies in individual training samples.

Random Forests offer several advantages: they are robust to noise, capable of capturing non-linear interactions and heterogeneous relationships, and provide feature importance scores that help in understanding variable influence and guiding feature selection. Moreover, they are relatively fast to train, easy to parallelize, and suitable for large datasets. However, one key limitation is that they are not inherently sequential models, and they do not account for the order or autocorrelation structure in time series data unless such relationships are explicitly encoded into the features. As such, effective forecasting with Random Forests depends heavily on thoughtful design of time-aware input features.

Mathematical Explanation

Random Forests work by combining the predictions of multiple decision trees.

The core steps of random forests are as follows:

1. Bootstrap Aggregating (Bagging):
    a. Draw a random sample with replacement from the training data.
    b. Size should be equal to the training data size.
2. Random Feature Selection:
    a. At each split in the tree, select a random subset of features and find the best split.
3. Grow Unpruned Trees:
    a. Each tree is grown fully or up to maximum depth.
4. Aggregate Predictions:
    a. For regression, average the predictions from all trees.

Mathematical Expression:

Given B trees $T_b(X)$, where each tree predicts the outcome based on its subset:

Final prediction:

$$\hat{f}(X) = \frac{1}{B}\sum_{b=1}^{B} T_b(X)$$

Key Mathematical Concepts:

- **Variance Reduction:** Averaging multiple trees reduces the variance of the model without increasing bias significantly.
- **De-correlation of Trees:** By using random subsets of features, trees are made less correlated, improving the ensemble's strength.

Feature Importance is usually computed based on:

- Decrease in node impurity (variance) weighted by node probability.
- Average across all trees.

Implementing the Math as a Python Function

In this section, let us implement a basic Random Forest Regressor using our earlier simple Decision Tree.

We will implement the **RandomForestRegressorSimple** class, which is a simplified version of the Random Forest algorithm for regression. This illustrates how ensemble learning combines multiple decision trees trained on different subsets of data and features to produce more accurate and robust predictions. This code will cover the key concepts from the Random Forest model, such as bagging, feature randomness, and model averaging.

Code:

```
import numpy as np
import random
```

In the preceding code,

- The class **RandomForestRegressorSimple** builds on NumPy for numerical operations and Python's built-in random module for sampling, simulating the internals of ensemble-based learning.

The class **RandomForestRegressorSimple** will have the following methods:

- **__init__**
- **_bootstrap_sample**
- **_random_features**
- **fit**
- **predict**

Code:

```
class RandomForestRegressorSimple:
    def __init__(self, n_estimators=10, max_depth=5, min_samples_
split=2, max_features=None):
        self.n_estimators = n_estimators
```

```
        self.max_depth = max_depth
        self.min_samples_split = min_samples_split
        self.max_features = max_features
        self.trees = []
```

In the preceding code,

The constructor **__init__** defines the following key hyperparameters:

- **n_estimators**: Number of decision trees in the ensemble.
- **max_depth, min_samples_split**: Tree-level hyperparameters to control complexity.
- **max_features**: Number of randomly selected features for each tree.
- **self.trees**: A list to store tuples of trained trees and their corresponding feature subsets.

Code:

```
    def _bootstrap_sample(self, X, y):
        n_samples = len(X)
        idxs = [random.randint(0, n_samples-1) for _ in range(n_samples)]
        X_sample = [X[i] for i in idxs]
        y_sample = [y[i] for i in idxs]
        return X_sample, y_sample
```

In the preceding code,

The **_bootstrap_sample** method samples data with replacement to generate a bootstrap dataset for each tree, introducing variability and reducing overfitting.

Code:

```
    def _random_features(self, X):
        n_features = len(X[0])
        if self.max_features is None:
            self.max_features = int(np.sqrt(n_features))
        feature_idxs = random.sample(range(n_features), self.max_features)
        return feature_idxs
```

In the preceding code,

- Each tree uses a random subset of features, which decorrelates the trees and allows the forest to explore different parts of the feature space.
- If **max_features** is not provided, it defaults to √(number of features).

Code:

```
    def fit(self, X, y):
        for _ in range(self.n_estimators):
```

```
            X_sample, y_sample = self._bootstrap_sample(X, y)
            feature_idxs = self._random_features(X_sample)
          X_modified = [[row[i] for i in feature_idxs] for row in X_sample]
              tree = DecisionTreeRegressorSimple(min_samples_split=self.
min_samples_split, max_depth=self.max_depth)
            tree.fit(X_modified, y_sample)
            self.trees.append((tree, feature_idxs))
```

In the preceding code,

For each tree:

- A bootstrap sample is drawn.
- A subset of features is selected.
- The corresponding **X_sample** is modified to include only those features.
- A **DecisionTreeRegressorSimple** is trained and stored with its selected features.

This process encourages diversity across trees, enabling the ensemble to generalize better than any individual tree.

Code:

```
    def predict(self, X):
        tree_preds = []
        for tree, feature_idxs in self.trees:
            X_modified = [[row[i] for i in feature_idxs] for row in X]
            preds = tree.predict(X_modified)
            tree_preds.append(preds)
    predictions = np.mean(tree_preds, axis=0)
        return predictions.tolist()
```

In the preceding code,

- Each tree makes predictions on the input data using only the features it was trained on.
- All tree predictions are aggregated via simple averaging.
- This ensemble strategy reduces variance and yields more stable and accurate forecasts than single decision trees.

This implementation illustrates how Random Forests mitigate overfitting and handle complex, nonlinear relationships through a combination of:

- Random data sampling (bagging),
- Random feature selection (decorrelation), and
- Model averaging (variance reduction).

Real-World Example

In a business scenario, such as forecasting daily sales for an e-commerce platform, Random Forests offer a highly effective modeling approach. Suppose the company wants to predict tomorrow's sales using inputs such as the sales figures from the past seven days, rolling averages over the last 3 and 7 days, and the day of the week (for example, Monday, Tuesday). This type of problem is well-suited for Random Forests because sales behavior can change abruptly due to events such as holidays or flash promotions, and the influence of past sales on future demand is often non-linear and context-dependent. Additionally, categorical variables such as the day of the week introduce external, cyclical patterns that impact outcomes. Random Forests excel in this setting by automatically learning interactions and nonlinear effects without requiring the user to manually define complex transformations or equations. Their ensemble nature allows them to generalize well across diverse conditions, making them a powerful and practical choice for demand forecasting in dynamic commercial environments.

Python Implementation on the Example

In this section, let us apply Random Forest to the e-commerce example for sales forecasting.

Code:

```
sales = [220, 230, 250, 270, 260, 275, 300, 320, 340, 330, 345, 365, 400]
```

In the preceding code,

- We have defined a sample sales data in the form of a list.

Code:

```
def create_features(data):
    X, y = [], []
    for i in range(7, len(data)):
        lags = [data[i-1], data[i-2], data[i-3]]
        avg3 = np.mean(data[i-3:i])
        avg7 = np.mean(data[i-7:i])
        features = lags + [avg3, avg7]
        X.append(features)
        y.append(data[i])
    return X, y

X, y = create_features(sales)
```

In the preceding code,

- The **create_features** function is defined to transform a univariate time series into a supervised learning format.

- It prepares input-output pairs that are suitable for regression models where historical data points are used to forecast future values.
- This approach captures short-term dynamics, smoothed trends, and seasonal behavior, all of which are common in real-world time series.
- This function converts a raw time series into a supervised format by generating meaningful predictor variables (X) and corresponding target values (y).
- It does this by constructing a set of features that reflect both recent activity and broader trends by using lags and rolling averages on the data.

Code:

```
rf_model = RandomForestRegressorSimple(n_estimators=10, max_depth=4,
min_samples_split=2)
rf_model.fit(X, y)
```

In the preceding code,

- It demonstrates the training step of the Random Forest model applied to supervised time series features.
- It marks the transition from data preparation to model learning, where the algorithm begins to understand the underlying structure of the data and forms the basis for future predictions.
- This code initializes and fits our Random Forest Regressor using previously created features X and target values y.
- The model is an ensemble of 10 decision trees trained on different subsets of the data, enabling it to learn from diverse patterns and reduce overfitting through bagging and feature randomness.

Code:

```
last_features = [[sales[-1], sales[-2], sales[-3], np.mean(sales[-3:]),
np.mean(sales[-7:])]]
predicted_sales = rf_model.predict(last_features)
print(f"Forecasted sales for next day: {predicted_sales[0]:.2f} units")
```

In the preceding code,

- This final code segment performs forecasting using our trained Random Forest model.
- It demonstrates how to prepare the latest observation into a format suitable for prediction.
- It then operationalizes the machine learning pipeline by transforming recent sales data into a feature vector and obtaining a forecast for the next time step.

Output:

```
Forecasted sales for next day: 396.50 units
```

In the preceding output,

The forecasted sales from the Random Forest model are printed, and they can be used for further sales planning and promotions.

Random Forest Regressors offer a robust and flexible framework for time series forecasting, especially when rich, structured features such as lagged values, rolling averages, and calendar effects are available. By combining the power of multiple decision trees, Random Forests inherit the ability to capture complex, non-linear relationships and automatically model interactions between variables, all while reducing overfitting through ensemble averaging. This makes them particularly effective in scenarios where high-dimensional data and irregular patterns are present.

Their key strengths lie in handling non-linearity with ease, managing large feature spaces, and delivering strong predictive performance with minimal tuning. Unlike single decision trees, Random Forests provide greater generalization due to reduced variance, making them more stable on unseen data. However, they also come with limitations. Multi-step forecasts often require recursive prediction strategies, which can introduce compounding errors over time. Additionally, they lack the native temporal modeling capabilities of classical methods such as ARIMA, and their interpretability is lower compared to simpler models, particularly when many trees are involved.

Despite these challenges, Random Forests remain an excellent choice for short-term forecasting tasks, anomaly detection, and scenarios where time series data is enriched with external regressors or engineered features. Their scalability, speed, and accuracy position them as a practical, modern alternative to traditional statistical techniques in a wide range of real-world forecasting applications.

Gradient Boosted Trees (XGBoost)

Gradient Boosted Trees (GBTs) and particularly their most prominent implementation, XGBoost (Extreme Gradient Boosting), represent one of the most powerful and widely used machine learning methods for structured data tasks, including time series forecasting. Unlike traditional decision trees or even Random Forests, XGBoost is based on sequential boosting, where multiple shallow trees are added iteratively, with each new tree aiming to correct the residual errors of the previous ones. This step-by-step refinement enables the model to focus on difficult-to-predict instances and achieve high accuracy.

While XGBoost is not inherently a sequential model, such as RNNs or LSTMs, it can be effectively adapted for time series forecasting by reframing the problem as supervised learning with feature engineering.

The key is to transform temporal dependencies into structured input features, such as:

- **Lagged values:** Previous day's or previous week's values.
- **Rolling statistics:** Moving averages, moving standard deviations.
- **Time-based indicators:** Day of the week, month, holiday flags, seasonality encodings.
- **External regressors (exogenous variables):** Weather, promotions, macroeconomic indicators, and so on.

This structured approach allows XGBoost to model the relationship between these engineered features and future values without explicitly relying on time order.

Unlike Random Forests, which train multiple trees in parallel and aggregate their predictions by averaging, XGBoost builds trees sequentially. Each new tree is constructed to minimize the residual error of the combined ensemble so far. This additive boosting strategy makes XGBoost highly efficient in converging toward minimal forecasting error, especially for complex, non-linear tasks.

Mathematical Explanation

At the heart of `XGBoost` is gradient boosting, where trees are added in a forward, stage-wise fashion to minimize the loss function.

Given:

A dataset $\{(x_i, y_i)\}^n_{i=1}$

A prediction model composed of K regression trees.

$$\hat{y}_i^{(K)} = \sum_{k=1}^{K} f_k(x_i), f_k \in F$$

Where:

- F: space of regression trees, and
- Each f_k is a decision tree.

The model is trained to minimize:

$$L(\phi) = \sum_{i=1}^{n} l\left(y_i, \hat{y}_i\right) + \sum_{k=1}^{K} \Omega(f_k)$$

Where:

- l: loss function (for example, squared error $(y-\hat{y})^2$),
- $\Omega(f) = \gamma T + \frac{1}{2}\lambda\|\square\|^2$: regularization term,

- T: number of leaves in the tree, and
- ω: leaf weights.

At step t, the model updates as:

$$\hat{y}_i^{(t)} = \hat{y}_i^{(t-1)} + f_t(x_i)$$

Each f_t is trained to minimize the **gradient** of the loss:

$$f_t = arg\ arg \sum_{i=1}^{n} [g_i f(x_i) + \frac{1}{2} h_i f(x_i)^2] + \Omega(f)$$

Where:

$$g_i = \partial_{\hat{y}_{t-1}} l\left(y_i, \hat{y}_i^{(t-1)}\right)(first - order\ gradient)$$

$$h_i = \partial^2_{\hat{y}_{t-1}} l\left(y_i, \hat{y}_i^{(t-1)}\right)(second - order\ gradient)$$

This second-order Taylor approximation allows efficient optimization using gradient descent on the function space of trees.

Implementing the Math as a Python Function

In this section, let us define a very simplified implementation of a basic gradient boosting algorithm with decision stumps (depth-1 trees) from scratch.

Let us define a SimpleGBDT class with methods: **`__init__`**, **`_fit_stump`**, **`fit`**, and **`predict`**. The SimpleGBDT class is a minimalistic implementation of a Gradient Boosted Decision Tree (GBDT) regressor, a powerful machine learning technique that builds an ensemble of shallow decision trees, where each new tree incrementally improves upon the predictions of the previous ones. This implementation illustrates the core concepts behind boosting: learning from residual errors, building trees sequentially, and applying a learning rate to control convergence and prevent overfitting.

Code:

```
class SimpleGBDT:
    def __init__(self, n_estimators=10, learning_rate=0.1):
        self.n_estimators = n_estimators
        self.learning_rate = learning_rate
        self.trees = []
```

In the preceding code,

The model is initialized with two key hyperparameters:

- **`n_estimators:`** Number of weak learners (trees) to train sequentially.
- **`learning_rate:`** Scaling factor that controls how much each tree's prediction contributes to the overall model, acting as a form of regularization.

Each weak learner is a decision stump, a simple one-level tree that splits on a single feature threshold.

Code:

```
def _fit_stump(self, X, residuals):
    best_feat, best_split, best_loss = None, None, float('inf')
    for j in range(len(X[0])):  # For each feature
        thresholds = set(row[j] for row in X)
        for t in thresholds:
            left, right = [], []
            for i, row in enumerate(X):
                if row[j] <= t:
                    left.append(residuals[i])
                else:
                    right.append(residuals[i])
            if not left or not right:
                continue
            left_mean = sum(left) / len(left)
            right_mean = sum(right) / len(right)
            loss = sum((r - left_mean)**2 for r in left) + sum((r -
right_mean)**2 for r in right)
            if loss < best_loss:
                best_feat, best_split, best_loss = j, t, loss
                best_left, best_right = left_mean, right_mean
    return (best_feat, best_split, best_left, best_right)
```

In the preceding code,

The **_fit_stump** method searches for the best one-level split (a decision stump) that minimizes squared error on the residuals, which represent the difference between true values and current predictions.

For each feature:

- It iterates through all unique values as possible thresholds.
- It splits the residuals into two groups and calculates the squared error for each.
- The split that results in the lowest total error is chosen.

This function encapsulates the core of boosting, focusing on examples that the model currently predicts poorly.

Code:

```
def fit(self, X, y):
    self.init_prediction = sum(y) / len(y)
```

```
        self.trees = []
        pred = [self.init_prediction] * len(y)

        for _ in range(self.n_estimators):
            residuals = [y[i] - pred[i] for i in range(len(y))]
            stump = self._fit_stump(X, residuals)
            self.trees.append(stump)

            for i in range(len(X)):
                j, t, left, right = stump
                update = left if X[i][j] <= t else right
                pred[i] += self.learning_rate * update
```

In the preceding code,

- The training process follows the gradient boosting model.
- Initialize predictions as the global mean of the target values.

For each iteration (tree):

- Compute residuals: the current error between y and the predicted values.
- Fit a stump to predict the residuals.
- Add the stump to the list of trees.
- Update the predictions by adding the scaled output of the stump (via **learning_rate**).

This **fit** method builds up the prediction gradually, improving accuracy with each iteration.

Code:

```
    def predict(self, X):
        pred = [self.init_prediction] * len(X)
        for j, t, left, right in self.trees:
            for i in range(len(X)):
                update = left if X[i][j] <= t else right
                pred[i] += self.learning_rate * update
        return pred
```

In the preceding code,

At prediction time:

- The model starts with the initial prediction (the training set mean).
- It adds the contribution from each learned stump, depending on whether the input satisfies the split condition.
- The result is a cumulative prediction reflecting the corrections made by all weak learners.

Real-World Example

In a real-world retail setting, forecasting weekly product demand often involves a mix of historical trends, seasonality, and external drivers such as promotions or holidays. For example, a retail store chain may rely on features such as lagged demand from the past three weeks, a rolling average of the previous four weeks to capture short-term trends, and calendar-based indicators, such as the week of the year or holiday flags, and binary indicators for store-level promotions. These variables often interact in non-linear and context-dependent ways. For instance, demand may spike near holidays, but only when promotions are also active. In such cases, lag features alone may be inadequate due to disruptive factors such as weather or marketing events. This is where XGBoost becomes particularly valuable. Its gradient boosting framework allows it to automatically capture complex interactions, model non-linear effects, and handle both categorical and numerical inputs effectively. As a result, XGBoost excels in forecasting scenarios where multiple factors interplay in unpredictable ways, offering high accuracy and flexibility without the need for manually specifying functional relationships.

Python Implementation on the Example

In this example, let us look at an example of how to use the XGBoost algorithm on a retail store's time series data.

Code:

```
demand = [150, 160, 170, 180, 190, 205, 220, 230, 240, 260, 275, 290]
```

In the preceding code,

We have started by creating a synthetic data set as a list.

Code:

```
def create_features(data):
    X, y = [], []
    for i in range(4, len(data)):
        lags = [data[i-1], data[i-2], data[i-3]]
        avg4 = sum(data[i-4:i]) / 4
        promotion = 1 if i % 5 == 0 else 0  # Promotion every 5th week
        week = i % 52
        features = lags + [avg4, week, promotion]
        X.append(features)
        y.append(data[i])
    return X, y

X, y = create_features(demand)
```

In the preceding code,

- This **create_features** function prepares data for a supervised learning regression model by constructing a feature matrix X and a target vector y for simulating the retail demand forecasting use case.
- It loops through the time series from the 5th observation onward (**i = 4**), ensuring that enough historical data is available to compute lag-based features and rolling statistics.

Code:

```
gbdt = SimpleGBDT(n_estimators=10, learning_rate=0.1)
gbdt.fit(X, y)
```

In the preceding code,

The first line creates an instance of the SimpleGBDT class with the following parameters:

- **n_estimators=10**: The model will build an ensemble of 10 weak learners.
- **learning_rate=0.1**: Controls how much each new tree contributes to the overall prediction. A smaller learning rate encourages slower but more stable convergence, reducing the risk of overfitting.
- Each estimator in the sequence will correct the residual errors left by its predecessors, aligning with the core.

The second line (calling the **fit**) triggers the training process, where the model:

- Initializes predictions with the mean of the target values.
- Iteratively computes residuals, the difference between actual and predicted values.
- Fits a one-level decision stump to the residuals in each iteration, identifying the best feature and threshold to split on.
- Updates the predictions by adding a scaled version of the new tree's output, scaled by **learning_rate**.

This sequential approach enables the model to gradually refine its predictions, with each tree learning to focus on previously mis-predicted observations.

Code:

```
last = demand[-4:]
avg = sum(last) / 4
promotion = 1 if len(demand) % 5 == 0 else 0
week = len(demand) % 52
new_features = [demand[-1], demand[-2], demand[-3], avg, week,
promotion]
```

```
pred = gbdt.predict([new_features])
print(f"Forecasted demand for next week: {pred[0]:.2f}")
```

In the preceding code,

The code block performs feature construction and prediction for the upcoming time step using the most recent observed values from the time series demand.

- It retrieves the most recent 4 weeks of demand data. The 3 most recent (**demand[-1], demand[-2], demand[-3]**) are used as lag features, and their average serves as a rolling statistic to capture recent trend/smoothness.
- It also simulates exogenous variables.
- A binary **promotion** flag, assuming promotions occur every 5th week.
- A cyclical calendar indicator, representing the current week of the year (**mod 52**).
- The complete feature vector mirrors the structure used during training, ensuring that the model sees input in the same format.
- The model makes a one-step-ahead prediction for the next week's demand using the trained SimpleGBDT ensemble.

Output:

```
Forecasted demand for next week: 261.10
```

The predictions are then printed as output covering the predicted value in a readable format, rounding to two decimal places.

Gradient Boosted Trees, particularly XGBoost, are among the most powerful and accurate machine learning models for time series forecasting when the problem is reframed as a supervised learning task using structured features. Their strength lies in the ability to model non-linear relationships and complex feature interactions without requiring explicit manual specification. XGBoost performs exceptionally well in handling mixed data types, incorporates built-in regularization to prevent overfitting, and supports efficient parallelized training and robust handling of missing values, making it a practical choice for real-world forecasting tasks.

However, XGBoost is not inherently designed for sequential modeling. It does not automatically recognize the temporal structure of the data, so we must explicitly engineer lag features, rolling statistics, and time-based indicators to capture temporal dependencies. Additionally, when used for multi-step-ahead forecasts, XGBoost typically relies on recursive strategies by feeding prior predictions back as inputs, which can introduce cumulative error over time. While less interpretable than simpler statistical models, its predictions can be made explainable using techniques such as feature importance.

In summary, XGBoost should be considered a go-to tool for high-accuracy forecasting, especially when working with rich, multivariate time series datasets and under constraints that demand quick, scalable, and flexible model training. Its performance and versatility make it a standout option for modern, feature-driven time series modeling.

Long Short-Term Memory (LSTM)

Long Short-Term Memory (LSTM) networks are a specialized architecture within the broader class of Recurrent Neural Networks (RNNs), explicitly developed to address the vanishing gradient problem, a major limitation of traditional RNNs when learning long-term dependencies in sequential data. Introduced by Hochreiter and Schmidhuber in 1997, LSTMs incorporate internal memory cells and a series of gating mechanisms (input, forget, and output gates) that regulate the flow of information over time. These mechanisms allow LSTMs to retain, update, or discard information dynamically, enabling them to learn both short-term patterns, such as recent spikes or drops in a time series, and long-term structures, such as seasonal trends or delayed responses.

In time series forecasting, LSTMs are especially powerful because they operate directly on raw sequences, and can handle univariate or multivariate inputs. Unlike classical models or tree-based methods, LSTMs do not require manual feature engineering. They learn temporal dependencies directly from the input data. This makes them well-suited for complex, high-dimensional forecasting problems where handcrafted features may be insufficient or infeasible.

LSTM networks have become a popular choice across various domains, including energy demand prediction, financial market forecasting, healthcare monitoring (for example, patient vital signs), and weather or environmental modeling. Their robustness, scalability, and ability to capture intricate temporal dynamics make them a leading deep learning solution for sequential prediction tasks, especially when the data exhibits both short-range noise and long-range structure.

Mathematical Explanation

An LSTM unit maintains a memory cell C_t and a hidden state h_t, which are updated at each time step through several gates:

Given input x_t, previous hidden state h_{t-1}, and previous cell state C_{t-1}:

1. Forget Gate:

$$f_t = \sigma(W_f \cdot [h_{t-1}, x_t] + b_f)$$

2. Input Gate:

$$i_t = \sigma(W_f \cdot [h_{t-1}, x_t] + b_i)$$

$$C\tilde{}_t = tanh(W_C \cdot [h_{t-1}, x_t] + b_C)$$

3. Cell State Update:

$$C_t = f_t * C_{t-1} + i_t * \tilde{C}_t$$

4. Output Gate:

$$o_t = \sigma(W_f \cdot [h_{t-1}, x_t] + b_o)$$
$$h_t = o_t * tanh\ (C_t)$$

Where:

- σ: sigmoid activation function,
- *tanh*: hyperbolic tangent function,
- *: element-wise multiplication, and
- W and *b*: trainable weights and biases.

Loss Function:

For forecasting:

$$L = \frac{1}{T}\sum_{t=1}^{T}(y_t - \hat{y}_t)^2$$

LSTM training uses Backpropagation Through Time (BPTT), just like RNNs, but the gating structure reduces vanishing gradients, enabling learning over long sequences.

Implementing the Math as a Python Function

In this section, let us implement a simplified LSTM from scratch for univariate input and single-layer forecasting.

Let us define the SimpleLSTM class with the methods: **`__init__`**, **`sigmoid`**, **`tanh`**, **`fit`**, and **`predict`**. The SimpleLSTM class is a minimalistic implementation of an LSTM (Long Short-Term Memory) network, which is a type of Recurrent Neural Network (RNN) specifically designed for sequence modeling tasks. We will illustrate the core computational logic of LSTMs, showcasing how they retain memory over time, regulate information flow, and generate predictions from sequential data. While simplified, it captures the essence of how LSTM networks operate and learn.

Code:

```
import math
import random
```

In the preceding code,

We have imported math and random libraries from Python that are used to perform computations in the **`SimpleLSTM`** class.

Code:

```
class SimpleLSTM:
    def __init__(self, input_size=1, hidden_size=1, lr=0.01, 
epochs=100):
        self.hidden_size = hidden_size
        self.lr = lr
        self.epochs = epochs

        def rand(): return random.uniform(-0.1, 0.1)
        self.Wf = [rand() for _ in range(2)]
        self.bf = rand()

        self.Wi = [rand() for _ in range(2)]
        self.bi = rand()

        self.WC = [rand() for _ in range(2)]
        self.bC = rand()

        self.Wo = [rand() for _ in range(2)]
        self.bo = rand()

        self.Why = rand()
        self.by = rand()
```

In the preceding code,

Upon instantiation, the SimpleLSTM model initializes the following variables:

- **`input_size, hidden_size`**: Determines how many inputs and hidden units are used. It is fixed at 1 for this example.
- **`lr`**: The learning rate, used to scale parameter updates.
- **`epochs`**: The number of training iterations over the dataset.

Weights for the four standard LSTM gates are initialized randomly:

- **Forget gate (`Wf, bf`)**: Controls how much past memory to retain.
- **Input gate (`Wi, bi`)**: Controls how much new information to write to memory.
- **Candidate memory (`WC, bC`)**: The raw memory update proposed.
- **Output gate (`Wo, bo`)**: Controls how much of the memory to expose as hidden state h.
- **Output projection (`Why, by`)**: Linear weights to transform the final hidden state into a scalar prediction.

Code:

```
def sigmoid(self, x):
    return 1 / (1 + math.exp(-x))
```

In the preceding code,

The **sigmoid** method squashes values to [0,1], ideal for gates.

Code:

```
def tanh(self, x):
    return math.tanh(x)
```

In the preceding code,

The **Tanh** methodbounds values between [-1,1], used for memory state and hidden state updates.

Code:

```
def fit(self, sequences, targets):
    for _ in range(self.epochs):
        for seq, y_target in zip(sequences, targets):
            h, C = 0.0, 0.0

            for x in seq:
                z = [h, x]
                f = self.sigmoid(sum(w * zi for w, zi in zip(self.
Wf, z)) + self.bf)
                i = self.sigmoid(sum(w * zi for w, zi in zip(self.
Wi, z)) + self.bi)
                C_tilde = self.tanh(sum(w * zi for w, zi in
zip(self.WC, z)) + self.bC)
                C = f * C + i * C_tilde
                o = self.sigmoid(sum(w * zi for w, zi in zip(self.
Wo, z)) + self.bo)
                h = o * self.tanh(C)

            y_pred = h * self.Why + self.by
            error = y_pred - y_target
            self.Why -= self.lr * error * h
            self.by -= self.lr * error
```

In the preceding code,

The **fit** method trains the LSTM over the input sequences and their corresponding targets (that is, supervised labels such as future values in a time series).

For each epoch:

- The model initializes hidden state h and memory cell C to zero.

For each timestep in the input sequence:

- It computes gate activations (forget, input, candidate, and output).
- Updates the memory cell C and hidden state h using standard LSTM equations.

At the end of the sequence, a scalar prediction **y_pred** is computed from the final hidden state.

A simplified gradient update is applied to the output weights (Why, by), based only on the output error, without full Backpropagation Through Time (BPTT).

Code:

```
    def predict(self, sequence):
        h, C = 0.0, 0.0
        for x in sequence:
            z = [h, x]
            f = self.sigmoid(sum(w * zi for w, zi in zip(self.Wf, z)) +
self.bf)
            i = self.sigmoid(sum(w * zi for w, zi in zip(self.Wi, z)) +
self.bi)
            C_tilde = self.tanh(sum(w * zi for w, zi in zip(self.WC, z))
+ self.bC)
            C = f * C + i * C_tilde
            o = self.sigmoid(sum(w * zi for w, zi in zip(self.Wo, z)) +
self.bo)
            h = o * self.tanh(C)

        y_pred = h * self.Why + self.by
        return y_pred
```

In the preceding code,

- The model then processes a new input sequence:
- It propagates through the sequence using LSTM cell logic.
- The final hidden state is transformed into a prediction.
- No learning or weight update occurs in the block.
- The predict method enables the model to generate forecasts for unseen sequences, such as one-step-ahead time series predictions.

Real-World Example

Imagine a solar energy provider aiming to forecast the next hour's solar power output using data from the previous six hours. Solar generation is influenced by immediate factors such as current output (lagged values), evolving conditions such as gradual cloud buildup, and broader patterns such as the typical daily cycle of sunrise, peak, and sunset. In this context, a Long Short-Term Memory (LSTM) network is an ideal modeling choice. Unlike traditional models that require manually crafted lag features or rolling averages, LSTMs can automatically learn both short-term fluctuations and long-term dependencies directly from sequential data. They are particularly well-suited for capturing recurring temporal patterns, such as the predictable ramp-up in solar output during morning hours or the drop in the evening, without explicitly encoding those behaviors. This ability to model complex, time-dependent dynamics makes LSTMs a powerful tool for forecasting in renewable energy applications, where output can be influenced by both immediate and slowly evolving atmospheric conditions.

Python Implementation on the Example

In this section, let us apply LSTM to the solar energy provider example.

Code:

```
solar_output = [20, 25, 28, 35, 42, 50, 55, 60, 65, 70, 74, 78]
```

In the preceding code,

We have started by creating a synthetic data set as a list.

Code:

```
def create_sequences(data, window=5):
    sequences, targets = [], []
    for i in range(window, len(data)):
        sequences.append(data[i-window:i])
        targets.append(data[i])
    return sequences, targets
sequences, targets = create_sequences(solar_output, window=5)
```

In the preceding code,

- The **create_sequences** function is a foundational utility for preparing sequential data—such as time series for models that learn from ordered observations, particularly Recurrent Neural Networks (RNNs) such as LSTMs. It transforms a 1D time series into a supervised learning format, where each training example is a sliding window of consecutive observations used to predict the next value.
- This function takes a univariate time series (**solar_output**) and restructures it into two parallel datasets:
- **sequences:** Each element is a list of consecutive past values within a window (for example, the last 5 hours of solar power output).
- **targets:** Each corresponding element is the value immediately following the window.

Code:

```
lstm = SimpleLSTM(input_size=1, hidden_size=1, lr=0.01, epochs=500)
lstm.fit(sequences, targets)
```

In the preceding code,

- This code initiates and trains a custom-built Long Short-Term Memory (LSTM) network using preprocessed sequence-target pairs derived from a univariate time series.
- It represents the training phase of this deep learning-based forecasting pipeline, specifically tailored for sequential prediction tasks such as one-step-ahead time series forecasting.
- The first line creates an instance of the SimpleLSTM class, which simulates the core logic of a real LSTM network using scalar weights and gates:
  - **`input_size=1`**: Each time step contains one scalar value (for example, hourly solar output).
  - **`hidden_size=1`**: The hidden state of the network is a single value, reflecting a simplified architecture.
  - **`lr=0.01`**: The learning rate controls how aggressively the model updates its weights during training.
  - **`epochs=500`**: The model will iterate over the training data 500 times, refining its internal parameters to minimize prediction error.

The **fit** method trains the LSTM on input sequences and their corresponding targets:

For each sequence (for example, the last 5 time steps), the LSTM processes one-time step at a time using its internal gated memory mechanisms:

- forget gate, input gate, output gate, and cell state.

At the end of each sequence, the LSTM outputs a single prediction, which is compared against the true target value.

The model updates its output weights (Why, by) using a simplified gradient descent update rule, based on the prediction error.

We have omitted full Backpropagation Through Time (BPTT) logic and multiple hidden units for simplicity, but it still demonstrates how LSTMs work:

- Accumulate knowledge across time steps,
- Encode memory through gating, and
- Learn to forecast future values based on historical patterns.

Code:

```
next_input = solar_output[-5:]
prediction = lstm.predict(next_input)
print(f"Forecasted solar output: {prediction:.2f} kW")
```

In the preceding code,

- This code illustrates the inference phase of our LSTM-based time series forecasting model, where the trained network is used to predict the next value in a univariate sequence such as solar energy output measured in kilowatts (kW).
- It demonstrates how a model that has learned temporal dependencies from past training can now be applied to make real-world predictions using the latest available data.
- This line extracts the most recent five time steps from the **solar_output** time series. These values serve as the input sequence for the LSTM model, mirroring the structure used during training with a window=5 sliding. This consistent input format ensures that the model receives the same type of data it was optimized on.
- The predict method of the trained **SimpleLSTM** model processes this sequence step-by-step through its internal memory and gating mechanisms.
- Using the learned weights from training, it calculates the hidden state at each time step and finally projects that hidden representation into a forecasted numeric value representing the solar output expected in the next hour.

Output:

```
Forecasted solar output: 65.93 kW
```

In the preceding output,

The prediction is formatted to two decimal places and printed with units (kW).

Long Short-Term Memory (LSTM) networks are among the most effective and widely used deep learning architectures for modeling time series data. Designed to overcome the limitations of traditional Recurrent Neural Networks (RNNs), LSTMs incorporate a memory cell and gating mechanisms that allow the network to retain information over both short and long time horizons. This enables LSTMs to capture complex temporal dependencies that are often missed by classical models or simpler RNNs, making them well-suited for forecasting tasks where trends, cycles, and delayed effects coexist.

LSTMs offer several advantages. They can learn non-linear and long-range patterns directly from raw sequential data, eliminating the need for manual feature engineering such as lag creation or smoothing. Their structure allows them to handle multivariate inputs and sequences of variable lengths, making them versatile across domains. However, these benefits come with trade-offs. LSTMs are computationally intensive, often requiring large datasets and careful tuning of hyperparameters such as learning rate, hidden units, and sequence length. Additionally, they function as "black boxes," with internal states that are difficult to interpret, unlike traditional statistical models or tree-based algorithms.

Despite the recent rise of Transformer-based architectures, LSTMs remain a foundational tool in sequence modeling, especially in fields such as finance, energy forecasting, healthcare monitoring, and natural language processing. When the goal is to build an end-to-end model that captures temporal dynamics without manual intervention, LSTMs continue to be a reliable and powerful choice.

Conclusion

In this chapter, we explored the evolution of time series forecasting from traditional machine learning models to deep learning architectures. Beginning with models such as Decision Trees, Random Forests, and XGBoost, we examined how engineered lag features and rolling statistics can convert sequential data into a supervised learning format, enabling highly accurate predictions even in complex, non-linear environments.

Transitioning to deep learning, we introduced LSTM, which extends Recurring Neural Networks (RNN) by providing mechanisms to retain information over long horizons, ideal for dynamic and evolving sequences.

Each model brings unique strengths and trade-offs. While tree-based models are intuitive and easy to interpret, deep learning methods thrive in data-rich, complex environments where long-term dependencies must be discovered automatically. Regardless of model type, effective time series forecasting demands a strong grasp of data structure, temporal validation, and proper evaluation metrics.

In the next chapter, we extend these concepts into the multivariate setting, where multiple time series interact, often influencing each other in non-obvious ways. We will explore how to model these interactions using Vector Autoregression (VAR), multivariate XGBoost, and advanced architectures such as Multivariate LSTMs and Transformers, and understand how to forecast systems where interdependence, causality, and external factors matter just as much as historical patterns.

References

- Breiman, L., Friedman, J., Olshen, R. and Stone, C. (1984) *Classification and Regression Trees. Wadsworth.*
- Hastie, T., Tibshirani, R. and Friedman, J. (2009). *The Elements of Statistical Learning*. 2nd edn. *Springer.*
- Géron, A. (2019) *Hands-On Machine Learning with Scikit-Learn, Keras, and TensorFlow*. 2nd edn. O'*Reilly.*
- James, G., Witten, D., Hastie, T. and Tibshirani, R. (2021) *An Introduction to Statistical Learning*. 2nd edn. *Springer.*
- Mitchell, T. M. (1997) *Machine Learning. McGraw-Hill.*

- Liaw, A. and Wiener, M. (2002) Classification and Regression by randomForest. *R News.*
- Chen, T. and Guestrin, C. (2016) XGBoost: A Scalable Tree Boosting System. *Proceedings of the 22nd* ACM SIGKDD.
- Ke, G. et al. (2017) LightGBM: A Highly Efficient Gradient Boosting Decision Tree. *NeurIPS.*
- Lundberg, S. and Lee, S. (2017) A Unified Approach to Interpreting Model Predictions. *NeurIPS.* (SHAP)
- Hochreiter, S. and Schmidhuber, J. (1997) Long Short-Term Memory. *Neural Computation.*
- Gers, F. A., Schmidhuber, J. and Cummins, F. (2000) Learning to Forget: Continual Prediction with LSTM. *Neural Computation.*
- Olah, C. (2015) *Understanding* LSTM *Networks.* https://colah.github.io/posts/2015-08-Understanding-LSTMs/
- Brownlee, J. (2017) Deep Learning for Time Series Forecasting. *Machine Learning Mastery.*
- Goodfellow, I., Bengio, Y. and Courville, A. (2016) *Deep Learning.* MIT Press.

CHAPTER 9
Multivariate Time Series Models

Introduction

In the real world, time series rarely evolve in isolation. From stock prices reacting to macroeconomic indicators, to electricity demand influenced by both temperature and time of day, to physiological signals interacting within the human body, multiple time-dependent variables often evolve together, influencing and responding to one another. This dynamic interplay forms the foundation of Multivariate Time Series (MTS) forecasting, where the goal is to capture not just the behavior of individual series, but the joint temporal dependencies across multiple variables.

Unlike univariate forecasting, which relies solely on a single variable's past to predict its future, multivariate models aim to learn from shared patterns, co-movements, and lagged interactions among multiple related series. This allows for a more comprehensive understanding of complex systems, where no single variable tells the full story. In many real-world scenarios, modeling this interdependence can significantly enhance predictive accuracy and decision-making.

This chapter provides a deep dive into the modeling landscape for multivariate time series. We begin with classical statistical frameworks such as Vector Autoregression (VAR) and Vector Error Correction Models (VECM), which generalize ARIMA logic to systems of equations across multiple series. We then explore machine learning approaches, including multivariate extensions of XGBoost, focusing on how to structure input features such as lags and exogenous variables across multiple dimensions.

Finally, we turn to deep learning architectures, where we will cover Multivariate LSTMs, which are capable of learning complex, non-linear dependencies over long temporal horizons.

By the end of this chapter, readers will understand the core differences between univariate and multivariate time series forecasting. The readers will be able to identify when multivariate modeling is beneficial, especially in systems where multiple variables influence each other over time. They will also be able to frame multivariate problems correctly for supervised learning, ensuring proper handling of temporal ordering, feature engineering, and validation schemes and gain practical insights on how to choose the right model class based on data characteristics, interpret model outputs, and apply these models to real-world forecasting tasks.

Structure

In this chapter, the following topics will be covered:

- Vector Autoregression (VAR)
- Vector Error Correction Model (VECM)
- Multivariate XGBoost
- Multivariate LSTM

Vector Autoregression (VAR)

Vector Autoregression (VAR) is a foundational model in multivariate time series analysis, particularly suited for systems where multiple variables exhibit dynamic interdependencies over time. Unlike univariate autoregressive models that only consider the historical values of a single variable to predict its future, VAR extends this concept to multiple variables simultaneously. Each variable in a VAR model is modeled not only as a function of its own past values but also of the past values of all other variables in the system.

Essentially, VAR consists of a system of interconnected autoregressive equations, where each variable is treated symmetrically as both a dependent variable and a predictor for others. This makes VAR especially powerful in contexts where feedback loops and mutual influence between time series are expected.

A key assumption of VAR is stationarity, that is, each time series should have a constant mean and variance over time. Given this assumption, the model leverages linear relationships across time-lagged observations to forecast future values. By capturing these intertemporal dynamics across multiple dimensions, VAR serves as a statistically grounded and interpretable framework for forecasting and analyzing multivariate time series systems.

Mathematical Explanation

Let y_t be a vector of K endogenous variables at time t:

$$y_t = [y_{1,t}\ \ y_{2,t} \vdots y_{K,t}]$$

A VAR(p) model (with p lags) is written as:

$$y_t = A_1 y_{t-1} + A_2 y_{t-2} + \cdots + A_p y_{t-p} + c + \varepsilon_t$$

Where:

- $A_i \in R^{K \times K}$: coefficient matrices for lag i,
- c: intercept vector, and
- $\varepsilon_t \sim N(0,\Sigma)$: multivariate white noise.
- Each variable $y_{i,t}$ is thus a linear combination of the lagged values of all K variables and a noise term.

For example, in a 2-variable VAR(1):

$$[y_{1,t}\ y_{2,t}] = [a_{11}\ a_{12}\ a_{21}\ a_{22}][y_{1,t-1}\ y_{2,t-2}] + [c_1\ c_2] + [\varepsilon_{1,t}\ \varepsilon_{2,t}]$$

Implementing the Math as a Python Function

In this section, let us implement a simplified version of VAR(1) for 2 variables using basic matrix algebra.

Code:

```
def estimate_var1(Y):
    n = len(Y) - 1
    X = [Y[t] for t in range(n)]
    Y_target = [Y[t+1] for t in range(n)]

    X_mat = [[x[0], x[1], 1] for x in X]  # Add intercept
    Y1 = [y[0] for y in Y_target]
    Y2 = [y[1] for y in Y_target]

    def ols(X, y):
        XT = list(zip(*X))
       XTX = [[sum(a * b for a, b in zip(row_i, row_j)) for row_j in XT]
for row_i in XT]
        XTy = [sum(xi * yi for xi, yi in zip(col, y)) for col in XT]
        import numpy as np
        coef = np.linalg.pinv(XTX).dot(XTy)
        return coef.tolist()

    coef1 = ols(X_mat, Y1)
    coef2 = ols(X_mat, Y2)

    return coef1, coef2
```

In the preceding code,

The **estimate_var1** function estimates a VAR(1) model for a bivariate time series, that is, a system where each variable at time t+1 is modeled as a linear function of both variables at time t.

Input and Transformation

- Y: A list of 2D vectors (that is, [[y1_t, y2_t], ...]) ordered in time.
- X: The set of lagged input vectors from time t = 0 to n-1.
- Y_target: The corresponding "next" vectors from time t = 1 to n.
- Each observation becomes part of a supervised regression problem:
- Predict [y1_t+1, y2_t+1] from [y1_t, y2_t].
- To account for the intercept, each input vector is extended with a 1, forming X_mat = [y1_t, y2_t, 1].

Estimation via OLS

Two separate OLS regressions are performed:

- One to predict y1_t+1 using the lagged values of y1 and y2.
- Another to predict y2_t+1 using the same lagged values.

This leads to two sets of coefficients:

- coef1 = [a11, a12, b1]: Coefficients for predicting y1 (autoregressive + intercept).
- coef2 = [a21, a22, b2]: Coefficients for predicting y2.

OLS is then solved using the normal equation implemented using NumPy:

$$\beta = (X^T X)^{-1} X^T y$$

The function returns a pair of coefficient vectors. Each represents one equation in the VAR(1) system, which can now be used for forecasting.

Real-World Example

In macroeconomic policy analysis, variables such as inflation and interest rates are deeply interconnected, each influencing and responding to the other over time. For example, a rise in interest rates by the central bank can help curb inflation by slowing down economic activity, while inflation expectations themselves often shape central bank decisions regarding future rate adjustments. These dynamics form a classic case of endogeneity, where no variable is strictly independent. In such settings, a Vector Autoregression (VAR) model is particularly well-suited. VAR treats both inflation and interest rates as jointly dependent time series, allowing each variable to be modeled as a function of its own lags as well as the lagged values of the other.

Python Implementation on the Example

In this section, we will look at a practical example of how to use the VAR model in macroeconomic analysis.

Let us start by defining a synthetic dataset for inflation and interest rates.

Code:

```
inflation = [2.0, 2.2, 2.5, 2.6, 2.8, 3.0, 2.9, 2.7]
interest_rate = [1.0, 1.2, 1.5, 1.8, 2.0, 2.1, 2.2, 2.3]
```

In the next step, let us combine this data into a multivariate time series.

Code:

```
Y = [[inflation[i], interest_rate[i]] for i in range(len(inflation))]
```

In the preceding code,

It merges the univariate sequences into a multivariate structure, where each element is a 2-dimensional vector: **inflation**, **interest_rate**. The Y list now represents the full history of the system as a sequence of vector-valued observations.

Code:

```
coef1, coef2 = estimate_var1(Y)
```

In the preceding code,

The **estimate_var1** function fits the first-order Vector Autoregressive model. In VAR(1), the value of each variable at time t+1 is modeled as a linear combination of both variables' values at time t. Specifically:

- coef1 holds the coefficients to forecast inflation, and
- coef2 holds the coefficients to forecast the interest rate.

Code:

```
last = Y[-1]
y1_forecast = coef1[0]*last[0] + coef1[1]*last[1] + coef1[2]
y2_forecast = coef2[0]*last[0] + coef2[1]*last[1] + coef2[2]

print(f"Forecasted Inflation: {y1_forecast:.2f}%")
print(f"Forecasted Interest Rate: {y2_forecast:.2f}%")
```

In the preceding code,

- Using the most recent observation (last), this code applies the VAR(1) formula to generate a 1-step-ahead forecast for both variables.
- This leverages the learned linear relationships to project inflation and interest rates forward in time.

Output:

```
Forecasted Inflation: 2.74%
Forecasted Interest Rate: 2.31%
```

In the preceding output,

The inflation and interest rates are both forecasted.

Vector Autoregression (VAR) models are important in the field of multivariate time series forecasting. By generalizing the principles of univariate autoregression to systems of interrelated time series, VAR provides a statistically sound and conceptually elegant framework for modeling dynamic interactions among multiple variables. Its capacity to treat each variable as both an outcome and a predictor of others makes it particularly well-suited for domains where feedback loops and co-movements are fundamental, such as macroeconomics, energy systems, and financial markets.

Throughout this section, we demonstrated how VAR(1), the simplest form of VAR, can effectively capture contemporaneous relationships by using past values of all variables to forecast future states. The matrix-based estimation procedure, built on Ordinary Least Squares (OLS), ensures that the model remains transparent and interpretable. This is a key advantage when compared to more complex machine learning models.

Additionally, VAR models support deeper structural analysis essential for uncovering causal linkages and assessing system behavior under hypothetical shocks. However, VAR's utility is bounded by its assumptions. It requires stationarity, linearity, and often a large number of observations to ensure parameter stability. As the number of variables and lags increases, the model can become overparameterized and difficult to estimate without regularization or dimensionality reduction techniques.

While newer machine learning and deep learning methods may offer enhanced accuracy in complex, non-linear settings, VAR is useful when we seek explainability, tractability, and strong theoretical foundations in multivariate forecasting.

Overall, VAR models strike a balance between statistical rigor and practical interpretability, making them a vital tool for understanding interdependent time series.

Vector Error Correction Model (VECM)

The Vector Error Correction Model (VECM) is a sophisticated extension of multivariate time series modeling that is particularly suitable when multiple non-stationary series exhibit cointegration, a statistical property indicating a stable, long-term equilibrium relationship among variables despite their individual trends. While each series may drift over time due to non-stationarity, a specific linear combination of them remains stationary, capturing an underlying equilibrium that ties them together.

VECM is designed to bridge short-term fluctuations with long-term stability. Unlike traditional Vector Autoregression (VAR), which requires stationarity and focuses solely on modeling short-term dynamics, VECM explicitly incorporates an error correction term that ensures deviations from the long-term equilibrium are gradually adjusted over time.

Mathematical Explanation

Let $y_t \in R^K$ be a K-dimensional time series. Assume each component of y_t is integrated of order 1 (I(1)), but there exists a stationary linear combination $\beta^T y_t$.

The VECM(*p*) representation is:

$$\Delta y_t = \Pi y_{t-1} + \sum_{i=1}^{p-1} \Gamma_i \Delta y_{t-i} + c + \varepsilon_t$$

where:

- $\Delta y_t = y_t - y_{t-1}$: differenced series
- $\Pi = \alpha\beta^T$: the error correction matrix
  - β: cointegration vector(s)
  - α speed of adjustment coefficients
- Γ_i: short-term lag effects
- ε_t: multivariate white noise

Cointegration:

- If $y_t \sim I(1)$ and there exists β such that $\beta^T y_t \sim I(0)$, then the system is cointegrated, and VECM should be used.
- The term Πy_{t-1} pulls the system back toward the long-run equilibrium whenever it deviates.

Implementing the Math as a Python Function

In this section, let us implement a 2-variable VECM(1) with a pre-specified cointegration vector.

Let us start by defining the **`estimate_vecm`** function as a simple and custom implementation of a Vector Error Correction Model (VECM) for a bivariate time series specifically designed to estimate short-term dynamics in systems where two non-stationary variables exhibit a long-term equilibrium relationship, also known as **cointegration**.

Code:

```
def estimate_vecm(Y, beta):
    delta_Y = [[Y[t][0] - Y[t-1][0], Y[t][1] - Y[t-1][1]] for t in
range(1, len(Y))]
    error_term = [beta[0] * Y[t-1][0] + beta[1] * Y[t-1][1] for t in
range(1, len(Y))]

    def ols(x, y):
```

```
        n = len(x)
        x_mean = sum(x)/n
        y_mean = sum(y)/n
        b1 = sum((x[i]-x_mean)*(y[i]-y_mean) for i in range(n)) / 
sum((x[i]-x_mean)**2 for i in range(n))
        b0 = y_mean - b1 * x_mean
        return b1, b0

    e = error_term
    dy1 = [dy[0] for dy in delta_Y]
    dy2 = [dy[1] for dy in delta_Y]

    alpha1, c1 = ols(e, dy1)
    alpha2, c2 = ols(e, dy2)

    return (alpha1, c1), (alpha2, c2)
```

In the preceding code,

The input parameters of the **estimate_vecm** function are:

- Y: A list of *[y1, y2]* observations over time.
- beta: A cointegration vector like [1,-1] which defines the long-term equilibrium relationship *(y1 - y2 = 0)*.

It then calculates the first differences, Δy_1 and, Δy_2 which capture short-term changes in each variable.

It then computes the lagged deviation from the long-term equilibrium. For the cointegration vector [1,-1], this term becomes *y1(t-1) - y2(t-1)*, indicating how far the system was from equilibrium in the previous time step.

Two OLS regressions are performed:

- $\Delta y_1 = a_1 \times \text{error}_t + c_1$
- $\Delta y_2 = a_2 \times \text{error}_t + c_2$

This gives the error correction coefficients (a_1, a_2) which quantify how each variable responds to disequilibrium.

A significant negative α indicates a correction mechanism that drives the system back to equilibrium.

Each tuple corresponds to one regression:

- The error correction coefficient and intercept for Δy_1 and Δy_2, respectively.

If $a_1 = -0.3$, then when the system deviates from equilibrium by + 1 unit, Δy_1 will decline by 0.3 units, restoring balance.

This model captures both short-term movements via first differences and long-term equilibrium behavior via error correction.

Real-World Example

A global investor wants to forecast the USD/EUR exchange rate and European interest rates. While both time series are non-stationary, they are known to move together over the long term due to arbitrage and policy coordination.

The investor believes there is a cointegration relationship, meaning:

$$\frac{USD}{EUR_t} - 0.5 = EUR\ Interest\ Rate_t \sim I(0)$$

By applying VECM, the model can:

- Enforce equilibrium constraints in forecasts,
- Allow short-term deviations while correcting over time, and
- Improve forecast stability and economic interpretability.

Python Implementation on the Example

In this section, let us look at a practical implementation of the Vector Error Correction Model (VECM) for forecasting two cointegrated economic time series: the USD/EUR exchange rate and a related EUR interest rate. It demonstrates how to model short-term deviations while preserving a long-term equilibrium relationship, which is at the heart of VECM modeling.

Let us start by simulating non-stationary data.

Code:

```
usd_eur = [1.10, 1.12, 1.13, 1.15, 1.17, 1.19, 1.18, 1.20]
eur_rate = [0.5, 0.51, 0.52, 0.53, 0.54, 0.55, 0.54, 0.56]
```

In the preceding code,

Both **usd_eur** and **eur_rate** are trending time series, representing two economic indicators. Both show upward drift and hence, are non-stationary.

Code:

```
Y = [[usd_eur[i], eur_rate[i]] for i in range(len(usd_eur))]
```

In the preceding code,

We combine the two univariate series into a bivariate sequence, where each observation is a vector at time.

Code:

```
beta = [1, -2]
```

In the preceding code,

- The model assumes a known cointegration vector, implying that is stationary, a long-run equilibrium relationship.
- For example, a central bank might target a stable ratio between currency value and interest rates.

Code:

```
(alpha1, c1), (alpha2, c2) = estimate_vecm(Y, beta)
```

In the preceding code,

Using the **estimate_vecm** function, the code calculates two regressions:

$$\Delta y1\_t = a_1 \cdot error_t + c_1$$

$$\Delta y2\_t = a_2 \cdot error_t + c_2$$

where $error_t$ is the deviation from long-term equilibrium in the previous period, computed from the cointegration vector.

Code:

```
error = beta[0]*Y[-1][0] + beta[1]*Y[-1][1]
dy1 = alpha1 * error + c1
dy2 = alpha2 * error + c2

y1_forecast = Y[-1][0] + dy1
y2_forecast = Y[-1][1] + dy2

print(f"Forecasted USD/EUR: {y1_forecast:.4f}")
print(f"Forecasted EUR Rate: {y2_forecast:.2f}%")
```

In the preceding code,

The model predicts how much each variable will change (Δy1, Δy2) based on the equilibrium error in the last observed period. Then, it adds this to the latest value to generate the next forecast.

Output:

```
Forecasted USD/EUR: 1.2083
Forecasted EUR Rate: 0.56%
```

In the preceding output,

This final output shows the one-step-ahead forecast for both variables, incorporating both short-term movement and long-term cointegration.

The Vector Error Correction Model (VECM) is a powerful tool for modeling the dynamic behavior of non-stationary time series that are cointegrated with long-term equilibrium despite short-term fluctuations. Unlike models that focus solely on temporal lags, VECM explicitly integrates both the short-run deviations and the long-run equilibrium relationship between variables, making it particularly well-suited for economic, financial, and many other applications where such relationships are both theoretically justified and empirically observed.

VECM is very useful in situations where understanding both immediate shocks and gradual adjustments is critical. It provides interpretable economic insights by quantifying how quickly deviations from equilibrium are corrected over time. Moreover, it often delivers more accurate forecasts than traditional Vector Autoregression (VAR) in systems where cointegration is present.

However, VECM comes with important considerations. Before applying the model, one must verify cointegration using techniques such as the Johansen test. The model's accuracy is sensitive to the chosen lag structure and specification, and it assumes a linear path to equilibrium, which may not always hold in real-world data. Despite these limitations, VECM remains an essential model when strong theoretical or empirical evidence suggests that variables evolve together over time, and the goal is to reflect both short-term dynamics and long-term relationships in forecasting.

Multivariate XGBoost

Multivariate XGBoost is a powerful extension of the XGBoost (Extreme Gradient Boosting) algorithm tailored for forecasting scenarios where multiple interrelated time series evolve simultaneously. Unlike the standard univariate application that relies on lagged and engineered features of a single variable, the multivariate variant utilizes lagged inputs from several correlated variables, each potentially serving as both predictors and targets, thereby enriching the feature space and capturing cross-variable interactions.

This approach transforms the multivariate time series problem into a structured supervised learning task. It constructs the training dataset by drawing on historical lags from all relevant series and optionally enhances it with external or exogenous variables such as weather, calendar events, or marketing promotions. Depending on the use case, it can train a single model to predict multiple targets or multiple models to individually forecast each dependent variable.

Multivariate XGBoost excels in environments where variables exhibit non-linear dependencies or shared dynamics, for instance, electricity usage influenced by temperature, holidays, and occupancy. It is particularly effective when long historical data, rich contextual metadata, or complex interaction effects are available, allowing the model to extract nuanced patterns.

Despite not being inherently sequential like RNNs or LSTMs, XGBoost remains a top performer in tabular and structured forecasting tasks. When equipped with well-designed lag and domain-specific features, multivariate XGBoost can surpass traditional statistical models and even rival deep learning models in predictive accuracy, making it a highly versatile choice for practical forecasting systems.

Mathematical Explanation

At its core, XGBoost minimizes the regularized loss:

$$L = \sum_{i=1}^{n} l\left(y_i, \hat{y}_i\right) + \sum_{k=1}^{K} \Omega(f_k)$$

where:

- y_i: actual values,
- $\hat{y}_i$: predicted values,
- l: loss function (for example, mean squared error),
- f_K: decision tree at iteration k, and
- $\Omega(f) = \gamma T + \frac{1}{2}\lambda||\omega||^2$: regularization term for complexity.

In the multivariate setting, we may use:

- Separate models per target (multi-output = multiple regressors)
- Joint model with a reshaped target matrix

For each target y_t, we use features:

$$X_t = [y_{1,t-1}, y_{2,t-1}, \dots, y_{k,t-1}, \textit{exogenous vars}]$$

XGBoost treats this as a supervised regression problem and learns mappings:

$$\hat{y}^j_{t+h} = f(X_t)$$

where h is the forecast horizon.

Implementing the Math as a Python Function

In this section, let us implement a simplified representation on Multivariate XGBoost algorithm.

Let us start by defining a class SimpleMultiXGB, which is a simplified implementation of a Gradient Boosting Decision Tree (GBDT) regressor, tailored for structured tabular data and intended to simulate the basic working principles behind algorithms such as XGBoost. This class is defined with the following methods: **`__init__`**, **`_fit_stump`**, **`fit`**, and **`predict`**.

Code:

```
class SimpleMultiXGB:
    def __init__(self, n_estimators=10, lr=0.1):
        self.n_estimators = n_estimators
```

```
        self.lr = lr
        self.trees = []
```

In the preceding code,

- The class begins with an initializer method **__init__** where the number of boosting rounds (**n_estimators**) and the learning rate (**lr**) are defined.
- These hyperparameters control how many weak learners (decision stumps) are added and how much each contributes to the final prediction. An empty list **self.trees** is used to store the learned weak models.

Code:

```
def _fit_stump(self, X, residuals):
        best_feat, best_split, best_loss = None, None, float('inf')
        for j in range(len(X[0])):
            thresholds = sorted(set(x[j] for x in X))
            for t in thresholds:
                left, right = [], []
                for i, x in enumerate(X):
                    (left if x[j] <= t else right).
append(residuals[i])
                if not left or not right: continue
                mean_left = sum(left)/len(left)
                mean_right = sum(right)/len(right)
                loss = sum((r - mean_left)**2 for r in left) +
sum((r - mean_right)**2 for r in right)
                if loss < best_loss:
                    best_feat, best_split, best_loss = j, t, loss
                    best_left, best_right = mean_left, mean_right
        return (best_feat, best_split, best_left, best_right)
```

In the preceding code,

The private method **_fit_stump** is responsible for building a single-level decision tree (that is, a decision stump) to fit the residuals of the current model. The procedure works by:

- Iterating through all feature indices **(j)** and their unique thresholds **(t)** to find the best binary split.
- For each candidate split, the residuals are separated into left and right nodes.
- The Mean Squared Error (MSE) of each split is calculated based on the average residual in each node.
- The split that minimizes the total loss (MSE over both left and right) is retained as the best split.

- The method returns the optimal splitting rule: the feature index, threshold, and predicted values for the left and right branches.

Code:

```
def fit(self, X, y):
    self.init = sum(y)/len(y)
    pred = [self.init] * len(y)
    for _ in range(self.n_estimators):
        residuals = [yi - pi for yi, pi in zip(y, pred)]
        stump = self._fit_stump(X, residuals)
        self.trees.append(stump)
        for i, x in enumerate(X):
            j, t, l, r = stump
            update = l if x[j] <= t else r
            pred[i] += self.lr * update
```

In the preceding code,

- In the **fit** method:
  - An initial prediction is set as the mean of the target **y** and used as a baseline.
- For each boosting round:
  - Residuals, the difference between actual y and predicted values so far, are computed.
  - A decision stump is fitted to these residuals using **_fit_stump**.
  - The model updates predictions by adding the scaled output of the stump, scaled by the learning rate, to the running predictions.
  - The stump is stored in **self.trees** for use in the prediction phase.

This iterative process forms the essence of gradient boosting. Each stump tries to correct the errors made by the ensemble so far.

Code:

```
def predict(self, X):
    pred = [self.init] * len(X)
    for j, t, l, r in self.trees:
        for i, x in enumerate(X):
            pred[i] += self.lr * (l if x[j] <= t else r)
    return pred
```

In the preceding code,

The **predict** method aggregates the contributions of all stored trees for each new input:

- Start with the initial prediction, the mean of y during training.
- For each tree, apply the binary rule and add the corresponding value, left or right, multiplied by the learning rate.
- This results in a final predicted value for each input.

Real-World Example

In the context of smart energy systems, multivariate time series forecasting is particularly valuable due to the interdependence between variables such as electricity demand and solar power generation. For instance, during peak daylight hours, solar generation can directly offset demand, creating a strong correlation between the two series. These relationships are further influenced by shared external factors such as ambient temperature, day of the week, and holiday effects. A multivariate XGBoost model provides a powerful framework to capture these dynamics by incorporating lagged values of both demand and solar generation, along with relevant exogenous features such as weather conditions and calendar variables. Such a model can simultaneously predict multiple outputs, such as the next hour's electricity demand and solar output, enabling highly accurate and interpretable forecasts. This approach supports real-time grid planning, improves load balancing, and enhances operational efficiency, making it well-suited for modern, data-driven energy infrastructure.

Python Implementation on the Example

In this section, let us demonstrate how a simple multivariate time series forecasting pipeline can be built using two separate gradient boosting models to predict electricity demand and solar output, leveraging their mutual interactions and external variables such as temperature.

Let us start by creating simulated time series data for this example.

Code:

```
demand = [100, 110, 120, 130, 125, 128, 135, 140]
solar = [50, 55, 60, 62, 65, 67, 68, 70]
temperature = [30, 32, 31, 29, 28, 27, 26, 25]
```

In the preceding code,

- The code begins by simulating hourly data for electricity demand and solar output.
- It also includes a dummy temperature series, which acts as an exogenous input.

Code:

```
def create_features(demand, solar, temp):
    X, yd, ys = [], [], []
    for i in range(2, len(demand)):
```

```
        features = [demand[i-1], demand[i-2], solar[i-1], solar[i-2], 
temp[i]]
        X.append(features)
        yd.append(demand[i])
        ys.append(solar[i])
    return X, yd, ys
X, y_demand, y_solar = create_features(demand, solar, temperature)
```

In the preceding code,

The function **create_features** constructs the supervised learning dataset by generating lag-based features:

- It uses the last two values of both demand and solar output, and includes the current temperature as an input feature.
- The target variables are the current hour's demand and solar values.
- This setup captures short-term dependencies and the influence of weather conditions.

Code:

```
model_d = SimpleMultiXGB(n_estimators=5)
model_s = SimpleMultiXGB(n_estimators=5)
model_d.fit(X, y_demand)
model_s.fit(X, y_solar)
```

In the preceding code,

- Two instances of **SimpleMultiXGB**, a custom lightweight implementation of **XGBoost** using decision stumps, are created:
- One for forecasting demand and another for solar output.
- Each model is trained separately on the same feature matrix **X** but with different target vectors (**y_demand** and **y_solar**).
- This separation allows for task-specific learning while still leveraging the same shared features, which is a practical strategy when target variables are correlated but not identical in dynamics.

Code:

```
new_input = [demand[-1], demand[-2], solar[-1], solar[-2], 
temperature[-1]]
forecast_d = model_d.predict([new_input])[0]
forecast_s = model_s.predict([new_input])[0]

print(f"Forecasted Demand: {forecast_d:.2f}")
print(f"Forecasted Solar Output: {forecast_s:.2f}")
```

In the preceding code,

- To forecast the next hour's values, the code prepares the latest input using the most recent demand and solar values, along with the last temperature value.
- Each model then predicts its respective output for the next time step.

Output:

```
Forecasted Demand: 132.53
Forecasted Solar Output: 66.39
```

In the preceding output,

- The predicted values are printed as forecasts for electricity demand and solar generation.

Multivariate XGBoost offers a powerful and pragmatic solution for time series forecasting when multiple interdependent variables are involved. Although originally designed for tabular data, XGBoost adapts well to time series settings when the data is thoughtfully engineered to reflect temporal dynamics. By transforming a multivariate time series into a supervised learning problem with carefully constructed lag features, rolling averages, and exogenous variables, it becomes possible to harness XGBoost's strengths in capturing complex, non-linear interactions.

This approach is especially advantageous in environments such as business forecasting, energy grid optimization, or supply chain operations, where fast and accurate predictions are essential. It excels at incorporating external signals such as holidays, temperature, or promotions and remains computationally efficient even at scale. However, because XGBoost does not inherently model sequences, the burden of temporal representation falls on manual feature engineering. It also lacks built-in mechanisms for long-range memory or autoregressive multi-step forecasting unless recursively structured.

Despite these limitations, multivariate XGBoost remains a benchmark tool in structured time series modeling. Its flexibility, speed, and accuracy often rival or exceed more complex deep learning models when applied to well-structured, feature-rich datasets. As such, it serves as an excellent baseline or even a production-ready model for many real-world forecasting problems where interpretability, robustness, and execution time matter.

Multivariate Long Short-Term Memory (LSTM)

Multivariate Long Short-Term Memory (LSTM) networks extend the capabilities of traditional univariate LSTMs by enabling simultaneous learning across multiple time-dependent variables. While univariate LSTMs focus solely on a single sequence, multivariate LSTMs process and model several interrelated sequences together, capturing both the temporal patterns within each variable and the interdependencies among them. This allows the model to forecast multiple future values from a common history, integrating short-term trends and long-range dynamics across a multivariate landscape.

The core strength of LSTMs, memory cells, and gating mechanisms that retain important patterns over long sequences is especially beneficial in the multivariate context. These models automatically learn which lags and seasonal structures are relevant, removing the need for manual feature engineering. They can forecast a single target or multiple outputs over varying time horizons within a unified framework.

This modeling approach is particularly impactful in complex domains where multiple factors co-evolve over time. In energy systems, for example, demand and weather variables interact nonlinearly. In healthcare, vital signs such as heart rate, blood oxygen, and blood pressure must be analyzed together to understand the patient's state. In supply chains, inventory levels, lead times, and demand signals jointly influence operations. Multivariate LSTMs provide a deep learning-based solution capable of handling such richly interwoven temporal systems.

Mathematical Explanation

Let $x_t \epsilon R^n$ be a multivariate input vector at time t, where n is the number of variables. The multivariate LSTM learns a mapping:

$$\hat{y}_{t+1} = f(x_t, x_{t+1,} \ldots, xt-\omega)$$

Where:

- ω: the lookback window, and
- f: the LSTM function that captures temporal and cross-variable interactions.

The internal mechanisms for each LSTM cell remain the same:

1. Forget gate:

$$f_t = \sigma(W_f \cdot [h_{t-1}, x_t] + b_f)$$

2. Input Gate:

$$i_t = \sigma(W_f \cdot [h_{t-1}, x_t] + b_i)$$

$$\tilde{C}_t = tanh(W_C \cdot [h_{t-1}, x_t] + b_C)$$

3. Cell State Update:

$$C_t = f_t * C_{t-1} + i_t * \tilde{C}_t$$

4. Output Gate:

$$o_t=\sigma(Wf \cdot [h_{t-1}, x_t]+b_o)$$

$$h_t=o_t * tanh\,(C_t)$$

Where:

- σ: sigmoid activation function,
- *tanh*: hyperbolic tangent function,
- *: element-wise multiplication, and
- W and *b*: trainable weights and biases.

Loss Function:

For forecasting:

$$L = \frac{1}{T}\sum_{t=1}^{T} (y_t - \widehat{y}_t)^2$$

LSTM training uses Backpropagation Through Time (BPTT), just like RNNs, but the gating structure reduces vanishing gradients, enabling learning over long sequences.

Here $x_t \in R^n$, and the **LSTM learns dependencies both within each variable and between variables over time**.

Implementing the Math as a Python Function

In this section, let us implement a simplified version of a multivariate LSTM. The **SimpleMultivariateLSTM** class is a simplified implementation of a multivariate Long Short-Term Memory (LSTM) network that captures temporal dependencies across multiple input features. While simplified, this handcrafted model illustrates the core mechanics of LSTM cells, including gating mechanisms and recurrent updates, and can be used for educational purposes or lightweight experimentation. This class is defined with the following methods:

__init__, **sigmoid**, **tanh**, **fit**, and **predict**.

Code:

```
class SimpleMultivariateLSTM:
    def __init__(self, input_dim, hidden_dim=1, lr=0.01, epochs=100):
        self.input_dim = input_dim
        self.hidden_dim = hidden_dim
        self.lr = lr
        self.epochs = epochs

        def rand(): return random.uniform(-0.1, 0.1)
```

```
        self.Wf = [[rand() for _ in range(input_dim + hidden_dim)] for _
in range(hidden_dim)]
        self.bf = [rand() for _ in range(hidden_dim)]

        self.Wi = [[rand() for _ in range(input_dim + hidden_dim)] for _
in range(hidden_dim)]
        self.bi = [rand() for _ in range(hidden_dim)]

        self.WC = [[rand() for _ in range(input_dim + hidden_dim)] for _
in range(hidden_dim)]
        self.bC = [rand() for _ in range(hidden_dim)]

        self.Wo = [[rand() for _ in range(input_dim + hidden_dim)] for _
in range(hidden_dim)]
        self.bo = [rand() for _ in range(hidden_dim)]

        self.Why = [rand() for _ in range(hidden_dim)]
        self.by = rand()
```

In the preceding code,

- The **__init__** method sets up the architecture and initializes all the weight matrices and biases with small random values.
- The model supports multiple input features (**input_dim**) and a tunable hidden state size (**hidden_dim**).
- Four gates are constructed:
    - **Forget Gate (Wf, bf):** Controls what information to retain from the past.
    - **Input Gate (Wi, bi):** Decides how much new information enters the cell state.
    - **Candidate Memory (WC, bC):** Encodes potential updates to the memory cell.
    - **Output Gate (Wo, bo):** Determines what information flows to the hidden state.
- Each gate is parameterized by its weights connecting past hidden states and current inputs, and a bias vector.
- Additionally, a fully connected layer at the output maps the hidden state to a scalar prediction using **Why** and **by**.

Code:

```
    def sigmoid(self, x): return 1 / (1 + math.exp(-x))
    def tanh(self, x): return math.tanh(x)
```

In the preceding code,

- **`sigmoid`** and **`tanh`** activation functions are standard nonlinearities used in LSTM cells.
- The **`sigmoid`** function compresses values between 0 and 1, essential for gating behavior.
- The **`tanh`** function ensures the internal cell values remain within a bounded range (–1 to 1), promoting stability.

Code:

```
def fit(self, sequences, targets):
        for _ in range(self.epochs):
            for seq, y_target in zip(sequences, targets):
                h, C = [0.0] * self.hidden_dim, [0.0] * self.hidden_dim
                for xt in seq:
                    xt = list(xt)
                    for i in range(self.hidden_dim):
                        combined = h + xt
                        f = self.sigmoid(sum(w * x for w, x in zip(self.
Wf[i], combined)) + self.bf[i])
                        i_ = self.sigmoid(sum(w * x for w, x in zip(self.
Wi[i], combined)) + self.bi[i])
                        C_tilde = self.tanh(sum(w * x for w, x in zip(self.
WC[i], combined)) + self.bC[i])
                        C[i] = f * C[i] + i_ * C_tilde
                        o = self.sigmoid(sum(w * x for w, x in zip(self.
Wo[i], combined)) + self.bo[i])
                        h[i] = o * self.tanh(C[i])

                    y_pred = sum(h[i] * self.Why[i] for i in range(self.
hidden_dim)) + self.by
                error = y_pred - y_target

                for i in range(self.hidden_dim):
                    self.Why[i] -= self.lr * error * h[i]
                self.by -= self.lr * error
```

In the preceding code,

The **`fit`** method trains the LSTM model on Sequence-Target Pairs over multiple epochs using a basic stochastic gradient descent loop.

For each training sequence:

- **Initialization:** Hidden state **`h`** and cell state **`C`** are reset to zero.

- **Sequential Update:** For each timestep **xt**:
    - Concatenate the previous hidden state **h** with the current input **xt**.
    - Pass the concatenated vector through the four gates.
    - Update the memory cell **C** using the forget and input gates.
    - Update the hidden state **h** via the output gate and the new memory state.
- After processing the sequence, the final hidden state is linearly transformed to yield a scalar prediction (**y_pred**).
- A simple squared error loss is used, and the gradients are backpropagated to update the final layer weights (**Why, by**).

Note: *This implementation does not update the LSTM cell weights (gates) and only trains the output layer.*

Code:

```
    def predict(self, sequence):
        h, C = [0.0] * self.hidden_dim, [0.0] * self.hidden_dim
        for xt in sequence:
            xt = list(xt)
            for i in range(self.hidden_dim):
                combined = h + xt
                f = self.sigmoid(sum(w * x for w, x in zip(self.Wf[i],
combined)) + self.bf[i])
                i_ = self.sigmoid(sum(w * x for w, x in zip(self.Wi[i],
combined)) + self.bi[i])
                C_tilde = self.tanh(sum(w * x for w, x in zip(self.
WC[i], combined)) + self.bC[i])
                C[i] = f * C[i] + i_ * C_tilde
                o = self.sigmoid(sum(w * x for w, x in zip(self.Wo[i],
combined)) + self.bo[i])
                h[i] = o * self.tanh(C[i])
        return sum(h[i] * self.Why[i] for i in range(self.hidden_dim)) +
self.by
```

In the preceding code,

- The **predict** method uses the learned LSTM to generate a prediction on unseen input sequences.
- It mirrors the forward pass used during training, iterating through each timestep to update the cell state **C** and hidden state **h**.
- The final hidden state is transformed into the predicted output using the trained output weights.

Real-World Example

In smart agriculture systems, accurate crop yield forecasting depends on synthesizing data from multiple dynamic and interrelated sources such as rainfall (in millimeters), soil moisture levels (in percentage), sunlight hours, and ambient temperature (in degrees Celsius). These variables interact in complex, non-linear ways over time, influencing plant growth, irrigation needs, and overall productivity.

A Multivariate LSTM (Long Short-Term Memory) model is particularly well-suited for this scenario because it can jointly learn from all input variables, automatically capturing both short-term fluctuations, such as a sudden heatwave, and long-term trends, such as seasonal rainfall patterns, without requiring manual feature engineering, such as lag creation.

The strength of a Multivariate LSTM lies in its ability to model temporal dependencies across multiple input streams, effectively understanding how factors such as soil moisture and temperature co-evolve and jointly affect yield. This approach allows for real-time, end-to-end forecasting as new data streams in from IoT sensors in the field.

As a result, stakeholders, including farmers, agronomists, and supply chain managers, can make more informed decisions about irrigation scheduling, optimal harvesting windows, and logistical planning. The integration of Multivariate LSTM into smart agriculture thus represents a leap forward in predictive precision, automation, and operational efficiency.

Python Implementation on the Example

In this section, let us implement the basic multivariate LSTM forecasting pipeline in Python using simulated sensor data for agriculture, specifically to predict crop yield based on rainfall and sunlight conditions.

Code:

```
rain = [10, 12, 8, 9, 11, 14, 15, 13]
sun = [5, 6, 5.5, 7, 8, 9, 9.5, 10]
yield_ = [20, 22, 21, 23, 24, 26, 27, 28]
```

In the preceding code,

This section defines three time series:

- **rain**: daily rainfall amounts,
- **sun**: daily sunlight hours, and
- **yield_**: corresponding crop yield values.

Each variable is aligned by time index, meaning **rain[i]**, **sun[i]**, and **yield_[i]** all refer to the same day **i**.

Code:

```
def create_sequences(X1, X2, y, window=3):
    seqs, targets = [], []
    for i in range(window, len(y)):
        seq = [(X1[j], X2[j]) for j in range(i-window, i)]
        seqs.append(seq)
        targets.append(y[i])
    return seqs, targets

X1, X2 = rain, sun
sequences, targets = create_sequences(X1, X2, yield_)
```

In the preceding code,

- The **create_sequences** function transforms raw time series into training-ready input-output sequences.
- Using a sliding window approach (here, of size 3), it creates input sequences of shape **[window, 2]** where each input is a tuple of **(rain, sun)** values over the past 3 days and matches each to the crop yield at the current day.
- This captures both temporal patterns and cross-variable dynamics.

Code:

```
model = SimpleMultivariateLSTM(input_dim=2, hidden_dim=2, lr=0.01,
epochs=300)
model.fit(sequences, targets)
```

In the preceding code,

- The simple multivariate LSTM is instantiated and trained:
    - **input_dim=2**: two input variables (rainfall and sunlight),
    - **hidden_dim=2**: two hidden units for the LSTM cell,
    - **lr=0.01**: learning rate, and
    - **epochs=300**: number of passes over the data.
- The **fit** method updates the model's weights through backpropagation based on each input-target pair in the training data, learning to map patterns of weather conditions to future yields.

Code:

```
latest_seq = [(rain[-3], sun[-3]), (rain[-2], sun[-2]), (rain[-1], sun[-
1])]
prediction = model.predict(latest_seq)
print(f"Forecasted Crop Yield: {prediction:.2f}")
```

In the preceding code,

- To generate a forecast, the model takes the most recent three days of data, forming a new input sequence for prediction.
- The **predict** method processes this sequence through the trained LSTM using memory cells to encode temporal and multivariate dependencies and returns the predicted crop yield for the next day.

Output:

```
Forecasted Crop Yield: 26.50
```

In the preceding output,

- The predicted yield is printed in a readable format, completing the end-to-end pipeline from multivariate sensor data to real-time agricultural forecast.

Multivariate Long Short-Term Memory (LSTM) networks blend the sequence-learning capabilities of standard LSTMs with the added advantage of modeling interactions across multiple input variables. These models shine in scenarios where several time-dependent features evolve together and influence future outcomes, especially when the dependencies are nonlinear, variable lags exist, or long-term temporal memory is crucial.

One of the core strengths of multivariate LSTMs lies in their ability to learn both temporal and inter-variable relationships without relying on manual feature engineering, making them particularly suited for complex systems such as energy demand forecasting, healthcare monitoring, and supply chain optimization.

They can support both one-to-many and many-to-many forecasting setups, making them highly flexible. However, their performance comes at the cost of higher computational requirements and the need for substantial data to generalize well.

Additionally, like most deep learning models, they tend to be opaque and less interpretable compared to tree-based methods such as XGBoost. Despite these trade-offs, multivariate LSTMs are considered a gold standard in deep learning for modeling intricate, dynamic environments where multiple signals interact over time.

Conclusion

In this chapter, we explored the rich and evolving landscape of multivariate time series forecasting, a domain where temporal dynamics meet inter-variable relationships to enable more accurate and intelligent prediction systems. Each modeling technique introduced serves a distinct purpose, grounded in different assumptions, mathematical formulations, and real-world applicability.

We began with Vector Autoregression (VAR), a classical statistical model that extends univariate autoregression to systems with multiple interdependent time series. VAR treats every variable symmetrically and models their dynamics through a system of equations based on lagged values. It is particularly effective for stationary time series and excels in domains such as macroeconomic forecasting, energy markets, and financial system modeling. The key strength of VAR lies in its interpretability and simplicity, making it a foundational tool for early-stage multivariate analysis and structural inference.

We then covered the Vector Error Correction Model (VECM) for balancing Short-Run Dynamics and Long-Run Equilibrium, where the time series are non-stationary yet cointegrated. VECM extends VAR by enforcing long-run equilibrium constraints through an error correction term, thereby preventing cointegrated variables from drifting arbitrarily apart over time. This model is vital in economic settings where theory suggests a stable relationship between variables such as exchange rates, inflation, and interest rates. VECM allows forecasters to model both short-term deviations and long-term corrections, making it a powerful tool for policy analysis, scenario modeling, and impulse response simulations.

Shifting from statistical modeling to supervised machine learning, we examined Multivariate XGBoost, a gradient boosting technique adapted to handle multivariate and exogenous features. By engineering lag features, rolling statistics, and external regressors, this model can efficiently learn complex nonlinear patterns in structured datasets. Although it lacks sequence memory like RNNs or LSTMs, XGBoost frequently outperforms deep learning models in tabular settings due to its speed, interpretability, and ease of tuning. It is particularly well-suited for applications such as retail demand forecasting, energy load prediction, and operational planning when data is feature-rich and well-structured.

Finally, we delved into Multivariate Long Short-Term Memory (LSTM) networks, which represent the deep learning standard for multivariate forecasting. These models are adept at capturing non-linear temporal dependencies across multiple correlated variables without explicit feature engineering. Their memory cells allow them to retain both short- and long-term patterns, making them suitable for high-dimensional, noisy, or sensor-driven environments such as smart agriculture, healthcare monitoring, and industrial IoT forecasting. While LSTMs demand more data and computational power, they unlock powerful capabilities for learning inter-variable dynamics directly from raw sequences.

References

- Hamilton, J. D. (1994) *Time Series Analysis. Princeton University Press.*
- Lütkepohl, H. (2005) *New Introduction to Multiple Time Series Analysis. Springer.*
- Enders, W. (2014) *Applied Econometric Time Series.* 4th edn. *Wiley.*

- Sims, C. A. (1980) Macroeconomics and Reality. *Econometrica.*
- Pfaff, B. (2008) VAR, SVAR and SVEC Models: Implementation Within R Package vars. *Journal of Statistical Software.*
- Johansen, S. (1991) Estimation and Hypothesis Testing of Cointegration Vectors in Gaussian Vector Autoregressive Models. *Econometrica.*
- Chen, T. and Guestrin, C. (2016) XGBoost: A Scalable Tree Boosting System. KDD.
- Brownlee, J. (2018) Deep Learning for Time Series Forecasting. *Machine Learning Mastery.*
- Rossi, R. A. (2020) Forecasting with Machine Learning Models in Python. *Towards Data Science.*
- Zhang, G., Eddy Patuwo, B. and Hu, M. Y. (1998) Forecasting with Artificial Neural Networks: The State of the Art. *International Journal of Forecasting.*
- Géron, A. (2019) *Hands-On Machine Learning with Scikit-Learn, Keras, and TensorFlow.* O'Reilly.
- Hochreiter, S. and Schmidhuber, J. (1997) Long short-term memory. *Neural Computation.*
- Karim, F. et al. (2019) Multivariate LSTM-FCNs for time series classification. *Neural Networks.*
- Lipton, Z. C. (2015) A Critical Review of Recurrent Neural Networks for Sequence Learning. *arXiv.*
- Goodfellow, I., Bengio, Y. and Courville, A. (2016) *Deep Learning.* MIT Press.

Index

E

G

I

K

L

M

N

P

R

S

T

V

W

Y

Z